POLAND

ON THE

PASSAIC

tales of a
New Jersey boyhood

POLAND
ON THE
PASSAIC

tales of a
New Jersey boyhood

Bill Michalski

GREYCOURT BOOKS
TUXEDO PARK
NEW YORK

ISBN-10: 0-9740968-0-6
ISBN-13: 978-0-9740968-0-3

Library of Congress Control Number: 2003107105

Edited and designed by Silk Purse Editorial Services
www.silkpurse.net   🐦   editor@silkpurse.net

"Charley" font created by Kevin Martin

Published by
Greycourt Books
P.O. Box 691
Tuxedo Park, New York 10987
info@greycourtbooks.com

Printed in the United States of America
Second printing, August 2005

Cover: Bill Michalski and Charley the crow, Camp Ocawasin, 1945

PULASKI PARK, 1935

I know we went to the river
when we shouldn't have . . .

And we didn't go to church
when we should have . . .

Rest in peace, Ma—all is well.

There's an old spinning wheel in the parlor
Spinning tales of a time long ago
There's an old spinning wheel in the parlor
Spinning tales of a time that I know

Sung to Billy and Joe by Aunt Annie

CONTENTS

Introduction	1
The Ambulance	5
Medicine	7
Pulaski Park	17
The Hospital	23
The River	26
Easter Egg Hunt	30
The Detective	33
The Dundee Canal	36
The Ice Man	39
The Palace	41
Christmas in the 1930s	44
Food	50
Dessert	59
Part II: Wallington	63
The First Day of School	72
79 Park Row	76
The Fourth Grade	84
The Coal Bucket	86
The Newspaper	90
The Attic	93
My First Dog	96
The Tanks	99
The Walk	105
The Wedding	109
The Promise	114
The Hunter	117

The Seventh Grade   *120*
Grandpa   *124*
The Sailor   *134*
World War II   *136*
The Bus   *147*
Poison Ivy   *150*
The Fourth of July   *154*
The Factory   *159*
The Railroad Tracks   *166*
The Chicken   *173*
Ice Skating   *176*
The Attack   *182*
The Dump   *188*
The Radio   *191*
The Great Fire   *195*
Tippy   *197*
The Carnival   *200*
The Nelkins   *206*
Walt Bednarz   *209*
Hot Dog Night   *218*
Charley the Crow   *222*
Camp Ocawasin   *228*
The Knife   *234*
Life at Camp Ocawasin   *236*
Welcome Home, Bill   *253*
World War II Surplus   *256*
The Robin Hood Gang   *260*
Work   *264*
My First Dance   *269*
A Christmas Present   *273*
Annie   *277*
Insurance   *280*
Epilogue   *283*

INTRODUCTION

I was born in Passaic, New Jersey, in an apartment house on the corner of Fourth and Bergen streets. The year was 1931. My mother's husband deserted her in 1930. At the time, she had a one-year-old son and was pregnant with me. She raised us both during the Great Depression, while also caring for her aged father. Her younger sister, Anne, also lived with us and helped out a great deal, as she had employment in a local cigar factory. This was our extended family, and it would remain this way until 1940, when my mother was able to remarry. After the marriage, we moved across the Passaic river to the small town of Wallington.

Fourth Street in the 1930s was mostly apartment houses, with a few two-family homes. There were three or four grocery stores, a bakery, and a stable for horses. Rounding out the picture were a barber shop, a couple of what we called "penny candy stores," and a few other small shops. Also on Fourth Street were a YWCA and a large church, which may have served some other immigrants before the neighborhood developed its current Polish character.

I never did observe much activity at the YWCA, although I lived right across the street. It is almost certain that very few if any of the area residents attended, as most of them were on hard times. Besides, they weren't the kind to shell out money to play games, exercise, and swim. To them, life was a more serious undertaking, and their main concern was getting by each day during a depression.

Fortunately for the people who lived in the area, there was a park nearby, called Pulaski Park. The name was very appropriate, as the entire neighborhood was mostly Polish or people of Slavic background. The park extended from Monroe Street almost to where Wall Street and Passaic Street met. It paralleled the entire length of Fourth Street and I believe a section of Third Street. It had a beautiful large pavilion with drinking fountains, park benches, and storage rooms for sports equipment. The park also had a baseball field and a large concrete wading pool for children. Many local events were held near the pavilion, including the annual Easter Egg hunt. The pavilion was the preferred place for the older men to congregate and converse in Polish about both America and Poland, a country they were still very much attached to, but that most would never see again.

There was a railroad track on the opposite side of the park that served as a boundary, separating the park from a small, unused area adjoining the Passaic River.

The Passaic River in the 1930s was badly polluted from both raw sewage and industrial waste. It was a river but it was also an open sewer. Yet fishermen would frequent the river to fish, although their catch would be mostly carp and eels. In spite of the pollution, they would take their catch home. This was the Depression and for many a very difficult time.

Market Street, two blocks away from Fourth Street, was the business district and the life blood of the neighborhood. Not only did it supply the local people with the necessities of life but it also served as a recreation area for kids, the unemployed, and those seeking diversion from the daily grind of their lives. These various categories of people could always be seen walking up and down Market Street, looking in store windows at goods they could not afford to buy. For many, this became a form of recreation and a regular ritual as the Depression continued to oppress people through the 1930s.

One of the main attractions on Market Street was the Palace Theater. It was here that we were introduced to the world of fantasy, which for us children was as real as any world that we knew. And here for five or ten cents many older people, the unemployed, and those just trying to escape the drudgery of their lives would come for a few hours of relief. Parents would also send their children here in order to escape from the chore of raising children and to have some free time of their own.

Next to the Palace Theater was a large, well-equipped hardware store. This store was a special attraction for children, as it had a very large area where one could view the merchandise behind glass. The display would usually have pocket knives, harmonicas, fishing tackle, BB guns, and other equipment to tantalize a youngster's imagination.

On Third Street was a library that youngsters would visit on a regular basis, especially if it was raining or very cold. Saturday was the day when most children attended. The library had a children's section and talking out loud was absolutely forbidden. This rule was strictly enforced.

A major portion of my life as a young boy growing up in Passaic was spent in the day nursery located at the corner of Jefferson and Columbia streets. It was here that my mother would deposit my brother and me while she worked during the Depression. As we became older, we would both attend Lafayette School # 6.

To many children who lived in the area, a real godsend was the Passaic Boys Club, which was located on Third Street right next to the library. This club also ran a summer camp called Camp Ocawasin. If ever a city was concerned about its citizens—and especially its children—during the Depression, that was Passaic.

Passaic during the 1930s was an industrial city, with many factories supplying work for the local population. Some of the major companies that employed many people from the Fourth Street area were Botany Mills, Forstmann Woolen Mills, Manhattan Rubber, U. S. Rubber, and Okonite. There were many other industries that contributed to the vibrancy of the area, besides providing a livelihood for many immigrant families. For many Polish and Slavic families the American dream began in the area around Passaic, New Jersey, especially Wallington—lovingly known as Poland on the Passaic.

THE AMBULANCE

It was a hot summer day, probably in 1936. I was playing on Bergen Street where it crossed Fourth Street and entered Pulaski Park. My brother and I were with a few older boys who had a scooter. The scooter was made from a two-by-four, one roller skate, a wooden box, and a piece of wood for steering. The skate would be separated into two sections, the two by four receiving a section at either end. The box would then be nailed upright to the two-by-four and a wooden slat placed across the top of the box to serve as a handle for steering. We were in the process of fixing one of the skates, which had come off, when people began to collect in front of the apartment house where I lived.

We continued working on the scooter, not paying much attention to the gathering people until we saw an ambulance arrive on the scene. Instantly we abandoned the scooter and took our place among the spectators. We watched as several men entered the apartment building, carrying a stretcher. The people standing around were very quiet and when talking to one another would only whisper. I managed to worm my way between people until I was in front, a ringside seat at the unfolding drama.

It wasn't long before footsteps could be heard coming downstairs from one of the upper apartments. The amount of noise indicated that the stretcher bearers were having a difficult time rounding the bends in the staircase. They finally reached the bottom and began the exit from the building. I was kneeling down at the time but as the stretcher bearers approached I stood up to get a better look.

It was my mother! Her eyes were closed and her face was ashen white. At that instant I thought she was dead. I dashed upstairs to our apartment and saw my aunt Annie conversing with some neighbors. Seeing me, she told me to go to the park and find my brother and bring him home. I left and went to Pulaski Park and found my brother shooting marbles near the pavilion. I told him everything and we headed back to the apartment.

After all the neighbors left, my aunt explained to us that our mother got sick and would be in the hospital for a few days. Life quickly went back to normal, with my aunt taking over for my mother, who returned about five days later. Many years would pass before I found out the reason behind my mother's trip to the hospital. She had collapsed from malnutrition and fatigue.

One of my youthful observations as a boy on Fourth Street was the handing out of food. It seems to me that from time to time a large stake-body truck would slowly proceed down Fourth Street. As I was there to see it and not in school, it was most likely a Saturday.

In the back of the truck were usually two men and stacks of large brown paper bags filled with stuff. The truck would occasionally stop and one of the men would pick up a bag and look at the name on it and then loudly call out the name to the people standing along the curb on Fourth Street. The person whose name was called would then go to the rear of the truck and would be handed the bag.

Much later in life, I asked my mother about the truck and the paper bags. She told me it was one of the forms of relief for people who were unemployed or had too many children to support for their income. She said that you had to sign up for relief and that she was on it for a short period of time until she found a job. She also mentioned that sometimes people would not go up to the truck to get their food as it was too embarrassing with all your neighbors looking.

MEDICINE

One of the main contrasts between the Depression period and what we generally refer to as modern times is in the field of medicine. Health care plans were virtually unknown and even those who were employed were not covered by health insurance. If someone was sick enough that a doctor was needed, you had to pay for his services. As money was usually in very short supply, the first line of defense against sickness was an array of home remedies. It was only after they were tried and there was no improvement or the condition worsened that a doctor would be notified. Since we had no telephone, my mother would have to locate one, probably in one of the local grocery stores, or wait until the doctor opened his office.

A child who was sick always knew when he was going to be taken to a doctor or a doctor was coming to visit him. Regardless of how sick he was, his mother would always change his underwear. In those days you took a bath only once a week and that's when you changed your underwear. Your mother didn't want the doctor to see your dirty underwear. Along with this procedure was a general cleaning of the parts of the house that the doctor would be exposed to. This was not done because the house was dirty but because anyone entering your house or apartment was entitled to a neat, orderly environment.

Many home remedies were in use in our Polish neighborhood during and after the Depression. I'm sure that each ethnic group and the neighborhoods they resided in had their own versions of "Mom's health care program."

To a young child, some of these home remedies could qualify as forms of torture or at the very least child abuse. Very often when suffering from some affliction we would be silent and try to endure the pain rather than take the cure.

Earaches

This usually ranked near the top of the list of treatments to be avoided if possible. Since the earache usually began quite slowly and the pain increased gradually, we would bear quite a bit before going to our mother for the treatment. Once she got involved, the following procedure would begin. She would take a teaspoon and fill it with oil, whatever kind was handy, usually mineral oil. The next step would be to light a wooden match and hold it beneath the teaspoon to heat the oil. My mother would then test the temperature of the oil with her pinky. If she thought the temperature was proper, you were then told to tilt your head to one side. She would now pour the hot oil into your ear. My mother's pinky must have been somewhat insensitive, as it always felt to us that boiling oil was being poured into our ears. A piece of cotton would then be used to plug up the ear and hold the hot oil inside. Usually after about an hour the cotton would be removed and the oil allowed to drain out. This home remedy usually worked, and you had immediate results as the hot oil melted the buildup of wax pressing on your eardrum.

Colds/Sore Throats

If any one illness plagued my brother and me during the Depression, it was colds and sore throats. This was probably a result of malnutrition, which we were at one time both diagnosed as suffering from by a physician. My mother coped with our problem as best she could under the circumstances, applying her array of home remedies with all the skills of a nurse. However, she had no thermometer to record our temperature, only her hand on our forehead. No aspirin, no reference books, only inherited folk remedies were her arsenal to protect her children against the ravages of disease.

At the first sign of a cold or sore throat my mother would concoct a drink which we always knew was coming at the first cough. She would begin the witches brew (this is how my brother and I referred to it) by finely chopping four or five cloves of garlic. These would be placed in a large glass, and added to this would be a large spoonful of butter. Very hot milk would then be poured into the glass. Drinking this brew when the glass was full was really not too bad. However, as the glass began to empty and you had to tilt it more, the butter and garlic would never flow out evenly with the milk. Rather, it would recede to the back of the glass. When the glass was empty of milk and tilted at its greatest angle, the glob of garlic and butter would now begin its slide down the glass towards your mouth. It was at this critical point that my mother would carefully watch you to make sure you swallowed it all. Lastly, she would examine the glass to make sure it was empty. If anything remained, it was scooped out with a spoon and the final act would be played out when you had to swallow what was on the spoon.

Bronchitis

During the Depression the medical knowledge of the average person was quite limited. That is, except on the subject of home remedies— where there was an overabundance of sages. During this period, bronchitis was more commonly referred to as a chest cold. However, most adults were fully aware that these so-called chest colds were potentially very dangerous, as they knew how easily they developed into pneumonia. At one point, my brother was hospitalized for a period of time with double pneumonia. Keep in mind that antibiotics had not yet been developed during this period.

The main treatment was bed rest, to be followed by having your entire chest area rubbed down with Vick's Vapo-Rub. Sometimes this would be covered by a towel, and a hot water bottle would be placed on top to speed up the development of vapor, which was supposed to be inhaled. For young kids, being in bed for several days at a time was trying indeed. There was no TV, daytime radio was not very appealing, and books at that time were not exactly household items. The only real relief from the drudgery of bedtime was the plentiful supply of what were then called joke books, or comic books. When either my brother or I was ill with bed time, to deal with this situation the other would have the chore of making trades with the other kids for different joke books, so that there was a constant supply of new material.

The only bright spot in being sick with either a cold or a sore throat was that at times you might be given cough drops. To young boys during the Depression a piece of candy was considered a treat, and to us cough drops were far closer to candy than to medicine. My brother always chose Vick's Cough Drops while my preference was for Smith Bros., as I had a liking for licorice.

Some of the other young boys that we knew told us of a different treatment they received when sick with a chest cold. Their mothers would apparently make some kind of a concoction using mustard, which was put on their chests. After hearing them describe its effects we were glad to settle for Vick's Vapo-Rub.

General Sickness

There were many times when we just did not feel well, the main symptoms being fatigue and lack of appetite. During the Depression a lack of appetite was a sure sign that you were ill, as food was a commodity that was always foremost on our minds. Whenever we were sick my mother would hurry down to Market Street where there was a chicken market. The place was quite an attraction, as you could watch through the window as they processed the live chickens.

The Jewish owners of the chicken market knew my mother well and always had free chicken feet for her. They seemed to know everyone who was needy, as the ones with money purchased whole chickens.

The chicken feet would be boiled for an hour or so with plenty of garlic added. The broth would be for the sick. Those not sick would feast on the chicken feet.

Much later, comedians and writers would refer to chicken soup as Jewish penicillin. Chicken soup was certainly a popular home remedy for all illnesses. However, most people made chicken soup using the whole chicken. As for us, during the Depression, we had chicken feet soup.

Constipation

As children growing up, we never knew anything about constipation or when we were constipated. However, what we did know was that adults seem to have an obsession with moving your bowels. It seems my mother was always asking, "Did you go Number Two today?" The nurse at the day nursery that I attended had a regular ritual for dealing with constipation. The children would all be lined up, then she would proceed down the line, pressing on each child's intestines to see how hard they were. And if she decided that you were constipated, you were required to endure the ultimate childhood torture— the dreaded soapy enema.

My mother rarely ever engaged in this practice. Rather than use enemas she would use other products which, when taken orally, weren't so traumatic. One of these products was Ex-Lax. It worked very well and it looked and tasted like chocolate, which made it more palatable to children.

Another product in common usage at the time was castor oil, although some families used mineral oil. It worked very well for constipation but also worked equally well as a punishment for misbehavior. The threat of a tablespoon of castor oil was enough to give any unruly child second thoughts.

Being children, we shared information as to the various conditions that adults subjected us to in order to keep us healthy or free from illness. One boy's mother followed none of the procedures as already described in the treatment of constipation. Rather, she would carve out suppositories from a bar of soap, and after placing them in warm water to soften them she would insert these in his rectum. Yes, it worked.

As kids, we were somewhat adaptable to the world of adults, and soon learned how to play the constipation game. When asked, "Did you go Number Two today?" you would reply, "Yeah, Ma, I went twice."

General Treatments

Our apartment was heated by a coal stove in the kitchen. Most apartments were heated this way, as central heating was not widely available. As a result of a hot stove in the kitchen, burns were a frequent occurrence among children, especially on very cold winter days when we played near the stove to keep warm. To young children there are not too many more painful experiences than having a burn. The usual treatment was to place the burned area under cold running water. This would result in immediate stopping of the pain and the crying. It was only temporary, though, and very often would have to be repeated. Next, either butter or lard was spread over the area and, depending on the size of the burn, sometimes a bandage would be used to cover it.

Cuts and scratches were a common occurrence for spunky kids growing up during the Depression. We generally had to create our own entertainment and sticks and stones were a part of our world. So were climbing trees and fences and a host of other activities that inevitably led to cuts, bruises, and abrasions. Virtually all cuts and abrasions were first cleaned with hydrogen peroxide. Depending upon the severity of the injury, it would very often be treated with a coating of iodine. Bandages would be used only if some bleeding continued; otherwise, it was exposed to the air so that a scab would form sooner.

In growing up, one of our main antagonists was splinters. The reason for this was that we were always playing with pieces of wood, as these served as the toys we didn't have. Almost all the kids carried sticks, the favorite usually being an old broom handle. There were many games that we played with these sticks which very often resulted in splinters. Even the pieces of wood stored behind the coal stove that were used to start fires became objects to play with when toys and other distractions were not available.

All splinters, regardless of the size and depth of penetration, were removed by my mother. First, she would get a large sewing needle and sterilize it with a match. She would then begin the operation of digging out the splinter. Naturally, this would be very painful, especially to a young boy. There was a natural tendency to jerk your hand as she continued her mining operations. How often I heard these words: "Dammit, be still." She always succeeded in removing every splinter she encountered, thus saving the money that would go to a doctor. The final act after removing the splinter was to clean the area with our old standby, hydrogen peroxide.

Boils, although not too common, occasionally did make an appearance in our young lives. These could get quite large and after a time they would emit a slowly oozing stream of pus. The area around the boil would be very tender and painful to any sort of pressure.

If the boil had not broken open my mother would lance it with our old friend, the hot sewing needle. She would then apply considerable pressure on the boil, squeezing out as much pus as possible. After this procedure was finished she would then apply a dark black salve called Ichthammol Ointment. Its purpose was to draw out the pus still contained within the boil, and it did its job quite well.

After several days of this treatment all was ready for the final stage. My mother knew it was necessary to remove the "root" of the boil or it would continue to fester. To do this she would sterilize a pair of tweezers with a wooden match. She would then do a little digging with the tweezers until she got a good grip on the root and was able to draw it out. This was not so simple, nor was it pain free; however, she always managed to get the root out. Once the root was out, healing occurred in a few days. She was truly a "Dr. Mom."

For bug bites, mosquito bites, or anything else that created an itch, the most popular remedy was witch hazel, although at times rubbing alcohol would be used. For poison ivy, a dark brown laundry soap called Octagon Soap or Fels Naphtha soap was used. Shavings from a bar of soap would be mixed with warm water, then made into a paste which would then be used to coat the poison ivy.

Cod liver oil was widely used during the 1930s, and in many cases it was used in conjunction with other treatments when illness struck. It was also used in a routine manner to prevent illness from occurring, similar to how vitamins are used today. At the day nursery that I attended for so many years, the dispensing of cod liver oil was a twice-weekly ritual. Mrs. Wallace would line up all of the attending children in a row. Then, starting from one end, she would proceed down the line with her bottle of cod liver oil and a spoon. To us, the spoon seemed as big as a serving spoon. After getting your dose of cod liver oil you were carefully watched to make sure you swallowed it. And the same spoon was used by everyone!

The Dentist

A common threat, when you misbehaved, was "You behave or you're going to the dentist." This was quite a threat, as we had a real fear of doctors and dentists.

Since this was the Depression era, and to say the least our food was not of the highest quality, we were seriously deficient in some nutrients. Early in life this would show up as the cavities with which we were plagued. After the age of about nine, going to the dentist became a regular ritual on Saturday mornings. To a young boy in the 1930s and 1940s, Saturday morning was not looked upon with fondness, as this was the time we went to the dentist, and also took a bath. The only exception to this Saturday ritual of visiting the dentist occurred while you were in school. I attended school #6, the Lafayette School, in Passaic, which arranged regular trips to the dentist for those who attended the school. The only difficulty was that if you had a toothache you had to wait until the scheduled visit.

Dentistry during the 1930s was not too different from the practice of dentistry today. The primary difference was in the quality and efficiency of technology applied to the equipment that dentists used.

The procedures were pretty much the same. The real difference was in what you had to endure as a patient.

For me, a trip to a dentist was a walk from Fourth Street to Market Street. My dentist was Dr. Fortgang, and he was just a few doors down from our family doctor, Dr. Weinert.

Upon arriving at the dentist's office you would prepare for a long wait, as even back then they were rarely on time. The worst part of waiting was that you could hear the low hum of the drilling machine. Saturday mornings were usually reserved for children, so you could be sure whoever was in the chair was quite young. The hum of the drill would occasionally be interrupted by the muffled sound of a child in pain. Sitting in the waiting room and listening to those sounds put you in a frightened state even before you sat in the dentist's chair. When you were finally called in, you were already in a mild state of shock.

After seating you and adjusting the chair, the dentist would examine your chart. This finished, he would inform you of what he was going to do. It would usually go something like this: "You have a large cavity in a lower molar." So far, so good. But if he said the following words you knew you were in for a rough time: "This may hurt a little." Translation: Hang on!

When he started the drill you would tense up and compress yourself in the dentist chair, a defensive measure, your last means of protecting yourself from the dreaded drill. Once the drilling began, the first thing you became aware of was the burning odor as the slow-turning drill bit chopped away at the enamel and decay. These slow drills generated a great deal of heat in the process of grinding away the tooth. The dentist would always carefully watch your face to detect any signs of discomfort. When he saw you beginning to squirm, he knew heat was building up in the tooth from the drilling. He would then stop, and taking a water jet he would spray the hot tooth to cool it off. This procedure would usually result in a sharp pain and a wish that you were somewhere else. His last words before beginning the drilling again were, "Rinse your mouth out."

Rarely was a large cavity filled in one visit. A temporary filling would be put in and sometimes it took several visits before a permanent filling was installed. The official reason behind the two or three treatments was that it was necessary to put medicine in the tooth. The people who paid had other ideas.

So, why didn't he use Novocain? I don't know. All I can say is that dentists did not generally use Novocain for filling teeth. It was almost exclusively used for the pulling of teeth. My suspicions are that Novocain was very expensive and considering the times and the amount of money that people had to pay, just too expensive to use in a general way.

So when you heard your mother say those dreaded words, "You're going to the dentist Saturday, it's time for a checkup," you knew a several-month cycle was beginning, as checkups always found cavities.

PULASKI PARK

Pulaski Park had a wading pool for young children. On those stifling summer days it was a favorite place for the younger kids to cool off for a spell. Apartments were very hot and we did not have the luxury of air conditioners or even a fan. The only consolation a child had when in the apartment was the icebox and the block of ice it usually held. On a very hot day a piece of the ice would be chipped off and it would be given to you to suck on. Yes, it was considered a real treat—so much so that if you misbehaved you would not get a piece of ice on a hot day. This was considered a severe punishment.

This particular day was very hot. To get relief, my mother took my brother and me to the wading pool. After about an hour she left to return home, but before leaving she asked one of our neighbors to watch us and to send us home in an hour. Since no one had a wristwatch, an hour was more or less a relative period of time. Everyone had a windup clock at home and some of the older people had pocket watches but wristwatches were scarce indeed. Sometimes it seems that the main contact with other people was in asking, "What time is it?" When your mother told you to be back at a certain time your only way to know the time was to ask someone who had a pocket watch.

After about an hour our neighbor informed us it was time to go home. We reluctantly wiped ourselves dry with a towel and headed back to our apartment. The main entrance was into the kitchen and there my mother was cooking supper on a hot stove in a hot apartment. Upon hearing us enter she turned to face my brother and me and immediately noticed I had no shoes on.

"Where are your shoes?" were the first words she uttered.

I didn't realized I had forgotten my shoes at the wading pool. Before I could even reply she ordered me to go back to the pool and find my shoes. In an obvious jab at my lack of responsibility she told my brother, "You go with him so he doesn't get lost."

My brother and I left the apartment and headed for the wading pool. Upon arriving, I immediately went to the place where I had left my shoes. My shoes were not there. I circled the pool several times, examining every pair of shoes, even looking at what the other kids were wearing, hoping they might have taken mine by mistake. They were gone. Reluctantly we headed home. I knew full well what my mother's reaction would be.

I entered the apartment crying, and between sobs tried to explain to my mother that I couldn't find my shoes, that someone must have taken them by mistake. She informed me that we would go back and look for them after six o'clock, when the pool closed.

At the appointed time, we left and went back to the pool to look for my missing shoes. When we arrived there were only a few stragglers left, and we circled the pool looking for my shoes. We didn't find them, but my sharp-eyed mother noticed that several pairs of shoes had been left behind by other forgetful kids. Examining each pair carefully, she selected a pair for me to try on. After I put them on, she pressed the front to see how much room there was, then she told me to walk in them. After walking a short distance I told her that they were too big for me. Her reply was, "You'll grow into them. Besides, they're better shoes than what you had."

Joe the Watchman

During the years that we lived on Fourth Street, Pulaski Park had a caretaker. His name was Joe and he was always referred to as Joe the Watchman. Everyone who used the park had a healthy fear of Joe, as he always carried a club and did not hesitate to use it. His job was to patrol the park and keep it orderly.

For us smaller kids who still loved to climb trees, Joe was a real threat. One boy would always have to serve as a lookout, as the worst imaginable situation was to be trapped in a tree with Joe ordering you to come down. You knew you would get one good shot across your buttocks before he let you go. If you were in a tree and the lookout shouted, "Joe's coming," there would be a mad scramble to get to the ground and exit the park.

In all fairness to Joe, he always had a pocketful of hard candies and if he saw you in the park and you weren't in a tree, there was a good chance that you would receive a treat.

The older boys—that is, those around seventeen—loved to play craps. Very often the games would be held in the park. They would pick one or two young boys and give them two cents each to circle the area and inform them if Joe was approaching.

Joe's favorite targets were bums and hobos that used the park. The hobos were pretty smart and avoided confrontations with the law, so they usually stayed at the hobo camps where no one would bother them. The bums, however, were another story, as many of them were alcoholics and troublemakers, who had very little regard for social norms. Unfortunately, some local people would have their Rock & Rye in a paper bag and would drink too much, after which they would pass out or just plain fall asleep on one of the park benches. All would receive the same treatment from Joe.

One day quite early, my brother and I were walking through the park when we came upon a bench with someone sleeping on it. His worn-out shoes were placed beneath the bench and his toes were sticking out of his dirty white socks. Joe the Watchman had also seen him and as he approached the sleeping man he removed the club from his belt. He then arranged himself so as to get a good swing, and struck the sleeping man across the soles of his feet. The man flew several feet into the air and came down on the ground. Looking up and seeing Joe with the club, he quickly got up and took off running, leaving his shoes behind.

The Parade

In the fall of 1939, I witnessed a strange parade taking place in Pulaski Park. A group of Indian dancers lead the parade, all dressed in buckskin and feathers. I was completely enthralled, as although I knew about Indians I had never seen any. The Indians were followed by a small band playing music which sent thrills through me. This was followed by a group of strange-looking soldiers wearing blue uniforms instead of the brown I was familiar with. Clearly, something unusual was taking place.

As I grew older I thought about this event many times. After I discussed the parade with some local Polish people, two possible explanations eventually presented themselves. One was that it was a ceremony honoring Gen. Pulaski, who fought on the American side during the revolution of 1776-1783. He served primarily as a cavalry officer, and he was killed at the battle of Savannah, Georgia. The second explanation was that the men in uniform were Polish citizens from the Passaic area who had volunteered to go to England and continue Poland's fight against Germany. They would fight for the Polish Home Army, whose headquarters were located in London. I was told that thousands of American Poles joined the free Polish forces, including a large number from the New York-New Jersey area. The parade might have been to honor them before they left.

Winter

During the winters, Pulaski Park was usually empty except for those kids and adults going down to the tracks with their buckets looking for coal. There were also a few small hills behind the apartment houses where kids would go sled riding on a piece of cardboard.

Behind one of the apartment houses was an empty shed which served as a hangout for the older boys, as there was precious little to do in an apartment, especially in winter.

I used to spend some time in the shed. The older boys would

only tolerate you if you were useful. The shed was very cold and did not have a stove, but these Depression kids were resourceful. This is where I came in. They took me down to the tracks and showed me how to remove "waste" from a box above the wheels on each boxcar. The waste was a cottony material that filled each box and was saturated with a special oil that would slowly drip onto the wheel bearings and lubricate them. Without this waste, there would be no lubrication of the bearings.

If I were in the shed and they needed waste, I would head for the tracks. This waste made an excellent fuel when lit and served to heat the shed. It would be placed in a five gallon metal can beneath a stovepipe that exited through the roof.

Railroads at that time were heavily patrolled by railroad "dicks" (detectives) and their special prey was young boys. Any boy along the tracks would immediately take off running at the sight of a grown man. If you got over the fence you were home free, as they never went off railroad property.

I was never caught but I have heard stories about those who were. I will end by saying they did not give you a lecture and they did not take you home to your parents.

Mushrooms

Polish people, especially those who came from the old country, seem to have a penchant for wild mushrooms. Polish mushrooms that were imported from Poland were much too expensive to purchase during the Depression. I was not introduced to these world-famous mushrooms until the late 1940s, when economic conditions vastly improved as a result of World War II. These mushrooms had a flavor that could make the most bland meal delightful, which in my book was either cabbage or sauerkraut soup.

Our only source of mushrooms was Pulaski Park. My grandfather, who came from Poland, was the mushroom expert. He would wait patiently for the proper weather conditions, which usually were accompanied by heavy rains. When mushroom growing conditions were at their best he would scour the park for mushrooms. The competition was fierce as there were a great number of unemployed and older folks searching for these prizes. However, he would always come back with a few, and at times he would fill a paper bag.

My mother would then cook meals around these mushrooms. The meals were pretty much limited to cabbage, sauerkraut, and barley. It seems my grandfather would always say the same thing after finishing his meal.

"Mushrooms from Poland are better."

THE HOSPITAL

It was a bitter cold day in February, sometime around 1937. Our apartment was very cold, as the small coal stove was unable to keep it warm. There were no storm windows and frost was on the insides of the window glass. We used to get up quite early, usually about 6 A.M. After getting dressed and having breakfast, we would begin our one-mile walk to the day nursery. Here we would be cared for while my mother would continue on to work.

On this particular morning my brother, older by a year and a half, was crying as he tried to get his shoes on. My mother, seeing him crying and not yet fully dressed, became very annoyed.

"Hurry up and get dressed, dammit," she said. "I have to be at work on time." But try as he might, my brother could not get his shoes on. His crying got louder, loud enough to attract my mother's attention.

"What's the matter?" she enquired, the tone clearly indicating that she was upset at the prospect of arriving late at work. My mother had a job during the Depression and she was determined to keep it.

Between sobs, as best he could, he tried telling her how his feet hurt. Impatiently, my mother reached down and began forcing his swollen feet into his shoes. His crying increased with the additional effort she made, but somehow she managed to get his shoes on. A quick breakfast of cold white rice which had been cooked the previous day and a glass of milk, which you could either drink or pour over the rice, was that morning's fare. My brother this morning did not participate in breakfast, a rare occurrence which indicated how ill he was.

Getting fully dressed for this wintry day, we began the one-mile trek to the day nursery. As we walked, my brother's crying changed to a low moan, punctuated by an occasional sob. My mother kept goading us to walk faster, as we were behind schedule and she had to be at work on time. Mercifully, we finally arrived at the day nursery and entered, to be greeted by Mrs. Wallace, who was a nurse and managed all aspects of the day nursery, including the cooking.

Immediately noticing the condition of my brother, she began to examine him and to take his temperature. There was a concerned look on her face. She told my mother to go ahead and go to work, saying, "He'll be all right."

My mother hurriedly left for her job, so as to be at work on time. As soon as she was gone, Mrs. Wallace went to the phone to call an ambulance. Within minutes an ambulance arrived and my brother was taken to St. Mary's Hospital.

It was 5:30 P.M. before my mother returned to the day nursery. It was only then that she received the details from Mrs. Wallace. My brother was in St. Mary's Hospital and he had rheumatic fever. It seemed very strange returning home without my brother walking beside me, and my mother's behavior clearly indicated that she was very worried.

It would be several days before I was allowed to visit my brother in the hospital. What I would see there made an impression on my mind that lasts to this day. In this hospital I saw some of the victims of polio. I had heard about it and it was one of the conditions of life that adults were always talking about. But to actually see young people living inside an iron lung, paralyzed and unable to move, was a real shock to a small boy. There was a strange rhythm to this awful machine as it pumped air into lifeless lungs. I remember the large mirror that was placed above the patients' heads so that they could see the person talking to them. They were helpless inside the iron lung and one could feel the agony of the parents who visited their children in this room.

My brother was located in the children's ward, a large room with perhaps ten or more patients. There was one particular child that both fascinated and terrorized me at the same time. His head was twice the normal size, somewhat like a watermelon, and I could see that he was having trouble controlling his movements. Yet I couldn't keep my eyes off of him, despite my mother's admonishments not to stare.

This was my first and last visit to the hospital, as I informed my mother that I didn't want to go back there. She understood and never pressed the issue, perhaps realizing that it was a mistake to allow me to see this world at the tender age of six.

THE RIVER

During our stay on Fourth Street in the 1930s, we lived in a two-bedroom apartment that had no bathtub or hot water. There were five of us cramped into this small apartment: my mother with two small children plus her aged father and a younger sister. My grandfather had one bedroom all to himself. The rest of us had the other, and all four of us shared the same bed.

Due to the cramped living conditions, my brother and I seemed to have developed a penchant for more open areas, which grew into wanderlust. At every opportunity we would be exploring Pulaski Park, and as we got older the bigger kids introduced us to the Passaic River.

My mother had a real fear of the river. Every time we left the house to go to the park she would invariably say, "I don't want you going near the river." At this time, to get to the river you had to climb an iron fence and then cross the railroad tracks. A few years in the future a young girl would lose her leg to a train and a bridge would be built over the tracks allowing people access to the river.

Our first trip to the river occurred when I was about seven. My mother was working and we were being cared for by my grandfather. He took us to the park where the swings were, then promptly left us to join a group of older men who spent all afternoon talking under the shade of the large trees that were all through the park. Some older boys that we knew came by and without much effort convinced us that we should accompany them to the river for some fishing. We had no difficulty getting over the fence.

These boys apparently spent a great deal of time there, as they had their fishing poles well hidden in some high grass and brush. Now, by a fishing pole I don't mean a fishing outfit with a rod and reel. It was simply a flexible stick about six feet long with a cord, a hook, and a Popsicle stick for a dobber. The river was at high tide and they had no trouble catching small minnows they called "killies." After they let us catch a few, my brother and I decided to head back to the park.

We arrived back at the swings and my grandfather was still engaged in conversation with his cronies. They always spoke in Polish, of which I learned very little considering that most adults still used it amongst themselves. Only the swear words seemed to come naturally to me.

At this point we were hooked on fishing and the river. It wasn't long before we had our own fishing poles, which we hid in the garbage can shed behind the apartment house. In the future, whenever we were sent to the park to play, and if it didn't arouse any suspicions and we had sufficient time, we would pick up our poles and head for the river.

At this time neither my brother nor I knew how to swim. We would learn a few years later when we became old enough to attend the Passaic Boys Club.

Despite my mother's constant warning about staying away from the river, it just never occurred to us that there was any danger in going there. We didn't know anything about drowning and all the other things that could happen.

This section of river was particularly dangerous, as the bank of the river was a six-foot wall that extended alongside a church. The river here was tidal, so that when the tide was high falling off the wall would put you in very deep water. When the tide was low, it exposed mud flats along the wall. Most of the fishing was done from this wall when the tides were high.

It was on a warm summer day in July that I snuck away from the park and headed for the river. The fence was no longer an obstacle, but I always kept my eyes open looking in both directions before crossing the tracks. Arriving at the river, I was surprised to see a large group of people and an ambulance nearby. For all these people it was strangely quiet and they were all standing and looking at something going on in the middle of the group. Being curious and not being able to see, I began working my way through the group towards the center. It was then that I saw a young black boy about ten years old lying on his stomach. A fireman was kneeling over him and pressing his back. Each time the fireman pressed down, water and vomit would leave the boy's mouth. I was now thoroughly upset and quickly left the scene to return to the park.

After settling down and thinking about the scene I had just witnessed and still not fully comprehending what had happened, I decided to return home. I knew the boy had drowned but I could not relate it to the wall or understand how it could have happened.

I arrived home a little late and my mother was already busy preparing supper, which happened to be potato soup. The bread and butter were already on the table.

Her first words were, "Where the hell have you been?" In a moment of forgetfulness I said, "Ma, there was this young black kid, he drowned in the river."

Her face turned an ashen gray, then a mixture of anger and fear entered her voice.

"Were you down by the river?" she demanded to know.

Instantly I realized my error and just as quickly made an excuse.

"No, Ma, Teddy K. saw the whole thing and told me about it."

She was still suspicious but ended the matter with a warning. "I don't ever want to find out or hear that you were near that damn river. Do you understand?"

"Sure, Mom, I'll never go near the river."

"Go find your brother. It's time for supper."

Another episode occurred near the same place that winter. This had all the ingredients of a real disaster. It was a Sunday morning in February and a very cold morning it was. My brother and I were on our way to Holy Rosary Church on Wall Street. The church was located on the Passaic River next to a bridge. A stone wall formed the river bank alongside the church property, the same stone wall I fished from and where the young black boy drowned. At the back of the church was another stone wall, two feet wide and topped with concrete that often froze over in wet or snowy weather. This wall tapered down towards the wall alongside the river. On that particular morning the church wall was covered with snow and ice, making it an excellent sliding pond to a young boy. Without thinking or being aware of the danger, I climbed onto the wall and launched myself down the frozen chute towards the river. I was very fortunate, as the ice stopped two feet from the edge of the wall and a plunge into the Passaic River. My feet were partly over the edge and I was looking down at a thin layer of ice four feet below me. Getting off of the sliding pond, and without even the slightest idea of how close this came to a tragedy, I headed off to church with my brother.

It was many years later that I would recall this event and realize how truly fortunate I was. Perhaps there is a guardian angel. As a young boy growing up, I never paid much attention to what my mother said. Today I remember everything she said, especially, "Don't ever let me find out that you went near that damn river."

EASTER EGG HUNT

It was the Saturday before Easter in 1938. A few days before, my mother had informed me and my brother that there was to be an Easter egg hunt in nearby Pulaski Park. She really didn't give any details except that a lot of prizes would be awarded. During the Depression, the word "prize" was enough to excite any youngster's blood. That Saturday morning, my brother and I went to the pavilion in the park and were surprised at the large number of kids and adults that had already arrived. We were all instructed to wait at the pavilion until the signal was given and then we should go out and find the hidden Easter eggs. While waiting for the signal I noticed several large tables had been set up that were completely covered with chocolate rabbits of different sizes. We never realized that those chocolate rabbits were the prizes for bringing in the eggs that you found.

Nine o'clock finally arrived, and at the signal hundreds of kids took off in all directions to look for those precious eggs. We did not fail to notice the number of grownups also out looking for eggs with their children. My brother and I headed for the nearest bushes, but we found nothing, as they had already been cleaned out. We tried another area that looked promising, but again we found no eggs. We were really too young to compete against these experienced scavengers.

Being pretty disappointed and disillusioned over not finding any eggs, we decided to return home. It was then that an old man came over to us and asked if we had found any eggs. The disappointment was evident in our manner as we told him that we had not found even one. Reaching down into a canvas bag that was slung over his shoulder, he removed four of those prized eggs and handed two to each of us. Then, with a wide smile, he walked away, no doubt looking for other youngsters who hadn't found any eggs.

My brother and I had never eaten an egg before and we were still unaware that these could be turned in for a chocolate rabbit. We were under the impression that the eggs themselves were the great prize, and we expected them to be a real delight. We had no idea what was inside and certainly no clue as to how to go about eating one. It was at this time that we noticed a group of older boys approaching. To protect our treasure, we hid our eggs next to a tree and covered them with grass. Even at our tender ages we were wise to the actions of rough kids and how they operated. One kid had a paper bag almost filled with eggs, so we knew they were most likely pirating them from younger kids. My brother and I both got our sticks ready just in case we had to defend our precious eggs from being taken by these bullies. Almost every kid during this period of time had a favorite stick that he usually carried. We referred to them as "shinny sticks." The boys asked us if we had any eggs; we told them no. Seeing our posture and the way we were holding our shinny sticks, they decided not to press any harder and moved on.

Since my brother and I were hungry, we decided to eat one of our precious eggs. Being older, my brother had the role of opening the egg so that we could partake of our much-awaited prize. He tapped it gently on a tree; a few cracks appeared. He then hit it harder—a little too hard—and ended up with a handful of mush. Somewhat confused by this mess in the palm of his hand, we decided to sample the flavor of our treasured egg. Now, it was not bad, but it was also not anything to get excited about. In point of taste, at least to us, it was on a par with a boiled potato with a little salt added. Since we grew up in a perpetual state of hunger, we decided to eat the other eggs, as we could see no point in carrying them around.

After finishing the eggs and hearing a great deal of noise at the pavilion, we decided to go over and investigate. Arriving at the pavilion, we noticed that the noise was being generated by very happy kids exchanging the eggs that they found for chocolate rabbits. The size of the rabbit depended upon the number of eggs. The four eggs that we had consumed were equal to a foot-high chocolate rabbit. My brother, being older and more outspoken, tried to explain to one of the officials that we ate our eggs because we didn't know they could be turned in for chocolate rabbits. He offered to get the eggshells to prove his case.

Needless to say, we never got even a little piece of chocolate. We watched the kids breaking off and eating pieces of chocolate from their rabbits and, somewhat heartbroken, left the park to return home.

Arriving home, we entered the kitchen where our mother was busy making our lunch, which happened to be cabbage soup. The bread and butter were already on the table.

"Ma," I asked, "how come we never get to eat eggs?"

To this day, I remember her reply. "They're too expensive. We can't afford eggs, they want fifteen cents for a dozen."

THE DETECTIVE

ne friend of our family—actually, his wife and my mother's sister were best friends—would always intrigue us with his stories. Whenever there was a get-together, most of the adults would listen for hours as Ed related his experiences as a detective for a nearby city. Since most of the listeners were ordinary factory workers, they had little to say that could compete with Ed's stories.

Ed was also an avid fisherman, and his fishing stories were a big hit amongst those factory workers, who had precious little opportunity to enjoy themselves. Ed was almost like a hero to them, as he added a dimension to their lives which in many ways gave them hope of a better future.

It was after one of Ed's exciting fishing stories that he turned to me and said, "William, how would you like to go bass fishing with me next Sunday?"

I turned to my mother with a pleading look on my face and was taken by surprise when she told Ed it would be all right for me to go. Since this was the Depression, and after hearing Ed's stories of his catches, I'm sure she was counting on us to bring home some fish.

At this point I informed Ed that I did not own a fishing pole. He said that this was not a problem, as he would buy me a complete outfit.

I was so excited that evening that I had trouble sleeping. So this is what happiness is like! For the rest of the week, my thoughts were dominated by this approaching adventure and I had all kinds of visions about the big bass that we would catch.

Sunday morning finally arrived, and after a breakfast of white rice and milk I waited patiently by the window for Ed to show up. A short time later he pulled up in front of our apartment house in his Dodge and proceeded to our apartment. My mother answered the door when he knocked and Ed strode into the kitchen. Upon seeing me standing there, his first words were, "Are you ready to go?" I nodded yes, and after a few words with my mother we left for our great fishing adventure.

Ed drove north and informed me that our destination was the Wanaque Reservoir. He parked on a dirt road and from this location I couldn't even see a lake. Then he went to the car trunk and removed my new fishing pole. It was a bamboo pole, all set up with a line and a red-and-white dobber, or float.

Leaving the car, we crossed the road, and I could not fail to notice the "No Trespassing" signs indicating reservoir property. There was a hole in the fence which we went through, and suddenly we found ourselves in a dense pine forest which blocked out the sun and made it very dark beneath the canopy. Ed told me to stay close to him as we made our way towards the lake, which I could now see. As I carried my new fishing pole the red-and-white dobber bounced in rhythm with each step I took.

All of a sudden, Ed stopped, and using his hand he motioned for me to be still. He was listening and looking intently towards a dark area covered with pine needles and broken branches. I began looking in the same direction and saw nothing of interest, but as my eyes began to adjust to the darkness I could now make out a clump.

"There he is," whispered Ed, pointing towards the clump about twenty feet away. "Hand me your pole."

I handed Ed my pole and asked him what the thing was.

"It's a big rattlesnake," he replied.

I watched as Ed approached the snake, which I could now clearly make out as the snake moved into a full coil and raised his head. As

Ed began stabbing it with my pole, the snake began to rattle furiously. This was followed by other snakes also making rattling sounds. Being so intent on the one rattlesnake, he had walked right into the middle of a half dozen. Suddenly realizing his predicament, Ed panicked and, dropping my new pole, red-and-white dobber and all, quickly ran from the area back to where I was standing.

Taking me by the hand he said, "Let's get the hell out of here."

"What about my pole?" I asked.

"Forget about it. I'll get you another."

With tears in my eyes, I looked back at my pole with the red-and-white dobber lying on the ground as I was being led back towards the car.

Ed didn't say a word about the snake or my pole on the drive home. He seemed like a different person after his encounter with the snakes. Upon arriving at our apartment house he took me upstairs and engaged in a private conversation with my mother. I had no idea what was discussed, but Ed left soon after. It was all very strange, as my mother never even asked me about our fishing trip or why we were back so soon. Or why we didn't have any fish.

I waited a long time for Ed to show up with a new pole for me— but he never did. And even though I saw Ed afterwards, he never mentioned either my fishing pole or the encounter with the rattlesnakes.

Later on in life I would see this incident in a different perspective. I would always be reminded of this event whenever I saw that famous flag used during the Revolutionary War. You know—the one with the coiled rattlesnake and the slogan "Don't Tread on Me."

THE DUNDEE CANAL

It was February of 1938, around the time of my seventh birthday. I was feeling ill that day and did not attend school. I was being watched over by my grandfather. My mother had gone to work and my brother, older by a year and a half, went off to school by himself. Usually we went together. These were difficult times as the Depression was in full swing and my mother was having a hard time raising two young boys by herself.

My mother returned home from work at 5:30 P.M. I was lying in bed when she walked into my room. Her first question was, "How do you feel?"

"I feel okay," I replied. This reply was conditioned on past experience, as a reply that you didn't feel well was usually followed by a dose of cod liver oil.

Her second question was, "Where's your brother?"

"I don't know, Ma," I said. "He hasn't come home from school yet."

"He should have come home a long time ago," she responded. A worried look began to cloud her face.

She began to busy herself preparing supper. This was usually a simple task, as the foods we ate were mostly soups and bread and butter. However, this evening she decided to make pancakes. First she made dough, and then using a rolling pin made pancakes about the size of a plate. They would then be fried in lard until brown. She would make a filling by frying sauerkraut in lard (or sometimes bacon fat, when that was available) and bringing it to life with some seasoning. The filling would then be placed into the pancake and rolled up. We always rated this a super meal, as the alternative was cabbage soup, beet soup, or perhaps potato soup. (Occasionally we would have chicken feet soup, made from chicken feet given to my mother by sympathetic butchers who understood her dire situation.)

My mother was occupied cooking when my brother walked into the kitchen crying and soaking wet. It being February, he was also almost frozen.

My mother's first words were, "Where the hell have you been?" Her second observation was, "Goddammit, how did you get so wet?"

My mother usually swore in Polish so as not to corrupt her two fine sons.

My brother, standing there totally wet and shivering, informed my mother through chattering teeth that after school he had been playing on the Dundee Canal and had fallen through the ice. He also told her that he had been afraid to come home, but after it turned dark he decided he'd better.

"Goddammit," she said in Polish. "I told you never to go near the canal, now look at you. Just look at your clothes."

Somehow it seemed never to have occurred to her how fortunate she was that her son was alive.

"Get your clothes off and go right to bed. No supper for you."

Now, this may not seem like much of a punishment, but let me tell you, missing a meal was a big time punishment to us. And this was extra hard on my brother, as he had a great love for those sauerkraut pancakes.

My brother crawled into bed with me and we pulled the feather-filled covering up to our necks to keep warm. The entire apartment was heated by a small coal stove and in the winter the temperature ranged from 40 to 60 degrees.

While my brother and I were conversing in bed he somehow convinced me to ask my mother if I could have another pancake.

I agreed. "Ma, I'm still hungry," I called out. "Can I have another pancake?"

All right," she replied, "but you eat it in bed as I don't want you walking around in the cold and getting sicker."

She brought the pancake into the bedroom and as I sat up she placed the plate in front of me and left the room. My brother had faked that he was sleeping and as soon as she left he reached over and took the pancake.

You should have see his face when my mother re-entered the bedroom and saw him with my pancake.

She left the room and quickly returned carrying a flat stick which was part of the kindling wood used to start the coal fires. She quickly pulled back the covers, grabbed my brother, rolled him over, and began wacking him on the rear end with the wooden slat. He began hollering and screaming way out of proportion to the damage that the little stick could have produced. It was when the blood began to show through his underwear and run down his legs that my mother decided to take a closer look. That was when she discovered that the innocent slat of wood contained a nail that protruded about an inch and a half. His rear end had four nail punctures.

It took a wipe down with some hydrogen peroxide and the promise of a sauerkraut pancake to make my brother's world well again.

Before retiring for the evening, usually after listening to Amos 'n' Andy, my mother would always fill the coal stove so that we could survive until morning. Since my brother's shoes were completely soaked, she decided to put them into the oven to dry out. The next morning, they resembled two dried out watermelon rinds.

Try as they might, they could not get my brother's feet into those shoes. Fortunately, it was a Saturday and the local shoemaker was open. His solution was to rub them with neatsfoot oil and bend them until they became pliable. He charged my mother twenty-five cents.

And so ended another episode during the Great Depression and we survived for another day. My brother is now 73 and he still loves those sauerkraut pancakes.

THE ICE MAN

It was one of those hot, humid days when even the tar on the roads becomes very soft. Even on days such as this, children could always be found playing outside, as the apartments without air conditioning or fans were almost unbearable.

In our area was an iceman who worked very hard delivering cakes of ice to the people who had iceboxes, which was everyone at this time. One of our pastimes, especially when it was very hot, was to follow him and his wagon as he was making deliveries of ice.

Occasionally, he would take his ice pick and chip off pieces of ice for us to suck on. On a day such as this one, this was a first-class treat.

We were sitting in the shade of a tree sucking on our pieces of ice when the iceman's horse, which was used to pull the ice wagon, suddenly fell over. We just watched as the horse lay there on the hot road. A group of bystanders soon gathered around the horse. It wasn't long before the ice man returned to find his horse lying in the road. Picking up the horse's head a little, he began talking to him as if it were his child. He then tried coaxing the horse to get back on his feet, but even though the horse made efforts to get up he would always fall back onto the road, breathing heavily.

The iceman gave up and stood there talking to some spectators about the horse. Apparently he was very much attached to the horse as it had been pulling his ice wagon for many years. He was lamenting the fact that without a horse he could not deliver ice, and how was he going to support his family as he couldn't afford to buy another.

It wasn't long before a motorcycle cop pulled up. He located the iceman, and a discussion began between them. After a few minutes, the cop removed his revolver from his holster and approached the horse. He ordered us away from the horse and then, taking aim, shot the horse in the head. There was a violent thrashing, then the horse lay still.

As a very young boy, I was mesmerized by the entire scene and will never forget the blood flowing from the horse's head into the gutter. The last thing I saw was the iceman crying over his dead horse, all the while holding its head and stroking it.

THE PALACE

The Palace Theater on Market Street was the main source of entertainment for young and old alike during the Depression. For the sum of five or ten cents you could watch two movies, two cartoons, a newsreel, and coming attractions. No one ever seemed to care what was playing; the thrill was in just being able to go to the movies.

A very special night for many people was Wednesday night, for this was the night when you received a free dish on attendance. If you went every Wednesday over a period of time, you would eventually have a complete set of dishes. There was no extra charge for admittance on this night and the lure of a free dish brought in many customers.

One family that lived nearby had six children ranging in age from six to fourteen. Using the Palace Theater, the parents devised a way to be free of the children and get a much-needed break during this stressful time. On Sunday, Mrs. Posluszny would make a lunch that would be enough for her six children, who would then leave for Market Street and the Palace to make the one o'clock movie. After they watched the complete program, Stanley, who was the oldest, would parcel out the food to his younger brothers and sisters. This would be eaten in the theater as they prepared to watch the entire program over again. They would return home at about 9:30 P.M.

My mother rarely went to the movies. My brother and I, like most of the kids, went on a pretty regular basis. I suspect it was the adults' way of getting a break from their kids and at the same time knowing where they were. On one particular day my mother joined us and took us to the Palace. When we went alone we were given the exact amount for admittance and no more. However, since my mother was there we were hoping that she might buy us a piece of candy—it only cost a penny.

I asked my mother what movie we were going to see, and she replied "I don't know what's playing. Whatever is playing is good enough." And it really didn't matter. When you decided to go to the movies you saw whatever the theater was showing. There were other "movie houses" besides the Palace. On Monroe Street was the Capital. The Montauk was on Main Street with the Playhouse. Also located uptown was the Lincoln. We never knew what was playing in these other theatres, and if we ever went uptown to take in a movie we would walk to every movie house to see what was playing before deciding which one to attend. Going to the movies in the 1930s was a big deal.

Just before we reached the theater, we saw a group of very strangely dressed men, women, and children congregating before a store and partially blocking the sidewalk. They were speaking loudly in a language I did not understand. What made them stand out so much to me was the color and brightness of their clothes. Compared to the drab clothes I was used to seeing, they looked like well-decorated Christmas trees. Before we got to them my mother took our hands and we crossed the street. Pointing to them, I asked my mother, "Ma, look at how those people are dressed. Where are they from?"

"Damn gypsies! They should ship them back to Europe where they came from. They're nothing but a bunch of thieves. You stay the hell away from them."

"Why, Ma?"

"My father told me that in Europe they steal young children and turn them into gypsies. Then they use the children to beg for money and to steal, because they're small and they can crawl into small places and through windows. And if one of them gets caught, the gypsies don't care. They just move on and steal more kids."

Somehow, that didn't seem dangerous to me, yet I held my mother's hand tighter as we crossed the street to avoid them.

A short time later, I was playing with some other kids, and when we got bored I suggested we sneak down to Market Street and see if we could locate some gypsies. One of the boys absolutely refused to go, reciting some grisly stories his parents from Poland had told him. After listening to him for a while, we decided to find some other way to amuse ourselves.

Oh, the movie we saw that day was "The Man They Couldn't Hang." As my mother said, "It doesn't matter what's playing. It's a movie."

CHRISTMAS IN THE 1930S

Christmas evokes pleasant memories of times gone by: the presents, the table of traditional foods a constant reminder of our Polish heritage, but most of all the entire family getting together. This solidarity of family was in its own way a security blanket for the youngsters growing up during that era.

But one lingering memory from those difficult times we now call the Great Depression is the constant disappointment of opening Christmas presents and never getting anything a kid would desire. The answer was obvious, though not to young children: times were tough, this was a struggle for survival, and we were growing up in a no-nonsense world that had little patience for trivial desires. In our minds as we opened the boxes would be pictures of toys, perhaps even a small train set; as we got older we imagined one of the boxes might hold a baseball glove or a few new comic books. On my mother's mind was food, clothing, and rent money. We would all receive something for Christmas but we learned at an early age not to expect anything that was not useful for our survival.

How those wrapped packages beneath the tree would stir the imagination. But the reality was that the box which looked like it might hold a football held a large winter sweater. The other box that must surely hold a baseball glove held a shirt and scarf. Soon you settled back into the old routine and mechanically opened your presents, knowing that there would be no surprises. The last box you received contained the standard Christmas gift until you were about eighteen: three pairs of underwear and three pairs of socks.

After a few years, the Christmases would come and go but no longer would our desires for toys and such dominate our imagination. We had been baptized into the world of the practical, and our presents would always be the necessary items that we would need during the year. A few times my mother did somehow get hold of a few used toys, which she carefully wrapped and placed under the Christmas tree—if we had one. We didn't know they were used and it really didn't matter; it was the excitement of opening a present and possibly having a dream come true.

A present that sticks out in my memory was the one my grandfather received every year. It was a large can of Prince Albert tobacco and it would always be accompanied by a box of wooden matches and pipe cleaners. This would constitute three separate presents. These were useful and practical, and they would be his presents from mother until the day he died. As we began to prosper during the 1940s, a bottle of Rock & Rye whiskey would be added. But even though the Depression was over by the 1940s and everyone was fully employed during World War II, it would continue to dominate the psychology of most people for years to come. In fact, fifty years later my mother's life would continue to be dominated by the effects of the Depression. Although the era might become distant garbled memories, it would continue to live within us, its effects artfully disguised under the terminology of "being practical."

One year we had a particularly bleak Christmas and we received no toys at all. Shortly after Christmas my brother and I walked over to Market Street, where all the stores were located. The Woolworth store, which was commonly called the five-and-dime store, was our favorite, as it had such a wide variety of items to look at. We spent most of the time there looking at toys, especially the toy lead soldiers. On the way home this day, in front of the bowling alley on Market Street, my brother removed a small, shiny car from his coat pocket and showed it to me. After a few questions from me he finally admitted that he had taken it from Woolworth's.

When we arrived home, my mother asked us where we had been. I told her that we had been on Market Street and that my brother had taken a toy from the five-and-dime. She became livid, as she had thought we were going to the library next to the Passaic Boys Club on Third Street. Turning to my brother, she demanded the toy. He was already crying when he handed it to her. She then put on her winter coat and, taking him by the hand, led him towards the door which led to the hallway. Before leaving, she turned to me with an angry look on her face and issued a stern warning: "You stay right here until I get back."

Half an hour later they retuned. My brother was still in tears. Her final words to him were, "Go to your room and stay there. No supper for you tonight." It may not seem like much of a punishment to miss supper, but in those days when there were no snacks and supper was usually bread and soup, it was a long time until breakfast.

My brother would later reveal to me what happened—that is, after he got over my squealing on him. He had been led back to the store by my mother, who asked to see the manager. She explained to him about the stolen toy. My brother was then required to hand it back and to promise never to steal again.

Another Christmas that sticks out in my mind occurred in either 1935 or 1936. This particular year we had no Christmas tree and very few presents. However, we did have a make-believe tree which was carefully decorated with some round balls, strings of popcorn, and a few pieces of tinsel salvaged from some previous Christmas in more prosperous times. There was at the bottom a thick layer of white cotton to represent snow. Our Christmas tree that year was a nicely decorated old Singer sewing machine. The popcorn hanging from the strings was a tempting target for two little boys who were always hungry and would eat almost anything. It was difficult to refrain from snatching an occasional piece of popcorn, but we didn't take too much as mother would notice and we always were careful not to upset mother.

Finally it was time for our traditional meal. Our diet during this period was really quite bland, dinner consisting of mainly bread and soups of various kinds while breakfast was a pretty consistent diet of white rice and milk. It was only at the day nursery that my brother and I would receive a nutritious meal, and this only during the week. So for us any food that varied from our usual fare was welcome. This day we would have pierogi, kielbasa (a real treat, as we rarely had meat) and the main dish, which would be sauerkraut soup with Polish mushrooms and chickpeas. This would be our Christmas feast, and we could not imagine a better meal. The drawback was that we would not eat like this again until next Christmas.

The day nursery was a home away from home for my brother and me from 1931 to 1939. Mrs. Wallace, who ran the establishment, was in many ways our surrogate mother. One year Mrs. Wallace convinced my mother to let me participate in a Christmas play to be held at the nursery on an evening just before Christmas. She gave my mother a script that I was supposed to memorize for the play.

Several weeks before the play my rehearsals with my mother began. I had to memorize about a page, which was to serve as an introduction to a scene in the play. Every evening around seven, before going to bed, I recited to my mother what I remembered. Several days before the play I had it completely memorized and had no difficulty reciting the entire page for my mother.

The night of the Christmas play finally arrived and my mother, my brother, and I began the walk from Fourth Street to the day nursery. After everyone was settled in, the play began, and since I was to introduce the opening scene I was the first one on the stage. Coming from behind a makeshift curtain I stood before the audience. My mother was in the front row and beaming as I stood before the group and began reciting what I had practiced so hard for. The first three or four sentences went very well, then suddenly I stopped. I could not remember any more of the script. I stood there fumbling around for the missing words for what seemed an eternity, then in a very agitated state I looked at my mother and called out, "Ma, what comes next?" I'll never forget the uproar of laughter when my mother replied, "I can't remember."

I was removed from the stage and an older kid was sent out to read from the script.

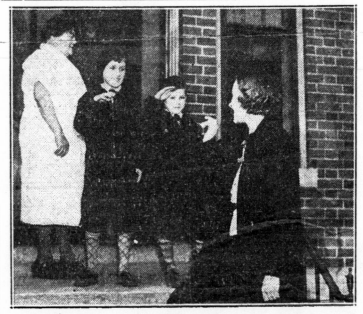

Bidding Good-Bye at Day Nursery

MRS. ARNOLD says good-bye at Nursery steps to her Joe and Billy.

From the Passaic Herald-News

How Day Nursery Cares for Their Children While Working Mothers Are Earning Living

MRS. MARY ARNOLD leaves her boys, Paul and William, at Passaic Day Nursery, to go to her job at the switchboard in the McLean Mills, earning her own livelihood and their upkeep.

From the Passaic Herald-News

FOOD

During the Depression, we ate to survive, and whatever made it to the table was consumed. There was no eating between meals, as there was nothing to eat. To us there were no such things as snacks. There never was any fruit on the table. There were no boxes of pretzels or potato chips, no raisins, nuts or for that matter anything to eat at all except what was available at mealtime. You never went to the icebox for something to eat, as whatever you found was most likely for your next meal. Come to think of it, all I ever remember seeing in the icebox was milk, butter, and some fresh vegetables. The foods that dominated our menu were mainly soups and bread and butter. If money was in short supply (which was very often), lard would be substituted for butter.

Food shopping in the 1930s wasn't a complicated process. Each street or block had its own grocery store and this was the store you usually went to. You didn't go to any other store; that is, unless you had cash. Most groceries would be purchased on credit and when pay day arrived you settled your bill; that is, if you had a payday.

The apartment house we lived in also had a grocery store. The owner of the apartment house and store was Mr. Glazer. I remember my mother sending me downstairs to get Jewish rolls. I believe they were called Jewish rolls because most of the grocery stores and bakeries were owned by Jewish people. Today we call these rolls hard rolls. Occasionally my mother would send me to Goodman's Bakery, which was located on Third Street, to pick up some fresh bread. Before I left, my mother would always warn me, "Don't you eat any." Returning home I would always open the bag and put my nose inside just to smell the odor of freshly baked bread. I never ate any. My mother was not to be trifled with.

Mr. Glazer was very kind to my mother and he always helped her out, as he knew the difficult time she was having raising two children during the Depression. We were always the recipient of the almost-stale Jewish rolls and bread. To us they were a real treat and when covered with a layer of butter and sprinkled with sugar would be our version of cake. If the rolls were very hard we would dip them in coffee containing milk and sugar.

One of my chores as a little boy was to go downstairs to our landlord's store to pick up items that my mother needed. Mr. Glazer would always write down whatever I needed in a book, using an indelible pencil. He extended credit to all of his customers and would generally be reimbursed on payday—if there was one.

One thing that always attracted my attention in his store was the constant buzzing of the flies that were stuck to the glued paper strips hanging from the ceiling. There was always a low hum from their frantic efforts to free themselves from the glue. One time, when Mr. Glazer was busy in the back room, I took a bench and placed it beneath one of the flypaper strips. In a moment of curiosity, or perhaps compassion, I tried to free one of the flies stuck onto the glue. Needless to say, my good intentions went awry when in the process of removal the fly's feet remained behind. I often think of this as my first lesson in biology.

Soup was to our diet what the infantry is to the military. We never asked "What's for supper?" Rather, the question would be "What kind of soup are we having for supper?" All soups would be accompanied by a plentiful supply of bread and butter. During the winter, however, the butter and milk would be stored outside on the fire escape. This way you saved a few nickels by not having to buy ice for the icebox. Trying to apply very cold butter to a slice of white bread usually resulted in the bread being torn apart, and what was left of the slice would hold a big glob of butter on one edge. But no matter, it would end up being dipped into the soup

There were four main soups that were a constant reminder that we were in a depression. Cabbage soup rated one star. It was the lowest on the soup rating scale. My mother would try all kinds of spices, but no matter what, it always ended up being cabbage soup. The only time the soup came to life was when my grandfather would bring home some mushrooms he had collected in Pulaski Park. Yet, despite my non-attachment for cabbage soup, my bowl was always empty, and you never heard the words "I don't like cabbage soup.'

Beet soup rated one star or two stars, depending upon the season of the year. When beets were fresh, they made an excellent soup which with a few spices rated two stars, especially if you had fresh bread from Goodman's Bakery. If you had to use canned beets (as we mostly did), it rated one star and fit into the same category as cabbage soup. Our general attitude towards cabbage soup or beet soup was that it was something that you dipped a piece of bread and butter into. Meanwhile you waited for tomorrow, when you knew there would be potato soup.

Potato soup was considered one of the better soups, perhaps because potatoes were never taken from a can (like beets) but were always fresh. Potatoes were always somewhat cheap, which meant that you had more potatoes and less water when making the soup. Garlic and onions plus peppercorns would be added to give some zest to the soup. My mother would always peel the potato before making the soup. She would save the potato peels for a poor family in the next door apartment house. I'm sure they made potato peel soup. With today's knowledge of vitamins we now know that we would have been better off if we had the potato peel soup, as most of the nutrients in the potato are just beneath the peel.

When there was leftover potato soup, which was quite rare, the pieces of potato would be removed from the soup and then mashed. This would be tomorrow's breakfast, and what a delight it was when the mashed potatoes were fried in lard then covered with buttermilk.

Potato soup rated three stars.

The favorite of almost everyone was chicken feet soup. Now, this was not chicken leg soup. This was the feet, the part with the toes and nails. There was no meat on the feet, only gelatin—but what a flavor.

To prepare the feet, my mother would begin by washing them off, then boiling them for an hour or two. She would then pull off the nails and allow the feet to cool. After they cooled she would peel off the scaly skin. Then what we considered a feast would begin. Celery, carrots, and onions, when in season, would be added to the broth to make chicken feet soup. And, if we were really in luck, she would find some rice to add to the soup. Of course, she would add peppercorns.

How well I remember the chicken feet cooking, and how on cold winter days the windows would steam up. Always the toenails would be sticking out from the top of the pot as the feet floated to the surface of the soup.

Sometimes while my mother was busy preparing the meal she would give us a couple of chicken feet to play with. If you pulled on the tendons at the top, the feet responded by opening and closing. This would usually occupy us for a while, or at least until supper was ready. Chicken feet soup: four stars.

There was another kind of chicken soup that we had occasionally. On some very special event my mother would cook a whole chicken. And after everyone had eaten, the bones would be collected from everyone's plate. These bones would then be boiled for several hours to make chicken bone soup. There was very little meat left on the bones before being boiled; however, it was very tasty and with the usual bread and butter made a very acceptable meal.

There was another kind of soup that we ate in a pinch. It also served as breakfast, especially in the winter when bread was not available. This would consist of boiled white rice and milk. If you were lucky, there might be some sugar in the bowl. Rating? Zero stars.

Although back then in the Depression I would eat almost anything, one food I simply could not tolerate was lima beans. The only place I was ever served these beans was at the day nursery where my mother dropped off my brother and me on her way to work. They had a strict rule: if it's on your plate, you eat it. Try as I might, I couldn't eat those damn beans. So for me, the question became how to get rid of them.

Once, I put them in my handkerchief with the idea of throwing them away when I went outside. However, they got crushed in my pocket and since we changed our pants only once a week, on Saturdays, this didn't go over too well with my mother. One time she said, "What is this damn stuff in your clothes?" I didn't dare tell her, and just shrugged my shoulders.

Another solution was to throw them, one at a time, under the table, always trying to get them near some other boys so as not to have anyone focus on me as the culprit. This worked for a while, until the caretakers realized it was me. Then they threatened me with the ultimate punishment if I didn't eat my lima beans. Since the punishment consisted of a tablespoon of cod liver oil, I realized I had to find a new way of dealing with these obnoxious beans. I finally arrived at a partial solution by crushing them and then mixing them in with mashed potatoes or anything else that was suitable. One boy offered to eat my lima beans for a penny. Rarely having a penny, we settled on five marbles instead. Many years later I would find out that he became a businessman.

When I was about six years old, I was sent to a camp in northern New Jersey called Camp Good Hope. Its purpose was to give poor kids a two-week vacation and help them along with some decent food. It was here that I had an encounter with a food I had never seen before. It was breakfast and we were all served with prepared plates. Now, I was familiar with pancakes, which I ate quite readily, although these were quite different from my mother's, which were fried in lard. However, the plate also held four or five strips that were blackened and curled up and I had no idea if they were animal, vegetable, or mineral. I refused to eat them or even try. Therefore, I was required to sit there until the next meal was served, which was probably about 11:30 A.M. Finally they removed the plate with a brief lecture on how good bacon was for you. It was years later when my mother's financial condition improved that she began substituting bacon fat for lard.

During the Depression, my brother and I participated in a ritual every few weeks or whenever my mother ran out of lard. As part of the ritual, my brother and I were required to sit patiently for several hours and not make a nuisance of ourselves. At the end of this time, if all went well, we would receive our rewards.

The ritual began with a piece of fatback, usually about eight inches by eight inches and about two inches thick. The reason it is called fatback is that it is cut from the back of a pig and usually consists of just two ingredients, skin and fat. My mother would cook the fatback in a large frying pan until it melted, which usually took several hours. She would then pour the fat into a can where it would eventually re-harden. This was now called lard and was a basic staple in our diets. In lean times it served as butter and was used in all cooking, including frying many of the vegetables before they entered the soup pot. One of the favorite foods we ate was sauerkraut fried in lard with some salt and pepper and served rolled up in large pancakes, which were also fried in lard.

You may wonder why we would hang around the kitchen waiting for this fatback to be cooked down into lard. The answer is quite simple but very revealing about how difficult times were for some people during the Depression. We were protein starved, as my mother's income did not allow for the luxury of eating meat or eggs, and after all the fat was cooked off the piece of skin, what was left was pure protein. My mother would cut the well-cooked skin in half and my brother and I would each receive a piece. Sometimes, depending on our behavior, she would cut it so it was not evenly divided and the larger section would serve as a reward. To us this was better than Christmas, as we usually only got underwear and socks, no toys.

If you wish to get an idea of what the skin was like, take a leather belt, cover it with Crisco, and fry it for a couple of hours. Now you will know what it was like. You will also know why footballs are made out of pigskin. But to our protein-starved bodies it was a real treat.

Today, I no longer eat the meals that were common fare back in the 1930s and 1940s. Gone is the cabbage soup, beet soup, potato soup, and chicken feet soup. No more white bread, Jewish rolls, and lard. Goodbye rolled-up pancakes with fried sauerkraut, and especially so-long to lima beans.

All of the above were primarily foods of the 1930s. Foods of the 1940s were somewhat better, as World War II was taking place and many homes now had two incomes. It was in 1940 that my mother was able to remarry, after raising two boys alone during the Depression. Most of the traditional foods of the 1940s are also rarely eaten now, except during Polish celebrations of Easter and Christmas.

At the top of the list were kielbasa, or polish sausage, and pierogi, which are small pancakes stuffed with potatoes, pot cheese, or sauerkraut. They were usually boiled, then fried in butter and served with sour cream. We also ate a sausage called kishka, which was a combination of pig's blood and buckwheat groats. It was a real delight when fried in butter. The only soup—or stew, depending on how you make it—that is still eaten on a regular basis is made of pork ribs, barley, and the ever-present sauerkraut, and it makes an excellent meal in the wintertime, especially when served with a dark rye bread and butter.

You may wonder how we ever survived on this diet, but in many ways we ate a more healthful diet than people do today. The only area that we were really deprived in was fresh fruits and vegetables, which today are available all year around. These were available to us only in the summer and fall; the rest of the year we relied upon canned vegetables. During the 1930s and 1940s, there were no supermarkets and very few refrigerators. We still kept what little food we had in an icebox.

Today, the old days are but distant memories and at times I need to revitalize the process of recalling the conditions under which I grew up. For this, I have a very special food that serves as the catalyst for restoring old memories that are fading into oblivion.

The main ingredient, if you can locate some, is head cheese, which is actually not a cheese, but a cold cut made from the remnants that are removed from a pig's head. In fact, whenever I travel I almost always eat this meal on the road. When traveling I always try to avoid restaurants, as a poorly prepared meal can have undesirable consequences—you know what I mean. There is no way that this meal can ever make you sick. Quite the contrary: if you are sick, it could make you well. The ingredients are simple: chopped up head cheese, chopped up raw onion, chopped up garlic, and lastly, apple cider vinegar. Don't forget the salt and pepper.

Not too many years ago while shopping in the supermarket, I wandered down an aisle I seldom frequent. It was loaded with pretzels, potato chips, nacho chips, and all kind of dead organic material brought back to temporary life by the use of fat and flavors. It was here that a strange looking bag caught my attention. Covering the bag in large gold letters were the words "Pork Rinds." This was the same stuff that as a kid I would sit waiting hours for, and now here it was being sold in supermarkets. All of the memories, tastes, and smells began to flood my mind as I fondled the package. Without thinking, and driven by the desire to recapture those times, I placed ten bags of pork rinds in my shopping cart.

While I drove home, my mind was constantly rehashing those early days in my childhood. On arriving at home, I put away all of my purchases except for the ten bags of pork rinds. I made a trip to the refrigerator for a cold bottle of Beck's dark beer. All was now ready for the grand moment, the opening of a bag of pork rinds.

Using a knife, I carefully cut open the top of the bag. Then I lowered my nose to the opening and inhaled deeply to capture the odor of freshly-cooked fatback. No odor came forth. I repeated the process with an even deeper inhalation. Still nothing came from the bag to reward my imagination. Deeply disappointed, I decided to examine the contents of the bag to unravel the mystery of these strange pork rinds that had no odor. Reaching in, I removed a few and began to look them over. I thought perhaps the company that manufactured them had made a mistake, as they resembled pine bark nuggets which had spent too much time in a microwave oven. A taste test was now necessary to justify my worst suspicions. Against my better judgment, I placed one in my mouth. It had virtually no taste and I kept it in my mouth longer than I should have, giving it every opportunity to redeem itself. When it failed the taste test I headed for the sink to give it a proper burial.

So much for my adventure into recapturing the pleasures of my early years in the Great Depression.

P.S. Having grown up in an era when waste did not exist, I just could not see throwing out those pork rinds. So I donated them to the local food pantry. I'm sure someone with no memory like mine was glad to have those bags of pork rinds.

DESSERT

During the Great Depression, desserts were unheard of unless you attended some special social function. It was never standard practice to have a dessert after supper, as it seems to be today.

It was 1937 and I was six years old. It was the day of my birthday, and just before supper, which was cabbage soup and bread and butter, my mother asked me what I would like for my birthday. Without a moment's hesitation I replied, "A glass of orange soda."

Notice I did not ask for a bicycle or a game or a baseball glove. Just a glass of orange soda. My mother removed a nickel from her purse and told me to go downstairs to Mr. Glazer's store to buy a large bottle of orange soda. I remember how happy I was with this wonderful birthday treat.

My brother recently came to visit, and the subject of desserts came up as we were discussing Depression foods. When I commented on how we never had desserts he began to laugh.

"What's so funny?" I asked.

"Bill, we often had dessert, don't you remember?'"

"No," I replied, "enlighten me."

"Don't you remember sometimes after supper, when Mom wanted to reward us, she would bring out the sugar bowl and two toothpicks. We would lick the toothpick and then dip it into the sugar bowl—that was dessert."

This treat once triggered in my brain a plan to cure my sugar deficiency. I deduced that the best way to get sweets was to purchase my own, so I had to think in terms of getting money, which was in very short supply during the Depression.

I had an idea, and it began with asking my mother for a penny. I remember her response: "Whaddya think, I'm made of money? Besides, what do you need it for?" I outlined my capitalist scheme to her, telling her how I would invest this penny and perhaps make a few dollars.

While handing me a penny from her change purse, she said, "What you're doing is crazy, but be careful you don't get hit by a car."

Step one was accomplished. Step two was a trip to the candy store to purchase a penny's worth of bubblegum. Next was a trip to Pulaski Park to find a five-foot-long stick that was straight. While looking for the stick I was furiously chewing the gum, preparing it for its job when the time was right.

All was ready as I walked towards Market Street, where all the shopping was done and where many people just walked around, looking in windows at things they couldn't afford.

There it was, my first challenge: the grate over the belowground storm drain.

While lying flat on the sidewalk, I tried peering down through the grates to see if I could spot any change that had fallen into the sewer pipe. Not being able to see too well, I decided to lie in the gutter for a better look. I couldn't see anything down there but all the rubbish, so I used my stick to push it around. Suddenly, there it was, a shiny new dime, defying me to remove it from its resting place and to hoist it the four feet needed to clear the grate.

My heart was pounding as I placed the gum carefully on the end of the stick. I carefully lowered the stick until the gum came in contact with the dime. I then gently pushed to embed the coin in the gum. It took three tries to finally lift the dime from the sewer. I felt like I had just raised the Titanic.

It was then that I noticed that a crowd of people had gathered around me and were watching. Damn, I thought, my secret's out. Two hours, twelve sewer pipes, and four pieces of gum later, I had a net gain of thirty-eight cents. That amount was considerably lower than what my imagination led me to believe I would find.

At supper that evening, which happened to be beet soup with bread and butter, my mother asked me how I made out with my experiment.

"Not so good," I replied. "Someone else must have had the idea before me, as I only made thirty-eight cents."

"Good," she replied. "When you go to church this Sunday, you can put your own money into the basket."

PART II: WALLINGTON

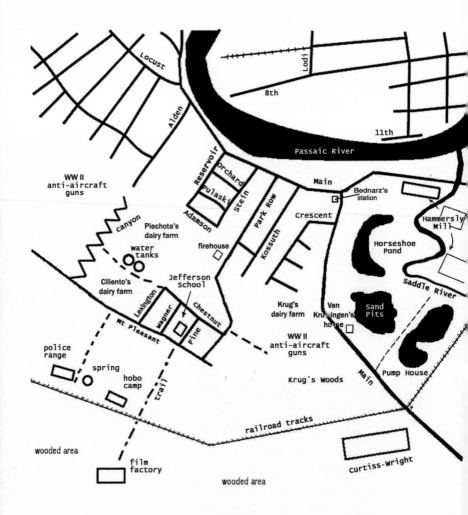

Wallington, 1942

WALLINGTON

In 1940, my mother remarried and we left Fourth Street in Passaic for our new home across the Passaic River in the small town of Wallington. This to me was like a move to another country. Whereas Passaic was a city, Wallington was still wooded in many areas, with fields and even a few farms. Wallington did not have a Palace Theater or a Market Street. The only thing the two areas had in common was that both were very Polish. Passaic was a city with a Polish neighborhood in the vicinity of Fourth Street; Wallington, however, was a town that was almost all Polish. So even though we moved, I was still living in Poland on the Passaic.

Wallington was about one and a half square miles in area. It was cut into two sections by a long, cigar-shaped hill, or drumlin, known as the Shohank Hill, probably a Delaware Indian name. The hill was a reminder that the area was once covered by glaciers. Looking west from the hill, in the distance you could see the Paterson Mountains. Closer by you could occasionally view the Passaic River as it wound its way through the great valley, a creation of eons of floods and erosion, a placid river but unfortunately very polluted as it served as an open sewer for the people and industries of the valley. Across the valley, large smokestacks jutted into the sky belching smoke, almost as if to serve as a beacon to guide those who worked there to their respective jobs. This was where the new immigrants came to work and still have the security of being among their own kind. This was necessary, as many could not speak English very well.

From the hill you could see three bridges joining Wallington to Passaic. On any work day they were alive with activity, as residents of Wallington went to their jobs in the factories and mills of Passaic. Two bus companies, Olympic and Comfort, were the main carriers to get people to their jobs and to return them afterward. During the 1940s, all three bridges—the Eighth Street Bridge, the Market Street Bridge, and the Acquackanonk Bridge (called the county bridge)—were drawbridges. At this time there was a great deal of barge traffic on the Passaic River. The river is a tidal estuary up to the first dam in Garfield and was heavily used by barges bringing material to Passaic's factories from ships in Newark Bay. The drawbridges were a real nuisance during the time that people were going to or coming home from work, as all traffic came to a halt while the slow moving barges made their way up river.

The Acquackanonk Bridge has a unique history, and its location dates back to the Revolutionary War. After General Washington's army was defeated by the British at the battle of White Plains, Washington decided to retreat to western New Jersey to regroup and preserve his army. His retreat took him through Wallington along the river road (now called Main Avenue) and across the Passaic River at the Acquackanonk Bridge to the relative safety of this very rural region of New Jersey. In this area the population strongly supported the revolution and Washington's defeated army could expect a great deal of help.

Visible to the east and parallel to Shohank Hill was another long hill about three quarters of a mile away, located mostly in the town of Wood-Ridge but extending into Hasbrouck Heights. Between the two hills was a railroad track that served as a boundary before curving towards Garfield. The area between the two hills was heavily wooded in parts, with many brushy fields and swamps. This area was very popular with rabbit hunters during the 1940s and many a Wallington boy's first experiences with hunting were in this area. From Jefferson School, located on the hill, was a panoramic view of mother nature, and it was here that I and other kids from the area of Park

Row, Kossuth Street, and the Star Homes, would spend much of our time while in the process of growing up.

The main access road to the hill was Park Row. On the top of the hill was Mt. Pleasant Avenue, which ran from Jefferson School all the way to the Paterson Plank Road. Sometime in the past an attempt had been made to make the hill more accessible by cutting through it at Alden Street. However, this failed and for many years the area was a raw wound constantly washing mud and debris onto upper Alden Street. The sides of this gigantic gully sloped more than 150 feet to a jumble of ice-age boulders in its eroded bottom. Needless to say, this area was a real magnet to the local kids and a first class playground. It was known as "the canyon."

Wallington in the 1940s had three dairy farms. At the base of the hill just below the water tanks was Piechota's dairy farm. It was at the end of Reservoir Road, one of the most beautiful roads in Wallington during the 1940s, a dirt road lined on both sides with gigantic oak trees. On hot summer days kids could always be found sitting or playing marbles in the shade provided by these beautiful trees. A paint factory was also located on Reservoir Road. It was destroyed in a spectacular fire about 1946. Also on Reservoir Road was a small company that bottled a soft drink called "Squirt."

On top of the hill, east of the water tanks, was Ciliento's dairy farm, a small farm located just off Mt. Pleasant Avenue. The largest of the dairy farms was Krug's, which ran from the "three corners" to Kossuth Street to the top of the hill, and included a large patch of woods known as Krug's woods. Much of his farm would be sold off to developers and about 1942 a large building project of single family brick homes was begun. It was known as the Star Homes and they sold for $3,333.

Also at this time there was a large vegetable farm just off Mt. Pleasant Avenue, very close to where Alden Street joins it. The farm extended towards the railroad tracks, and located just behind it was the Wallington Police pistol range. Kids were always picking lead here to make a few extra nickels, as most of us during this period were scavengers. Nearby was also a spring, and tucked in the woods was a well-used hobo camp. The Wallington police never bothered the hobos as they did the bums that sometimes made their way through town by following the tracks.

On the other side of the tracks in the town of Wood-Ridge was a factory that processed movie film. We always referred to it as the film factory. It was located in a wooded area and was prominent in the lives of many local kids.

A big industry in the 1940s was raising flowers. Near where Mt. Pleasant Avenue joined the Paterson Plank Road was a large nursery called Roehr's. Across the Plank Road was Bobbink and Atkins. Many young Wallington boys would earn their first paycheck working at these two nurseries. The nature of the business allowed them to hire 14-year-olds and they needed large numbers of young kids to help out at Easter and Christmas. I worked there a short time as a helper on a truck delivering flowers to New York City. The driver was Mr. Gasper, who lived on the hill section of Willow Avenue. As we went through the toll booths he always handed free flowers to the attendants. To this day I am amazed by how a flower can alter a person's disposition, especially a toll collector's.

Even though Wallington was a small town in the 1940s, there was almost no mixing of kids from different sections. Boys from two blocks away were total strangers, as they went to different schools. The three public schools (Washington, Lincoln, and Jefferson) were grade schools and served their immediate areas. Jefferson School was on the hill and it served all children from Stein Avenue north, including the Star Homes. However, there was a glitch, as all pupils south to the Plank Road living along Mt. Pleasant Avenue also attended. We had no contact with them except during school. The area from Mt. Pleasant Avenue to the Plank Road was referred to as the Morrissey or "Marcy" section. At this time Mt. Pleasant Avenue was very rural, with very few houses.

Wallington in the 1940s did not have a high school. If you lived in the southern part of town you attended East Rutherford High

School. If you lived in the northern part you attended Lodi High School. Also available was Bloomfield Technical High School for those who were more interested in following a trade.

For those of us who lived from about Stein Avenue northwards towards the three corners and including the Star Homes, there was close by our own private playground. And what a playground it was. Behind Van Kruiningen's brick house, which was located on Main Street, there was a large sandpit which covered several acres and was filled with water. This was the local swimming hole, as the Passaic River was far too polluted even for us. Sometime around the middle of the 1940s, the factories began filling in the sandpits with material from the paper mills and other industries. Van Kruiningen's sandpits now became Van Kruiningen's dump. This dump became an important part of our lives, for we were all Depression babies and our parents had all borne the brunt of the Great Depression. Money was always scarce and this dump was one of our primary sources of money. Today this area is covered by apartments houses and is called Jasontown.

Near to the sandpits, alongside the railroad tracks, was another lake that was used to supply water to the nearby Hammersly paper mill. A dirt road separated the sandpits from the lake, which we always referred to as the Pump House. The dirt road ended where the Saddle River wound behind the Hammersly Paper Mill just before entering the Passaic River. As the sandpits became polluted from the material being used as fill, we transferred our swimming to the Pump House. Wallington boys would swim on one side and kids from Garfield would swim on the other side, where the railroad tracks were located. We never associated with each other as we unconsciously followed that ancient dictum, "Stick to your own kind."

The three corners at this time held a gas station (to become Bednarz's Gulf), Reggie's Tavern (located where the Polish restaurant is today), and a greenhouse. Next to the greenhouse was another tavern. A large vacant lot next to the tavern was a favorite place for ball games, but more important it gave us access to a large pond which was always referred to as the Horseshoe Pond. This pond was an "oxbow lake," created when the Saddle River changed course on its floodplain. Over the years it began to fill in, until its depth was one to three feet during the 1940s. The Horseshoe Pond was a favorite area, especially in the winter, as its shallow depth allowed it to quickly freeze. It attracted many ice skaters, and during the evening bonfires were always burning along its shore as the skaters tried to stay warm. Many a boy learned how to trap muskrats along its banks, as they were very plentiful around the pond and the nearby Saddle River.

Several of us young boys, 13 to 15, owned .22 caliber rifles during the middle 1940s. One of our favorite pastimes was shooting rats at the developing dump and along the banks of the Saddle River just behind the Hammersly waxpaper mill. The dump also supplied us with bottles and cans which we would shoot as they floated down the river. Ammunition was always difficult to come by as we were too young to purchase our own. However, one store on Outwater Lane in Garfield could always be counted on when we needed ammo.

Sometime around 1948 the Horseshoe Pond disappeared. The Passaic River was being dredged up to the Eighth Street bridge to allow the barges to continue using the river. The material dredged from the river was sent via large hoses to the Horseshoe Pond and Van Kruiningen's dump, where it was used to fill in the entire area.

World War II had a large impact on Wallington. In 1942, the U.S. Army moved into town, with hundreds of soldiers being stationed on the hill. Barracks were built and almost the entire hill was covered with anti-aircraft batteries, from Krug's woods past Alden Street almost to the Plank Road. They were there for about a year before being transferred.

During the 1940s, almost every street in Wallington had a grocery store or two, the Star Homes and Reservoir Avenue being the exceptions in the northern part of town. It also seems that they all had a tavern, or—as they were called during this period by some—gin mill. People said that the only place with more gin mills for its size was Hoboken. It was almost a ritual for many going to their factory jobs in Passaic to have a "shot and a beer" before arriving for work. The procedure would be reversed after work as they would stop for a "shot and a beer" before returning home. It was this habit that kept many of these small gin mills in business. It was said that during the 1940s, Wallington had forty-nine gin mills, and that this was our contribution to the industrial revolution.

Although Wallington did not have a high school or a high school football team, it did have a town team, the Wallington Bulldogs. During the 1940s most towns had a football team composed of local players, hence the name "town team" although it was not in any way connected to the town government. Towns and cities would compete with each other and very often drew large crowds with teams like the Lodi Rams, Paterson Panthers, and Passaic Red Devils.

The population of Wallington in the 1940s was about six thousand. Yet during World War II, it supplied over nine hundred servicemen to the war effort, of whom forty-one would make the ultimate sacrifice. In relation to population, this small town of mostly Polish people whose parents and grandparents were immigrants made a contribution during World War II probably unequaled anywhere in America.

All the surrounding communities—Passaic, Garfield, Clifton, Lodi—had sizeable Polish populations, but Wallington was more than just a Polish town, it was the heart and soul of Polish New Jersey. The Wallington borough flag is based on the flag of Poland. Wallington is a Polish-American town, and the residents are proud to be both.

THE FIRST DAY OF SCHOOL

My mother remarried in 1940, and this required that we move to a larger apartment. We moved from the city of Passaic to Wallington, a small town across the river. This town had a large wooded area, which over the next ten years would become my second home. A double-track railroad bed cut through the woods and also served as the boundary between several small towns.

The move was made on a weekend, and on Sunday night my mother informed me that the next day she would be taking me to school. Monday morning began in a very strange way, as my mother wanted me to take a bath. In those days, we only took a bath once a week, on Saturday mornings. Since we had no hot water, the water was heated in a large bucket on the stove, then dumped into the bathtub. After the bath I was required to dress in my Sunday clothes and instead of the usual beat-up sneakers I wore shoes, the only pair that I owned.

We left the apartment at 8:30 A.M. and headed up a road that eventually became a curved steep hill. My mother informed me that the name of the road was Park Row. On the top of the hill stood Jefferson School, a large brick building which overlooked a valley on either side. On one side of the school the valley held the town that I had just left. On the other side, the valley contained nothing but woods and fields and the railroad tracks.

Finally arriving at the school, my mother took me to the closest entrance. It was at this time that she gave me the following instructions: "When you leave school at 3:15, I want you to come directly home. Now, look at the front of the school." Which I did. "Okay, now turn around and look in the direction we came from." Which I did. "When you come out of this door you are to go straight ahead until you come to the road which will lead you downhill to the house, understand?"

"Yeah, Ma, I can get home all right."

She then led me into the school to meet the principal and to register. At this time I was eight years old and was placed in the third grade. The rest of the day was uneventful except for the fact that I was uncomfortable being examined by strange kids whose clothes did not resemble my Sunday finery. I had the distinct feeling that they thought I was some kind of pansy based upon the clothes I was wearing, although it would not be long before they would find out otherwise, much to their regret.

The school day finally came to an end and we all lined up by classes waiting for the 3:15 bell to sound, which was followed by an orderly exit from the school. After leaving the school I paused to examine the entrance to make sure everything was familiar. It perfectly matched the previous image I had established when I had arrived in the morning with my mother.

However, there was a small detail that I failed to notice. When I arrived in the morning, the entrance had the word "BOYS" carved into the stone above the door. When I left in the afternoon the entrance had the word "GIRLS" carved into the stone above the door. Otherwise, the front and back of the school were identical. Even the landscape was similar, for upon leaving either entrance you would be walking downhill towards a valley on either side.

I lined myself up with the door and headed in the direction my mother had told me to take. The only problem was that they had dismissed my class on the opposite side of the school from which I had entered, and I was heading for the woods and the railroad tracks instead of the town.

It didn't take me long to realize that something was wrong when I began crossing a field filled with briar bushes that were tearing at my pants. The field ended at a shallow swamp and on the other side I could see a road, which I thought was the road I was looking for.

Making my way through the muddy swamp, I finally arrived at the road, which turned out to be a railroad bed. I had tried crossing the swampy area by jumping from grassy hummock to grassy hummock but about half the time I ended up in knee-deep mud. In a particularly deep muddy place one of my shoes came off and I had a most difficult time extracting it from the muck.

I stood on the railroad tracks, confused, covered with mud, but more worried about my mother's reactions if I ever got home. The thought of my mother's anger caused tears to flow down my cheeks.

At this point, I decided to walk down the tracks a short distance, hoping to find a way back to the school without having to cross the swamp again. From where I was I could still see the top of the school and it served as a beacon to a very confused boy who felt trapped in a wilderness. After a few minutes of walking I saw three men sitting in a small clearing in a patch of woods. Approaching them, I noticed a lot of stuff hanging from branches. There were pots and clothes and it looked like it was very heavily used.

Walking over to them, still crying, I explained my dilemma: I was lost and needed to get home, as my mother would be very upset. One of them asked a lot of questions about where I lived, trying to get some information to help me out. Since I didn't know much about where I lived I wasn't very helpful. By a sheer stroke of luck I happened to remember Park Row, and he was familiar with the road.

"C'mon, young man, follow me. I think we can get you home." He led me to a trail that went around the swamp and up the hill right past the school, to a place where the opposite side of the hill overlooked the valley with my town in it. Pointing to a road which I now recognized, he said, "That's Park Row. I'd take you down there but townsfolks don't take to us hobos." Gratefully I thanked him and left, secure that everything was now all right.

I knew what my mother's reaction would be on seeing the mess my good clothes were in. In vain I tried cleaning myself up, even to the point of removing my shoes and knocking them against a tree to remove the mud. It was a hopeless task and to make matters worse, I didn't realize it was already almost 5 o'clock.

My mother's reaction when I entered the kitchen was predictable.

"Just look at your clothes! Where the hell have you been?"

I tried to explain what had happened, but she really wasn't listening. She was extremely upset over the condition of my clothes. After she had cooled down, which took quite a while, I again tried to explain what had happened.

"Ma, I did just what you told me to do. I left the building by the same door and headed down the hill just like you told me to do. Excepting everything was different and I ended up in this swamp by the railroad tracks and I met these hobos and they showed me how to get home."

When I mentioned the word "hobos," my mother's face suddenly changed. With a new burst of anger she began another tirade.

"Don't you ever go near those damn people again! They're nothing but a bunch of lazy bums, all they do is drink and steal things." By the time my mother finished with her verbal attack on the hobos she created the feeling in me that I should be glad I had escaped with my life.

As I grew older and spent most of my spare time around the woods by the tracks, I would learn that many of my mother's beliefs were, to say the least, highly exaggerated. Some of the hobos were professional people, others were businessmen, and others were simply unemployed. They were all casualties of the Depression. And even at my young age, this period in the country's history would leave its mark on me just as it left its mark on them. Very few Americans would escape the effects of the Great Depression.

79 PARK ROW

iving in Wallington opened up a whole new world for me that was unavailable on Fourth Street in Passaic. The house we moved to had a large back yard with apple and pear trees. It also had a large chicken yard with several dozen chickens trying to get by on kitchen scraps and whatever insects or other living things were unlucky enough to enter their domain. Next to the chicken yard was a mad dog that was always on a chain. His name was Poochie. This dog was so mean he would bite himself for entertainment. Pity the poor rats that lived under the chicken house near where he was tied up. Even the rats hated this dog.

We rented the upstairs apartment in Sura's house, which was very nice compared to Fourth Street. However, like Fourth Street, our sole source of heat was a large cast iron cooking stove with a small coal box on one end that provided the heat. It was very inadequate, and the living room was closed off all winter to keep the heat in the kitchen. We were able to survive the winters because we always wore heavy sweaters indoors, and the beds had thick feather quilts. Although there was running water we had no hot water, and all water for washing dishes, clothes, and even taking a bath had to be heated on the stove in either a large bucket or a roasting pan.

This arduous process was kept to a minimum as we only took a bath once a week—usually on Saturday. This was the time of our weekly change of socks and underwear. We did have a bath tub, which we did not have on Fourth Street. Since I had an older brother, protocol allowed him to have the first bath. I would follow him using the same water, which by the time I got in was usually cool and dirty.

During the winter when it got dark early, the kitchen became the social room. We had one radio, which was moved from the living room to the kitchen so we could listen to our favorite programs with some heat provided by the coal stove.

The owner of the house, "OK" Sura, was a Wallington police officer. There are several stories about how he got the name "OK." All are related to his job as a policeman and his inability to write well in English; that is, if he could write at all. It was said that anything written down was "OK" by him. OK was once called to an incident on Kossuth Street which was serious enough to require an accident report. Since he couldn't spell Kossuth, he substituted Main Street, which he could spell.

OK's favorite pastime was racing pigeons, as it was a very popular sport in this area in the 1940s. Almost every garage had a pigeon coop built somewhere on the top, and at almost any hour of daylight flocks of pigeons could be seen flying overheard as they were being exercised and trained for the next race. When they were not flying, a constant cooing sound emanated from the dozen pigeon coops in the area of Park Row.

These pigeons were primarily racing birds, although there was a pigeon referred to as a "tumbler" which when flying in a flock (pigeons from the same coop always flew in flocks) would suddenly begin to tumble towards the ground for no apparent reason. After falling for perhaps fifty feet it would regain its balance and return to the flock.

The pigeons used for racing were all banded, meaning they had metal tags on their legs which identified the owner and the bird. On race day, usually a Saturday or Sunday, a flatbed truck would pick up all the birds in the area that were entered in the race. Each owner had a special wicker crate to transport his pigeons in. Some crates would hold as many as ten pigeons. The truck would proceed to the starting point, which was usually hundreds of miles away. The birds would then be released to return home, which is why they were often referred to as "homing pigeons." When a pigeon returned to its coop (many did not), its owner used a special clock to record the number on the band and the time. The fastest pigeons won money; as for the others, they often ended up as pigeon stew.

Apparently OK was not very adept at breeding quality racing pigeons, as it seems an inordinate number of his pigeons ended up as pigeon stew. I remember watching him pull the heads off pigeons that had failed to perform. As he so often said, "Slow pigeons make the best stew."

OK was a big guy at a time when people were much shorter than they are today. He stood 6′4″ and was very intimidating; yet in many ways he was a kind and understanding person. He was not always around during World War II, as he volunteered for the merchant marine. One ship he served on during the war was sunk by a German submarine. I heard that he had also been on a ship that was sunk in World War I.

Sura's house had a large attic on the third floor, and one of the windows overlooked the chicken yard—which was also the home of many rats. Often while playing we would glance up and see OK at the attic window with his .22 caliber rifle, patiently waiting to shoot any rats that showed themselves. Poochie always knew when OK was at the attic window and he would position himself so as to be able to catch any wounded rats.

Yes, Wallington was quite a change from Passaic.

Across the street from Sura's house lived the Kopecs. There were a large number of Kopecs, but only Butch (Daniel) was my age.

My introduction to Butch occurred a few days after we arrived in Wallington. An empty lot stood between Sura's house and the Kudlacik house. There was a large, four-foot-high boulder on the lot and I was playing on it when Butch and a few other kids came over. The episode went something like this:

Butch: Hey, kid, where you from?

Me: Fourth Street.
Butch: Where's that?
Me: Passaic.
Butch: So you're from across the river, huh?
Me: Yeah.
Butch: What's your name?
Me: Billy Arnold.
Butch: What brings you here?
Me: None of your business.
Butch: A tough guy, huh?
Me: Yeah!

I'm not sure what triggered the fist fight, but it ended quickly with one punch. Butch was taller than me and the punch I threw, instead of hitting him in the face, caught him in the throat. He fell to the ground as if he had been hit with an axe handle. He lay there for a full minute, gasping for air. I was getting very worried when all of a sudden he got up, looked at me, and ran home. After this incident we became good friends and never had another problem.

The Kopecs' backyard in the 1930s and early 1940s could pass for that of a very rural house anywhere in America. They had their own milk cow to supply their needs. Kopec chickens would wander from behind the old firehouse (where the present firehouse is) up to Dolack's property just below the hill. It was Butch's job to collect the eggs that the chickens laid in the brushy area behind his house. Since they were free range, the eggs could be anywhere. He seemed to know pretty much where they would lay their eggs.

As with so many of their neighbors, the Kopecs had a pigeon coop above the garage. They also had roosters, as did many of the other families that raised their own chickens for food. I never could decide which was the worse noise, Kopec's roosters or the firehouse siren.

Then, in the early 1940s, a new noise began to erupt from the Kopec household. This new noise caused a complete reassessment of all local noises that were judged to be irritating. Displaced on the scale of annoying sounds were the roosters and the wailing siren. The noisy pigeons now began to sound like a symphony orchestra. Even Mrs. Novack's yelling out of the window for her son Matt was now a tolerable sound. This new noise could permeate the neighborhood at any hour. Even the local animals were affected by the sound. All in hearing distance would agree: this noise was god-awful. Butch Kopec had begun taking lessons on the saxophone.

In addition to all the farm animals, the Kopecs also had a large cherry tree in the front yard. All the local kids feasted on cherries when they were ripe, and it was a close call who had the best ones. The sweetest cherries came from the Kopecs' tree. However, the largest cherries came from the Dolacks' tree, which was located on the first bend in Park Row as it began the steep climb towards Willow Avenue.

The Dolack house was set back a good distance from the road. The house was originally a large chicken coop before being converted to a house. At that time chicken coops had to be a good distance from a road, which explains why it was so far back from Park Row.

Cherries were not the only fruit on the menu for us perpetually hungry kids. On Kossuth Street next to the Byras' house were two large mulberry trees. One produced white fruit and the other blue fruit. It was not unusual when the fruit was ripe to see a half dozen kids in the trees filling paper bags with mulberries to bring home. The blue mulberries would make a stain on anything they touched, including the skin. A kid with a blue mouth was a dead giveaway that the mulberries were ripe.

Between Sura's house and the Kudlaciks' house was a vacant lot. The Kudlaciks' house was almost on the Park Row bend next to the Krolls' house. They didn't keep cows and pigeons but they did have chickens. It was Cassey (Casimir) Kudlacik's job to keep the coop clean, and it was a job he despised.

The Kudlaciks had the only swing set in the neighborhood. It was made by Cassey's father from scrap wood, and on any nice day the children could be seen using the swings—that is, after all the work was done.

They usually had a large vegetable garden that was pretty standard for the area except that they grew a large amount of rhubarb. Cassey said that his mother made rhubarb pie, and told me to eat some raw. I tried several times, but it was so sour it hurt my mouth. I never did understand how someone could make a pie from that awful plant.

By the time we were fourteen, most of us kids from the neighborhood owned a gun, usually a .22 caliber rifle or a single-shot shotgun. In many cases our parents did not know we had them. The exception was Cassey, who had no interest in guns and never hunted. The following incident might explain his lack of interest in guns.

Sometime around 1937, Tom Pirog, who was about five years old, and his sister Claire, who was about six, were playing near their house on Kossuth Street. Claire found a revolver hidden beneath the porch of the house. The gun had been there a long time, and when she gave it to her younger brother it was not in the best of condition. Tommy was playing with the gun when his friend Cassey Kudlacik came over. Using two hands, he pointed the gun at Cassey and the gun fired. The bullet struck Cassey in the stomach area. The impact of the bullet knocked him off his feet and tumbled him to the ground. Although stunned, he jumped up, looked at Tommy holding the gun, and ran home to his house on Park Row.

The area where the bullet struck was badly discolored and his mother could not determine the extent of the damage. Back then you could not just call the police, as no one had a telephone; someone had to go to the butcher store on the corner of Park Row and Adamson Avenue to use their phone. A short time later the police arrived and took Cassey to the General Hospital in Passaic. After an examination and X-ray, no bullet could be found. The police concluded that the rusted barrel of the gun and the deteriorated condition of the gun powder saved Cassey's life. Somewhere on his run home the bullet must have become dislodged and lost.

My friend Louie lived in Szymanski's house across the street from the Kudlaciks and next to the Kopecs. He was my age and was involved in most of the events that occurred while I was growing up during the 1940s. He was always big on hunting and fishing and by the time he was thirteen owned a shotgun and a Springfield single-shot .22 caliber rifle. During hunting season (which was whenever we felt like hunting) he could always be found hunting with Dick Koster (Kossuth Street), Dicky Miskuff (Pine Street), or me. The favorite area was below Jefferson School where there were extensive areas of briar bushes that continued all the way to the Plank Road.

We were not always sensible in our use of the guns that we owned. In fact, we were often downright careless—and today I wonder how we ever escaped being injured.

One day during summer vacation in 1945, Louie and I decided to go down to the Saddle River and do some shooting with our .22 caliber rifles. Since we didn't have enough ammunition on hand we had to first walk to Outwater Lane in Garfield, where even as youngsters we could purchase ammo. After returning, we picked up our guns and headed for the Saddle River. We began the afternoon by shooting a few rats on Van Kruiningen's dump, which was located near the river. After tiring of this we decided to shoot at bottles and cans thrown into the river. The Saddle River at this point made several sweeping bends behind the Hammersly mill, which was located in Garfield. We would take turns throwing in bottles and shooting. At times the bottles would be very hard to hit, as they would sink too deeply into the water, revealing only the bottle's neck. And they would float a long way down the river, unbeknownst to us changing the angle at which the bullets struck the water.

We had been shooting for well over an hour when our attention was drawn to a large dust cloud on the dirt road leading from Main Street to the Hamersly pumping station located near the river. Someone was speeding down the dirt road to where we were shooting and they didn't seem to care about all the ruts and bumps.

Before we could even react, a Wallington Police car pulled up within fifty feet of us. Out came two police officers who were angry as hell, and one of them was my old landlord OK Sura. All six-feet-four-inches of him showed his displeasure at finding Louie and me standing there with our rifles. His first words were, "What the hell are you doing?"

"OK," I replied, "we're just shooting bottles in the river. We're not doing anything wrong."

He took our rifles and removed the bullets from the chambers. He then scanned the area to get a better understanding of the situation that had brought him there. Turning to us, he informed us that the police had received a report from the Hammersly factory that bullets were shattering the windows and that the workers were lying on the floor and hiding to avoid being hit.

"OK, I swear we never shot at the factory. We're only shooting at bottles in the river."

At this time he pointed out to us that as we shot the bottles farther down the river, the bullets would ricochet off of the water—going back up into the air and striking the factory.

"I've a good mind to tell your mothers about this," he said.

Louie and I both became very scared. Nothing could be worse than to have our mothers find out what had happened, and that we had guns they didn't know about.

"Please, OK," I begged, "don't tell our mothers. I promise we won't do this any more."

"All right, but I don't want to hear any more about you two getting into trouble, you hear me?

We both nodded our heads.

The police officers began to leave and I decided to broach the subject of getting our rifles back, as they were leaving with them.

"You want your rifles back, we'll take you down to the station and your mothers can come down and get both you and the rifles."

We both agreed that we didn't want them back that badly.

OK Sura was a master of psychology, as he knew the fear we had of our mothers during this time period. I don't know what kind of a report he filled out—that is, if he even filled one out. But our mothers never did find out, thanks to OK Sura.

THE FOURTH GRADE

My fourth grade teacher's name was Mrs. Saul. In a small town where most people worked hard in factories and were usually quite thin, this woman to me was a 300-pound monster. I admit that from the start I had a bitter dislike for her.

Part of the teaching method at that time was to have pupils stand before the class to read paragraphs from a story in a workbook. Needless to say, this was a very humiliating process for some of the kids. One boy was from Poland and could hardly speak English. Mrs. Saul always gave me the feeling that she didn't care for the Polish kids in class. And since my name ended with "ski," I always felt as though I were the object of her special attention.

Another boy had a slight stutter, so when he read before the class he would almost literally fall apart. We even had a girl who was left back twice because she was slightly retarded. She stayed in the elementary grades until she left school at sixteen. No one was spared the ordeal of reading before the class regardless of his or her limitations. We would all be equally crucified on the cross of education.

One hot day in May, I had just taken my seat after noon recess. I was sweaty and hot from our outdoor play. While waiting for Mrs. Saul to settle in, I popped a clove of garlic into my mouth and began to chew it. During the early 1940s there was a polio epidemic. With no medicine to combat it, it was up to every family to use their own devices to stave off the disease. My mother's solution was two garlic cloves in my lunch and a bag of camphor around my neck.

After Mrs. Saul settled her 300-pound body behind her desk, she announced in her flat, unemotional voice, "William, take your book and read before the class, page seventeen, second paragraph."

Removing the book from inside my desk and quickly swallowing the remains of the garlic, I headed for the front of the classroom. I fumbled around until I found page seventeen, then wiped my sweaty hands on my knickers. I was the only kid who still wore knickers, my mother taking all the hand-me-downs from the Kobscenskis. I began to read, but didn't get very far before I ran into a word I had never seen before. Stopping to study it very carefully, I finally pronounced it: "ren-dev-on-ous."

Mrs. Saul gave me one of those dirty looks that served to remind me of my heritage and said, "Read it again."

Starting over at the beginning of the sentence, I read: "The trappers agreed to have a ren-dev-on-ous again next year at the same location." In a loud voice, she demanded that I read it again. Studying the word carefully and searching for a phonetic variation of the way I was saying it, I tried once more. Needless to say, it came out the same: "ren-dev-on-ous."

In a voice that carried overtones of a superior culture, she informed me that the word was "rendezvous." She then ordered me to stand in the corner until school was out. That was bad enough, but when she ordered me to put on the dunce cap I began to seethe with rage.

The bell finally rang indicating school was over. Walking past me was a bright, attractive girl named Helen. With a superior smile, the little witch informed me that I should keep the dunce cap on so that she would be able to recognize me "when we have a ren-dev-on-ous in the future."

At supper that evening I asked my mother, "Ma, what kind of word is rendezvous?"

She paused for a moment, a frown covering her face.

"I don't know," she replied, "but it sounds to me like it's Hungarian."

THE COAL BUCKET

ne of my jobs as a kid during the winter was to make sure the coal bucket was always full. I did not like this chore, as I had to go from our upstairs apartment all the way to the basement to get a bucket of coal. It wasn't bad during the fall when it stayed light longer but when real winter set in and it got dark at 5 P.M. I disliked going to the basement. It seemed that the bulbs never gave off enough light (40 or 60 watt bulbs were often used) and the low level of light created all kinds of scary shadows. My imagination was always operating at full speed when carrying out this chore and those shadows took on a realism which was frightening.

One day Poochie, OK Sura's mad dog, somehow got free from his chain. This dog had never been free of his chain and in his temporary state of freedom somehow managed to get hit by a car. There were very few cars on the roads in the early 1940s. For a dog to be hit by a car, either he was very stupid or he was mad and had attacked the car. Poochie was a dog that would attack a car if it got in his way. After the accident he was put in the basement to recover or die. Since he was never taken to a veterinarian, I doubt if anyone knew what his true condition was.

This dog did not like anyone, but especially me. I am somewhat responsible for his attitude as I must admit I did not always behave properly towards him. It was a mutual dislike, but I was in a more advantageous position as I was not encumbered by a heavy chain. I will admit to this: whenever I finished eating an apple or pear I would always throw the core at him. Also, when no one was looking, the water hose would sometimes spray him. He disliked water.

The area of the yard that he could reach was very well worn from his dragging the chain back and forth through it. One day I got careless and strayed too close to his coop. Before I could react, he dashed out from the coop and headed straight for me. He managed to get a hold of my pants leg before he reached the end of his chain. Pulling away from him left a good portion of my pants in his mouth. He was in a frenzy and continued to tear at the cloth until it was in shreds. My fear turned to anger when I realized I would have to explain my missing pants leg to my mother.

Without thinking, I decided to get even with this mad dog. I had been shooting with my homemade bow and arrows that day. Taking my homemade hickory-wood bow, I loosed a few arrows at him just to let him know I was not to be trifled with. It was lucky for him that I missed, as the arrows were tipped with ten penny nails that had been flattened on the railroad tracks. (Unfortunately, there was no way I could get my arrows back.)

One evening around 7 p.m., the coal bucket had to be filled. This full bucket of coal would be for the morning fire which was usually started by my mother about 5 A.M. I picked up the empty bucket and headed for the basement. Arriving at the staircase that led to the basement, I switched on the lights and descended the wooden stairs. Making a sharp turn at the bottom of the staircase I immediately froze when I heard the sounds of a dog growling at me. I was very familiar with this sound—it was Poochie. I did not know at this time that Poochie had been injured and put in the basement. I quickly retreated back up the staircase. There was no way I was going into the basement with that dog down there.

I went back to our apartment with an empty coal bucket. It wasn't long before my mother inquired as to why there wasn't any coal in the bucket. I made up a fib and told her the lights were out in the basement and I couldn't see where I was going. I breathed a sigh of relief when she walked away. However, panic returned a few minutes later when she came back and handed me a flashlight.

Again I descended the stairs to the basement. However, I developed a strategy this time based upon my knowledge of flashlights. I did not put the lights on, but upon entering the basement I shined the flashlight into Poochie's eyes to blind him—and most of all to keep him from seeing who I was. I had never realized the extent of the hatred in this dog until he was focused in the beam of a flashlight. I slowly walked around him, about ten feet away, keeping the coal bucket ready to be used as a weapon should he attack.

After making my way to the coal bin and filling the bucket I looked around for some better way to make the return trip. I decided to leave by way of the outside cellar door. Damn, it was locked. No way out except to go past Poochie again. Going out would be difficult, as I was now burdened by a large bucket of coal which made me walk with a lean to one side and a very awkward gait, as the heavy coal bucket kept hitting my legs. I could not carry a weapon on the return trip as one hand had the flashlight and the other gripped the wooden handle of the coal bucket, so I had prepared for Poochie's attack by placing large pieces of coal on the top of the coal bucket just in case I had to throw them to defend myself. My pocket knife (most kids carried them) was opened up and lying on the top of the coal as I began my journey past Poochie.

The light going back struck Poochie at a different angle. He was in exactly the same position except that from this new viewpoint I could plainly see that he was badly injured, as his legs stuck out in a most unusual posture. As I got to the point nearest to him a low growl and bared teeth brought back all my fears, but he made no attempt to get up. Soon I was past him and rapidly heading upstairs.

The next morning I was able to fill the coal bucket by using the outside cellar entrance, which was only locked in the evenings.

Returning from school that afternoon, I heard a shot as I got close to my home. I went to the back yard to see if OK was shooting rats. Instead, he was in the process of digging a hole, his 22-caliber rifle resting against a pear tree. Poochie was lying on the same old rug that I had seen him on in the basement—except now he was dead. I watched from a distance as OK finished digging the hole and without ceremony put Poochie and the rug inside.

That evening going downstairs to the basement for coal, despite having seen him buried, I checked beneath the stairs to see if Poochie was there. He wasn't. I was relieved. Now I could concentrate all of my fears on those damn shadows.

THE NEWSPAPER

It was June of 1942, and World War II was well under way, when six of us local (Park Row-Kossuth Street) kids decided to help the war effort. Of course, if we could make a little money at it, so much the better.

One of the only items that wasn't being collected for the war effort was newspaper. Since everything else was donated and collected in scrap drives, we opted to collect newspapers and sell them.

The only place that we had for storage was the coal bin in Sura's house. There were actually two coal bins as each apartment had its own. Coal bins were usually empty this time of year and our coal bin would be a perfect place for storage.

There were six of us and three wagons to pick up the papers with. We would go to all the people in the neighborhood and ask for any old newspapers. We were surprised at the amount we collected. All the newspapers had to be tied in bundles so they could be carried into the basement and stacked. In a week the coal bin was half full. Our imaginations began to rise in relation to the rapidly filling coal bin. After many hours of work our favorite topic of conversation was how we were going to spend all the money that we planned on getting.

Things slowed down considerably the second week, and the third week was a struggle to get newspaper. Since we only had a limited radius that we could work we were going back to the same people, and it was apparent even to us insensitive kids that some of them were getting annoyed.

Actually, the coal bin was about full when we got tired of the project. It was now time to reap the rewards of our labors and we also felt good about helping the war effort.

Now we had to explore the question of how to sell all of the papers. Since no one had a telephone to call and enquire, several of us walked over to River Road by the Passaic Stadium where we knew that there were scrap dealers. The first two dealers were not even interested unless we brought the newspapers to them. This was impossible considering the amount that we had. The third dealer agreed to pick up the papers if we loaded the truck and then informed us that he would have to charge us for the use of his truck. We agreed. What the hell, with the amount of paper we had and the money we would make, we would still be able to afford his truck.

It was a Saturday when he arrived with a large stake-body truck. All six of us were waiting when his truck pulled into Sura's driveway. He came downstairs into the coal bin to see how much paper we had collected. He was quite surprised. He then began to supervise the loading of his truck. All six of us began carrying the bundles from the coal bin upstairs to the driveway and onto the bed of the truck. The driver stacked the bundles evenly, as he could see that he was going to have a full load. After two hours of hard work he closed the gate on his truck—we were finished! It was then that he told us that he couldn't pay us until he had the truck weighed. "When will that be?" I asked. He promised to be back in an hour. We did not like seeing him drive off with our valuable newspapers without having received our money. We patiently awaited his return.

True to his word, he returned. Not in the large truck but in a car. We all gathered around him as he got out of his vehicle. "Who's in charge?" he asked. "I am," I replied. He took out his wallet and removed some bills.

"The newspaper market is very bad," he announced. "You're lucky I took your papers." Somehow I instinctively knew we were about to get screwed.

"Newspaper," he continued, "is selling for two dollars a ton. Since you had three tons, that comes to six dollars." He handed me the money. We were all in a state of shock and disappointment. He got into his vehicle and before pulling out of the driveway informed us with a smile that he didn't charge us for the use of his truck.

Without a word I handed each kid his dollar. No one said anything. They all left to go home. We were all richer by a dollar but our spirit was left much impoverished.

THE ATTIC

Our apartment at 79 Park Row was quite small. This necessitated that the large attic be used for a considerable amount of household activity. It was primarily used as a storage area. On rainy days it would be a play area or a place where wooden model airplanes were built. In the winter, clothes would be hung there to dry out. Clothes lines were always located in the kitchen near the coal stove. In wet or snowy weather one could always find wool gloves, socks, and shoes drying out near the stove.

In the 1940s most items that were made from cloth had to be ironed, as the material was very prone to wrinkling. Pants, shirts, dresses, and blouses all went through this process in order to look presentable. Curtains required a special process and were dried on large wooden racks to avoid having to iron them. These racks were adjustable and could be spread to hold curtains as long as six feet. The curtains would be held in place by sharp nails driven through the rack from the opposite side. As many as six or eight curtains could be placed on the rack at any one time, the thickness of the fabric determining how many would fit over the nails.

One of the pastimes that we kids engaged in in the 1940s was shooting at each other with what we always referred to as "pooty blowers." Some kids from other areas called them bean shooters or pea shooters, but we never shot beans or peas—we ate them. The instrument to shoot the "pooties" consisted of a hollow metal tube about 12 inches long with a hole about ¼" in diameter. On one end was a wooden mouthpiece.

What we called pooties were actually green chokecherries, which when not ripe were very hard. During the season we would collect several bagsful before they had a chance to ripen and turn soft.

I was out gathering chokecherries one day with Pete Stagg when he informed me of another use for chokecherries that I had never heard of. He told me that some people made chokecherry wine. Being curious, I inquired as to how this was done. He did not go into any great detail but simply told me that you put the chokecherries in a jar and add some sugar. Then find a warm place to store them for a couple of weeks—and presto, you have a jar of chokecherry wine.

I filed this information away until the time that the chokecherries became ripe. Meanwhile, I kept my eyes open for a large one-gallon jar. If I was going to make wine I might just as well make a lot. It wasn't long before I found a one-gallon jar being thrown out by Belski's butcher store. Several weeks went by and the chokecherries were now ripe. I had never eaten one before, so I gave them a try and quickly learned why they were called chokecherries. They were about as bad as Kudlacik's rhubarb.

All was now ready. I filled the one gallon jar about half full with chokecherries. I then added about two cups of sugar. (Getting the sugar represented a problem as we rarely had that much sugar in the house. I had to pilfer it a spoon at a time over several weeks to keep its disappearance from being noticed.) I took the jar up to the attic to hide it. Before putting it in a place that was not likely to be discovered I made sure the cap was on tight.

Several weeks went by. I was sitting at the kitchen table with my mother having lunch one day when there was a loud bang. My mother was startled by the loud noise and jumped up, inquiring "What was that?" Since I had no idea what had happened I shrugged my shoulders to indicate that I didn't know anything, which was quite true.

Several hours later my mother went to the attic to check on the curtains that were on the drying rack. I was still in the kitchen listening to the radio when I head my mother swearing loudly in Polish. In a few minutes she returned to the kitchen still swearing and carrying all the curtains that had been stretched on the drying rack. I immediately saw that the curtains were covered with dark blue stains and rotted chokecherries. It then occurred to me that the loud sound we heard was my jar of chokecherries exploding. I quickly left the kitchen to go outside and get away from the scene of my crime and my mother's furious state.

Sitting on the porch, I heard my mother discussing what happened with one of our neighbors. They came to the conclusion that someone had been making wine in the attic. I believe that I was saved by the fact that my mother could not believe her good little boy was entering the winemaking business. She evidently thought it was OK Sura, our landlord. She was not about to question OK concerning the damage to her curtains.

The last I saw of the curtains, they were soaking in a tub of hot water on the stove. The color of the water had turned to a dark blue. Taking a fork, I lifted a section of curtain out of the water to check on its color. It was no longer white but was light blue with dark spots.

I saw Pete in school the next day and told him what had happened. His answer explained everything: "Oh, I forgot to tell you, never screw the cap on tight." Thanks, Pete.

MY FIRST DOG

It was Sunday, some time in October of 1942. I dreaded Sundays, as I always felt constricted by the opposing effects of God and the Devil. My mother, being a devout Catholic, insisted on my attending church. I, being a boy of eleven, had other ideas and interests.

Sunday would always start out with good intentions. I would leave the small town I lived in and begin the walk to church about two miles away. Somewhere about the mile mark I would cross a railroad track that led to a large woods that even had a hobo camp. It was at the railroad crossing that the Devil always confronted me to test my resolve. He always had that cocky smile on his face, as if he knew he couldn't lose.

He would begin by reminding me that after church I would have to attend one hour of catechism class. (Children under sixteen were only allowed to attend eight o'clock mass, and after mass the nuns and brothers would surround the exit and bring us to the basement of the church, where classes were held.) Sitting in church and having to put my precious nickel in the basket was taxing enough for a young boy who would rather be in the woods, but catechism classes were pure agony.

The Devil would usually clinch the deal by informing me that by not going to church I would be able to keep the nickel. Now, back then that would be a couple of candy bars. I did possess deep feelings of guilt, though. One time when the basket was passed I kept the nickel and put a cookie in the basket. I had no pleasure in spending that nickel.

Believe me, I used to struggle with the Devil, and you should not get the idea that I was a pushover. However, I did lose quite often. I sometimes wondered why God didn't have the power of the Devil. God never once met me at the tracks to give me a hand. Perhaps that's why I resented putting the nickel in the basket.

I made the right turn to follow the tracks—the Devil always smiled when I followed the railroad tracks. I followed them to a small pond where there was an ideal place to sit and watch the red-wing blackbirds. As I was sitting and aimlessly throwing pebbles into the pond I noticed a small beagle looking me over and very cautiously approaching. Even to me, it was obvious that he was either lost or abandoned. His tail was curled beneath his legs, his head was lowered in a posture of submission, and he had a sort of sideways shuffle. I made believe I was eating something and was finally able to coax him close enough to begin petting him. Instantly his tail came from beneath his legs and began to wag furiously. It was love at first touch.

Without really thinking about how my mother would react, I decided to bring my new friend home. Never having had a dog before, it just seemed like the natural thing to do. I had to wait the required time allowed for church and catechism class before heading home. It was imperative that I not arouse any suspicion in my mother about how I really spent my Sunday mornings.

Passing through the hobo camp, I found some rope which I used to tie up my newfound friend. I decided he needed a name, as I would give him a proper introduction to my mother. This was a difficult decision but I finally settled on "Charley."

I remember so well leaving the woods with Charley and having to tug on the leash as if he had regrets about going to his new home. We finally arrived at the house and there was my mother right in front, sweeping the sidewalk. She didn't see us approaching and was quite startled when I said, "Hi, Mom." She suddenly turned around, and she just stood there staring at me and Charley, who was half hidden, cowering behind me with his tail tucked between his legs.

My mother finally broke the silence. "Where the hell did you get that thing from?" She didn't have to explain what "thing" she meant.

"Ma," I began, "this is Charley. I found him walking along the road and he began following me home." Notice I left out that it was the railroad bed where I found him.

"Ma, he's lost and hungry. Can I keep him?"

Her reply was short and sweet and branded into my memory. "You take that thing back where you found him and I mean right now."

I had prepared for this possibility with a response that I hoped would save my relationship with Charley.

"If you don't let me keep Charley, I'm going to run away," I said, while wiping tears from my eyes.

Totally unmoved by my threat, she replied, "Go ahead and go, and take that damn thing with you."

I was beaten. With that, I turned away and headed for the woods. Arriving at the location where I found him, I played with him for a few minutes then untied the rope that bound us together. As soon as he was free from the rope he took off running and I never saw Charley again.

The only reason I can come up with to explain his behavior is that after meeting my mother he considered himself a lucky dog to get out of there.

THE TANKS

ocated on the top of Shohank Hill were two large water tanks that supplied Wallington with water. In the 1940s, a dirt road ran from Chestnut Street past the tanks and ended at the canyon (the present Alden Street). The grass around the tanks was usually a lush green and on hot summer days it was usually a little cooler near to the tanks as the large volume of water they held served to cool the air. They also provided shade, which was another attraction.

The area around the tanks not only served as a refuge from the summer heat it was also the battleground for the kids from Jefferson School who decided to settle their problems with their fists. There was a very well-developed protocol regarding fist fights. If a situation broke out in school (usually during recess or lunch) and both parties agreed, the word would quickly be spread that a fist fight would take place after school.

If by some chance you were slighted by another kid and he challenged you to a fight and you refused, the other kids in your class would be unmerciful on you. They would flap their arms like wings and make sounds of a chicken. It came down to fight or suffer humiliation from your classmates. Some kids lived in a constant defensive posture, always behaving in a way that would cause the least amount of friction with their classmates.

When the word began to spread of a fist fight, it spread through the school like wildfire. When school was over (about 3:15) the combatants, each surrounded by his supporters, would begin the quarter-mile walk to the tanks. The girls were some of the most enthusiastic supporters of the boy gladiators, each having her own favorite. These future Clara Bartons would often bring the combatants water. Whether this was to ease their thirst and suffering or to keep them fighting I do not know. However, considering their zealous attitude, I suspect the latter.

On this particular day, after an incident which occurred on the ball field, I would be one of the boy gladiators. It was so trivial; yet, to growing boys preparing for the rigors of life, it was a good enough reason to exercise our fighting skills and to establish our position of dominance within the group structure. The boys from the Morrissey Avenue area that attended Jefferson School were not a large part of the overall school population and formed a distinct group. We always referred to them as the kids from the "Marcy" section. Today would be a double header. Two kids from the Morrissey Avenue area would be fighting two kids from the Park Row area.

School was now over and the walk towards the tanks began. A large group of kids headed down Chestnut Street, the atmosphere being full of merriment. That is, except for the combatants. On the walk your friends would be giving you all kinds of advice as to how to beat your opponent, even though most of them couldn't fight their way out of a paper bag. At times there was a strange ritual of one kid's putting a stick on his shoulder, and if you knocked it off the fight would begin. There was one part of fist fighting protocol that I never saw broken; you never took a swing at another person until he had his hands up to defend himself. All fights ended when the person being beaten dropped his hands or his friends stepped in to stop the fight. At times one of the fighters would be better at wrestling than boxing, and if he were successful he would try to grab you to change the contest into a wrestling match. This does not mean that punches were not exchanged while wrestling. Rather, a free-for-all brawl took place. However, regardless of the procedure, the best puncher usually won.

Arriving at the tanks, the first pair of gladiators began to get ready by stripping off some of their excess clothes. If you wore glasses someone would hold them (usually one of the girls). When all was ready, a large circle of onlookers would form a ring. The two fighters would enter the ring and when ready would commence fighting.

The first fight on this day would be Eugene Castileone from the Marcy section vs. Pete Stagg from Main Avenue. I was very friendly with Pete but he had very poor skills (if any skills at all) when it came to fist fighting. In fact, I had never seen him have a fight. I do not know how these two most improbable combatants could even have arrived at the conditions that would cause them to fight. I can only assume that lower echelon chickens (lower in the pecking order) only fought other lower echelon chickens. This must be so, as it was generally frowned upon for kids that were known to be good at fighting (and everyone knew who was good) to pick on someone who wasn't very adept.

The first fight ended very quickly with Eugene the clear winner. It was over so fast the girls did not even have time to get their emotions into play. However, by the time the second fight had begun their emotional frequency was at its peak.

The circle opened slightly to allow the next two gladiators into the center. The first in was Eddie Nieglos from the Marcy section. From the opposite side of the circle came Bill Michalski from Park Row.

We both put up our hands, and feeling one another out began to circle each other. I was at a clear disadvantage, as I was much smaller and lighter than my opponent. I also knew he was a good wrestler and that if he ever got his hands on me I was done for. My strength lay in the boxing skills that I had developed at the Passaic Boys Club, which had a boxing program.

He was very aggressive, constantly moving towards me. My strategy was simple; keep backing up, don't let him get hold of you, stop suddenly, take a few swings, then back up. This made for a very long fight. In fact, it was so long we had to take rest breaks. During this time one of the Clara Bartons would go down to the spring near the railroad tracks and bring us some cold water to keep us in fighting trim. Boys fighting was one of the more exciting episodes in their lives.

The fight came to a halt when a Wallington Police car came up the dirt road to the tanks. We quickly dispersed into the woods, everyone heading home as it already was well past 4 o'clock.

Arriving home, I immediately went to a mirror to asses the damage. There were a few bruises above my eyes but not much else. I had heard that placing a cold knife blade on a bruise would cause the swelling to go down. This was important, as my mother would be home from work about 5:30 P.M. and I didn't want her to be asking any questions. At the supper table she did notice, and inquired how I got the bruises. I made up a story about falling in Krug's woods and a branch hitting me across the face.

I was very apprehensive about going to school the next day with bruises on my face. After arriving at school and taking my seat I glanced over to where Eddie sat. I was delighted to see that his face was worse than mine—including his black eye.

We never had a problem after this, as rarely did two people who had a fist fight ever fight again.

The area around the tanks also served another function besides as an area for fist fighting. Actually, this other function was the exact opposite—it also served as a lovers' lane. In the 1940s very few people had cars, especially those of the age that would be interested in a lovers' lane. So it would be more exact to say that most of the love taking place there was illicit love.

It was a warm spring evening, the sun just beginning to set behind the Paterson Mountains, when my friend and I noticed a car approaching the tanks from the dirt road. This was most unusual, so we decided to hide in the woods adjacent to the road. The car drove by very slowly and we noticed the driver was a male and that he had a passenger—a female. His cautious driving was a dead giveaway that he was not familiar with the road. He drove beyond the tanks and parked the car where the wooded area came closer to the road. He was not aware that he had stopped about one hundred and fifty feet from the edge of the canyon.

My friend and I watched the car for half an hour from our concealment in the woods. Then we slowly and cautiously moved to new positions to get a better look. However, other than a few giggles that we could hear, we could see nothing. We decided to get closer to the vehicle and to approach it from the rear. Sneaking carefully through the woods so as not to make any noise, we slowly made our way to the rear of the car. It was an older model Ford with a high rear window and we could see nothing from our position by the trunk. The giggles and noises were beginning to affect our hormones, which made us somewhat careless. Without thinking, we both at the same time stepped on the rear bumper to get a better look through the rear window. The car immediately sagged under our weight and the leaf strings gave out a loud squeal. Instantly there was a shuffling of bodies as pandemonium broke out on the front seat. A few seconds later the motor roared to life and in a blaze of spinning wheels the car headed down the dirt road towards the canyon. The lights finally came on. Standing in the road, paralyzed by the rapidly changing events, we watched as the lights—and the car—disappeared over the edge of the canyon.

We were well aware of the steepness of the sides of the canyon and the badly eroded bottom. We were plainly worried about the outcome of our sexual curiosity and what it had led to. Before going home we swore each other to secrecy. The next morning, curiosity got the best of me and I decided to investigate the previous night's episode. Rather than go to the tanks I walked up Alden Street to where it ended at the canyon. Half way up the canyon was the car, piled up against a large boulder. I walked past the car, uphill towards Mt. Pleasant Avenue. As I passed the car I noticed that both doors were open. Apparently they were both able to exit the car and had not been injured.

I continued my walk towards Mt. Pleasant Avenue, all the time pondering what could they have been doing in the car that caused them to panic so much. By peeking through the back window of the car we had expected to see some necking and petting—but that was it. We were young kids and in many ways the 1940s was still the age of innocence. The most sexually graphic magazine at this time was the Sears, Roebuck catalog.

THE WALK

The day started out and progressed quite normally until bedtime. My brother and I shared the same bed, and we both retired to the bedroom shortly after listening to our favorite radio programs. As it was getting dark a little early, there was precious little to do after listening to the radio. There was no television, no phone, we had no books to read, and what little conversation we engaged in was quickly exhausted or degenerated into personal squabbles.

We were not very long in bed when my brother became upset, complaining to me that he had a pain in his belly. We were in a constant rivalry, and I teased him about eating like a pig and stuffing his mouth. As the evening progressed, however, so did his pain, and his tossing and turning also kept me awake, although I eventually did fall asleep.

After about an hour his crying woke me up, and I saw him get out of bed and go over to my mother's bedroom. My mother worked very hard as a sewing machine operator in a factory in Passaic. This was World War II and she was making uniforms for the military. She always went to bed quite early, usually 7 or 8 P.M., and was always up some time between 4 and 5 A.M. She was quite disturbed at having her precious sleep interrupted by a bellyache. Getting out of bed, she gave my brother a superficial examination while standing next to the coal stove to keep warm. As she was pressing on his abdomen to see if he was constipated he let out a loud howl.

"You need an enema," she announced—as if the whole world was waiting for her diagnosis.

Of all the treatments administered by our parents, none was more dreaded than that rubber bag filled with soapy water. My mother first had to heat the water on the stove. Next, Ivory soap was dissolved in the water, then cold water was added until the water became the proper temperature (lukewarm). I prepared myself, for I knew what was coming—but it arrived much sooner than expected. He began howling in pain as soon as the warm soapy water began to flow, and did not cease until the enema was over with. After cleaning up she pronounced him cured and sent him back to bed.

He was still crying when he returned to bed and all night long I listened to his low sobs and his constant tossing and turning as he tried to find a position that would ease his pain.

My mother got up at her usual time, and after dressing and starting a coal fire she came to our bedroom to check on my brother's condition. He was awake and quietly sobbing. It was then that my mother realized he would have to go to the doctor. However, they would have to wait until 8:15 to leave, as Dr. Weinert's office opened at 9.

My mother cleaned my brother up as best she could and had him change his underwear. Finally 8:15 arrived and they began the two-mile walk from Park Row in Wallington to the corner of Market and Mercer streets in Passaic where Dr. Weinert had his office. The trip was very difficult for my brother, as the walking aggravated his condition. Upon their arrival, Dr. Weinert immediately examined my brother. At the conclusion of his examination he told my mother, "Mary, take him immediately to General Hospital and I will meet you there. Understand?"

My mother quickly left to get to the hospital as soon as possible with my still-sobbing brother in tow. General Hospital was a mile and a half away. When they finally arrived at the hospital an hour later, Dr. Weinert confronted my mother, furious.

"Mary, where the hell have you been? I told you to get here as soon as possible!"

"Dr. Weinert," my mother responded, "we walked as fast as we could."

They quickly prepared my brother for surgery, as he had an acute attack of appendicitis and, as Dr. Weinert later informed my mother, his appendix was about to burst.

"Mary," he asked, "why didn't you take a cab?"

"Dr. Weinert," she responded, "they cost too much."

So even though conditions had improved greatly in the early 1940s, my mother was still living under the effects of the Great Depression. And this would continue until the end of her life.

About ten years later my brother would visit Dr. Weinert for a physical required by his company in order to become a long-distance truck driver. After the physical he and Dr. Weinert discussed his ordeal of getting to General Hospital and conditions during the Depression.

"I also had a hard time during the Depression," Dr. Weinert told him. "Most of my patients were Polish people who lived right around Market Street and worked in the local factories. Many of them became unemployed during the Depression. I never made any money during this period, although I was able to get by all right. Most of them couldn't pay their bills and I accepted whatever they could afford.

"Although," Dr. Weinert added, laughing, "I wouldn't accept any chickens."

He told my brother that if he charged a patient three dollars for his services, he would often receive only fifty cents, or perhaps a dollar if he were really lucky.

"Joe, I never made any money during the 1930s, but I did very well in the 1940s. It was during World War II when people went back to work and began to earn a good living that they remembered me. I began getting many letters from people I didn't even recall. The letters would contain anywhere from five to fifty dollars for services I gave them during the Depression. So many of the letters were written in Polish that I had to get someone to translate them for me. Those people couldn't pay me during the Depression and I had written it off as a loss, but by-and-large these hard-working local people had an ethic about paying what you owe that compensated me very well during the 1940s."

THE WEDDING

K Sura had only one child, a daughter by the name of Josie. In 1943, when we were living in his house, Josie was dating Bill Broska. They had two things in common: both were Polish and both were big.

One day Josie got me in a corner and asked me if I would be a ring bearer at her pending wedding. Without any hesitation I flatly refused, even though I had no idea what a ring bearer was supposed to do. There was ingrained in me a natural tendency to avoid adults and their gatherings and to me a wedding should be avoided at all costs.

Josie decided to sweeten the pot. "You'll get a very nice, useful present if you'll do me this little favor."

A present. Now I had to give this offer some consideration. "What kind of present?" I asked.

"Why, it's a secret," she replied, "but I know you'll like it."

Damn, she was shrewd. I wondered how she knew that I would like it. Besides, if it was so good why didn't she just tell me what it was, or, better still, if it was so important for me to carry the ring why not let me pick the present that I wanted.

"You think about it and I'll get back to you in a few days."

That evening and the next day all I could think about were the possibilities that this secret present might have. Flowing through my mind were pictures of ice skates, BB guns, fishing poles, and a wide assortment of other acceptable presents that I would consider useful and appropriate for an active young boy. Slowly I was convincing myself to accept this unpleasant chore just to please my runaway imagination.

However, the very next evening, the decision of whether to be a ring bearer or not was taken out of my hands.

My mother: Josie asked you to be a ring bearer?

Me: Yeah.

My mother: What did you say?

Me: I'll think about it.

My mother: You're going to carry the damn ring, there's nothing to think about.

Me: Aw, Ma, do I have to?

My mother: She's OK's daughter, if you don't do this they could ask us to leave and get another apartment.

I could say no to Josie, but my mother was a totally different ball game.

After a brief pause, she ordered me to go downstairs right then and inform Josie that I would be happy to be the ring bearer. "And dammit," she continued, "look like you're happy to do it!"

I went downstairs to where Josie lived with her father. I knocked on the door and while waiting for an answer I practiced smiling. Soon Josie came to the door and her look informed me that she knew I was there to surrender. Smiling, I informed her I would love to be the ring bearer at her wedding. In a not-so-subtle fashion I also reminded her about this useful present I was to receive.

Over the next several weeks the agony I had anticipated began. First there were trips to the store to be fitted with proper clothes for the occasion. This was a black suit with coattails. Completing this costume was a white shirt with a cast iron collar and a black bowtie.

The little blonde girl that I was matched up with loved her part as a flower girl and always acted as if this were a dress rehearsal for her own future wedding. Only slightly worse than being fitted in those godawful clothes was having to go to church and practice walking down the aisle with this little blonde twit that had the aura of Joan of Arc when in church. Whenever the organist played the wedding march during rehearsal her face would light up like a candle. However, everything went well during the wedding ceremony despite my belligerent attitude towards the whole affair.

After the wedding a reception was held at the Polish People's Home in Wallington, across the street from the Eighth Street bridge. After the bride and groom had settled in at their table, people began to go crazy, banging on their plates with spoons and carrying on in a most unusual fashion. The bride and groom then kissed each other and proceeded to the dance floor where they were the only ones that danced. After their dance, other couples began to dance to polkas, the music being supplied by a Polish band.

By obligation I was sitting at the main table with the blonde Joan of Arc. She leaned towards me and asked me if I would like to dance with her. I curtly informed her that I knew nothing about dancing and that I was there only to get a present and to participate in the feast of roast beef. We never conversed after that. Apparently I didn't fulfill her expectations for the evening as it was quite plain that I was more interested in the roast beef than in dancing with her. After my fill of roast beef, I walked home.

I had expected my present from Josie to be delivered in a day or two. No present arrived. I asked my mother about it and she told me that they would be gone for a week or so, as they had gone away on their "honeymoon." I didn't know what a honeymoon was so I asked my mother out of curiosity. She informed me that when people got married they went away to a place to learn how to cook. It sounded reasonable to me.

When they returned from this cooking program, I had expected prompt delivery of my present. I was very disappointed as time went by and no present was ever delivered. The time eventually came when I no longer gave it any thought; I was getting tired of my own imagination.

Then one evening there was a knock on the kitchen door. I was sitting in the kitchen on a platform rocker listening to the radio when my mother opened the door. There stood Josie with a large, nicely wrapped box in her hands. Finally, I thought, the payoff. She entered the kitchen and, seeing me sitting in the rocker, walked over to me and handed me the box. I stood up and took the box but I wasn't sure if I was supposed to open it right then.

"Go ahead and open it," she urged. "I want to see if you like it."

Out of habit I shook the box to get a clue to what might be inside. No sound came forth so I began unwrapping the package as all of my old imaginings began to return. At this time I could see that my brother had a jealous look on his face, as I was getting a present and he wasn't. After removing the ribbons and paper I placed the box on the table to remove the cover. The box cover came off and I found myself staring at a piece of black rubber. My first impression was that it was a rubber life raft that you blow up.

I was confused and dumfounded when I heard Josie tell me to remove it from the box. When I finally got the rubber thing unraveled I was—to put it mildly—horrified. Where were all those things that I had thought of getting? I found myself staring at a black rubber raincoat. Josie then insisted I try it on. I had no will to resist. Total humiliation occurred when they had me put on the black rubber fisherman's hat that came with the raincoat. I felt like a freak as the two women beamed with pride, and my brother had difficulty controlling his laughter.

My mother and Josie went through a ritual of checking out the rubber suit to make sure everything fit. The last part of the program in humiliation was the most difficult. I had to thank Josie and act as if I were glad to receive this thoughtful present. In this department I did have a lot of experience from past Christmases, as all I ever got was underwear, socks, sweaters, and scarves, yet I always had to behave as if that was exactly what I wanted.

I never wore the damn thing. It eventually passed into the no-man's-land of useless presents put away to be given to someone else as a thoughtful gift at a later date. The box with the rubber raincoat remained in the attic for years, finally falling victim to time as the rubber dried out and became brittle. No one could ever be found who would appreciate it. With a collection of other useless presents it was thrown out to spend all eternity in junkyard heaven.

And not long after I received my present we were told we had to move—Josie and Bill wanted the apartment.

THE PROMISE

It was on one of those hot, humid days in July that I found my-self in the kitchen sitting in a platform rocker trying to cool off. I was very overheated and thirsty. I remembered my mother's constant admonition that I shouldn't get overheated as there was a polio epidemic occurring at this time. Using a knife, I chopped off a piece of ice from the large block inside the icebox. I put it in a glass of ice cold water which I got from the pan beneath the icebox that collected the melted ice.

The early 1940s were a time of fear for most parents. Polio (infantile paralysis) was devastating many families throughout the area. Swimming pools were closed and most activities involving children were cancelled. At this time little was really known about polio and the doctors were powerless to help. It was up to each individual family to cope with the disease as best they knew how. In this neighborhood, garlic and a bag of camphor mothballs worn on a string around the neck were the preferred means of preventing the disease. It seemed as if there was always the sound of the ambulance siren to remind you that this invisible killer was lurking in your area.

This was the climate at the time that I was sitting in the rocker drinking cold water in my overheated condition. My mother's warnings had gone unheeded.

The sitting position I had assumed in the rocker was unusual for me. I was sitting on my right leg, which was tucked under my other leg so that my full body weight rested on it. I was in this position for perhaps ten minutes when I decided to get another glass of cold water. Jumping up, I immediately fell to the floor.

Something was clearly wrong, although I didn't feel any pain. I tried getting up but I could not feel the floor with my leg, and I stumbled back down. I now touched my leg with my hands, and could not feel my hands on my leg. With great difficulty, by hanging on to the edge of the rocker, I managed to pull myself into a sitting position.

All of a sudden it struck me—I had contracted polio! I was very well acquainted with the ravages of this disease, as one of my friends had contracted it. I was also familiar with that godawful machine that was called an "iron lung." I knew that people could spend the rest of their lives in it, as they needed it to breathe. With the help of my imagination I was now completely terrified. Why didn't I listen to my mother?

I slowly lowered myself to the floor and took a kneeling position with my elbows on the rocker cushion, and with my head in my hands I began to pray.

"Dear God, I know I don't always do things right but I really don't think that I was so bad to deserve this kind of punishment. I know I lie a little and I even swear using your name. But all the kids do this and how come *they* didn't get polio? I know why you're punishing me—it's because I keep skipping church on Sundays and going down to the railroad tracks and then lying to my mother about where I've been. Look, God, let's make a deal. You cure me of this polio and I promise I won't skip church anymore to go down to the railroad tracks. I'll even attend catechism classes."

I knew I wouldn't get a verbal answer, as I had occasionally talked to God in the past and he never answered. So after a few minutes I decided to try walking. Very cautiously I placed my right leg on the floor. It felt normal. I began to walk. Hallelujah! I was cured.

I was overjoyed, no polio. Boy, I thought, God can sure work fast when he has a mind to. And I had all the best intentions of keeping my promise.

Weeks went by, and one Sunday morning I found myself walking along the railroad tracks with my older brother instead of going to church. I was feeling somewhat guilty about being there, and I told him the story about my polio. He looked at me as if I were an idiot, then informed me that my leg had fallen asleep from the position I was sitting in.

How was I to know? This was the first time I had come in contact with this "fall asleep" syndrome. This may also have been the first time I came in contact with that old saying, "The road to hell is paved with good intentions."

THE HUNTER

I t is 1943. The boy is thirteen and in the seventh grade. The teacher stands at the blackboard explaining rules of grammar and illustrating how they work. Her attempt to hold the boy's interest in the subject is futile. He struggles to pay attention but the subject matter continues to elude him and he simply cannot understand what she is trying to teach. In his mind he can find no practical reason why anyone should learn how to diagram a sentence.

His attention continually drifts towards the large windows that overlook a wooded valley. This valley serves as his second home and whenever free time allows he spends his time here. It is the main attraction in his life, and for a young boy this is where the action takes place. He raises himself to get a better view, but hopefully not enough to attract the attention of the teacher who is struggling in vain to teach him grammar.

He notices a hunter following his two beagles trying to flush rabbits. The dogs begin yelping, which means they have found a trail.

He looks at the large clock on the wall to check the time; another hour to go before the school day ends. He can't wait until school is over so that he can head into the valley with his 410 shotgun. He is always afraid his mother will discover the two guns he has hidden in the cellar. He also owns a single shot Springfield .22 caliber rifle. His 410 folds down, reducing its length by half. It is hidden in a model airplane box and whenever he goes hunting he informs his mother that he is going over to a friend's house to build model airplanes.

This strategy is only necessary on weekends. During the week both his parents work long hours in a defense plant, and when he goes hunting after school it is not necessary to hide his shotgun. He does occasionally get rabbits or squirrels and he always has to give them away, as he can't bring them home to be cooked. He looks forward to the day that he will be old enough to bring his game home and have it prepared for supper.

The boy hears two shots and without thinking stands up to get a better view. Suddenly, reality strikes: "William, come up to the blackboard and diagram this sentence!" The tone of the teacher's voice is a clear indication that she has observed his lack of attention and now it is time for retribution. A strange mixture of fear and hate overcomes him as he approaches the blackboard. Some of the girls begin to giggle in anticipation of his embarrassment, as they are well acquainted with his lackluster performances in school. The teacher seems menacing as she holds out the hand containing the chalk, and with the look of a successful gladiator she instructs him to underline the verb. He takes the chalk and turns to the blackboard to study the sentence. Viewing the sentence with a dumb look on his face, he is aware that the giggles are getting louder. With developing anger he turns towards the class to face his tormentors in a defiant posture. This only serves to fuel the fires, as giggles now break out into laughter. Only one girl, Sophia, shows a hint of compassion as he is being roasted.

"Since you don't know what a verb is," the teacher announces, "try underlining the pronoun." He is no longer looking at the blackboard but simply staring down at his shoes, hoping this whole scene will just go away. The spell is finally broken when the teacher announces, "William, you will remain after school for extra instruction. Is that clear?" He nods his head and starts back towards his seat, all the while tightening his jaws, preparing to run the gauntlet of the giggling little witches.

Back in the security of his seat, he realizes it isn't necessary to pay any more attention to the class instructions. He turns to look out of the windows the way some people turn towards God—to find relief from the trials and tribulations of life.

Then it dawns on him. Damn, there would be no hunting after school today.

THE SEVENTH GRADE

Of all the classes that I attended in grammar school, the most memorable—and most important—was the seventh grade. This particular class had profound effects upon me that would serve me well in the years to come. In this grammar school, the seventh grade teacher was also the principal of the school. We had a strange mixture of ethnic groups, as the principal was German, the teachers were mostly Jewish, and the pupils were Polish. I also remember a couple of very pretty Dutch girls.

Miss Rymarcik, the principal, was a no-nonsense woman, and she had a special kind of toughness that was common in the 1940s but very rare today. She was generally liked and although single she did not convey the bitterness that seemed to possess some of the other single teachers.

Even though she was traditional in her teaching, there were some aspects of her class that were completely different from all others and it was one of these differences that had such an important influence on my life and thinking.

In her class, everyone was seated according to that month's grade average. So the person with the highest grade average would sit in row #1, seat #1, and the one with the next highest in the seat behind. When all was complete, the students would be seated one behind another according to their test results. Every month the seating would change, reflecting changing grade averages. The surprising thing was that over the period of a school year pupils rarely changed places by more than a seat or two. This system was a constant reminder of how you were doing compared to everyone else.

The first five seats were always held by girls. In fact, the whole first row was almost always filled with girls. Steve Shaw was the only boy in the class who ever entered that magic circle, the first row. Rows one and two were dominated by girls, while rows three and four were considered boys' territory. Yours truly was usually in the first seat of the third row. It would be safe to say that attention in school was not one of my strong points.

However, this story is about the fourth row, and a couple of individuals who resided there. By all reasoning, one would have to conclude that their future would indeed be bleak. This row, and in particular the last seat, was obviously a place to be avoided if you wished to avoid the ridicule of your classmates. If you were a boy it didn't matter to the other boys, as long as you were good at sports. To the girls it was a different matter. Yes, little girls at that age are not always sweet and nice.

John Pandorf was one of those pupils who were always in contention for that last seat. He was not very academic, but he was a fine athlete and excelled in most sports. He became one of the major players on our local football team, the Wallington Bulldogs. My best friend back then, who is still my best friend fifty-five years later, was often the other front runner for the last seat in the last row. Stanley Posluszny is now a multi-millionaire, living a life that would be the envy of his classmates, especially those who once inhabited the first row.

When Stan was a 16-year-old high school student, he took a job in a bakery. He had to arrive at the bakery at 3:00 A.M. to prepare for the morning customers. He would leave the bakery at 7:00 A.M. and ride his bicycle home to prepare for school. After school he would return home, have a bite to eat, and pedal his bicycle back to work, a distance of two miles. He had to be back at work by 3:30 P.M. and he would work until 7:00 P.M. When he finished he would return home on his bicycle for some much-needed sleep. He continued this routine for two years, until he graduated.

A few of our seventh grade classmates went on to college, some went into the trades, others went to work in factories. A few, like myself, went into the military. Upon graduation, Stan was a master baker, and he found an excellent job immediately. Stan worked as a master baker for ten years before saving sufficient money to buy his own business. He worked very hard and soon owned two bakeries.

One of the problems he faced in the bakery business was what to do with all the leftovers that eventually went stale. He resolved the problem by raising hamsters in the basement of his home and feeding them the stale bread. At one time he had two hundred pairs of breeding hamsters in his basement. If you know anything at all about biology and hamsters you have some idea of the number of offspring they could produce. Laboratories and hospitals were the main purchasers of the young hamsters. (Stan's wife, Dorothy, deserves a great deal of credit, as it was she who cleaned the cages and kept the whole operation going.)

After ten years in the bakery business, with people now doing more and more of their purchasing in supermarkets, Stan decided it was time for another profession. He sold his bakeries at a good price and entered school to become a stock broker. His motto was simple: "If you have to do something, you may as well choose that which will make you money."

After graduating he found it impossible to get a job, as the companies all wanted someone with experience. Finally he was given the chance that he needed. There was a stipulation that he had just six months to show his abilities. Today he is senior vice president of a well-known brokerage firm and a wealthy man.

So if by chance you should someday end up in the fourth row, or your situation in life feels like the fourth row, do not despair. For in America, no one with a well-developed work ethic will ever suffer due to lack of opportunity. If you look carefully at the immigrants who gave up their past attachments to become Americans—the Irish, Germans, Italians, Poles and a host of others—the most important commodity that they brought with them was a strong work ethic. It was this quality that could not be measured in school, and that defied the stigma of the last seat in the last row.

GRANDPA

My grandfather was born in 1865 on a small farm near the city of Lwów in southern Poland. This area has been under the domination of several different countries at various times during Polish history. Today, Lwów is a city in the recently independent country of Ukraine. Before Ukrainian independence it was a province of Russia, which received it at the end of World War II from Poland. The Poles even today are very bitter at the transfer of their homeland to the Russians by the Americans and British at Teheran.

Sometime around the year 1900, my grandfather left his farm and emigrated to America. His purpose was to find a good job, save some money, and then send for his family that remained behind in Poland. His oldest son, Joseph, who was fifteen at the time, would care for the family and work the farm with the help of some money being sent back from America.

My grandfather was living on Fourth Street in Passaic and working at the Hammersly waxpaper mill in Garfield when tragedy struck. He was informed that his wife and three of his four children had burned to death when their house caught fire. Only the eldest son, Joseph, survived. My grandfather would later describe the cottage as being made of wood with a straw roof and dirt floor. He returned to Poland, but after comparing Poland with America he gave the farm to this son and returned to his new and now-permanent home.

He married another immigrant, a Polish woman, and this union produced three children, one of whom was my mother. He continued living on Fourth Street and working for the Hammersly company.

An unfortunate accident occurred while he was employed at Hammersly that would have profound effects on all of his family. While working on the loading docks, he fell off the dock and broke his leg. He was out of work for over a month. When he returned, his supervisor warned him not to go out onto the loading docks but to remain in the warehouse. It wasn't long before the supervisor found him outside on the loading docks that he had been warned to stay away from. The supervisor fired him on the spot. My grandfather had six months to go until retirement, and his stubbornness cost him his pension. He and his wife, who died shortly afterward, moved in with two of their children, my aunt and my mother, who at this time was separated and had two young children of her own.

We were living in Wallington at 51 Stein Avenue when we became aware of a strange relationship between my grandfather and another man who lived nearby. What I gather from the discussions about my grandfather and Mr. Zigmund was that they hated each other, and whenever they bumped into each other on their almost-daily walks they would go through a ritual of spitting at each other as they passed. Apparently there was some deep-seated bitterness from an unusual source, as this strange behavior began almost as soon as they became neighbors.

The reason for their behavior came to light when a very knowledgeable local woman informed my mother of the history of Lwów at the time my grandfather lived there. Apparently, Mr. Zigmund came from the same general area as my grandfather. The woman asked my mother for some details about how her father had lived. I was quite surprised how little she knew about her father's life in Poland. Other than his being a poor farmer, she had some vague recollection of his being connected to a Polish cavalry unit at a very young age.

The woman, with my mother's information and assisted by a good education, was able to piece together a creditable story to explain the men's strange behavior. She explained that the area around Lwów was not always Polish, but also Russian, Ukrainian, and Austrian. And that as the countryside changed hands new immigrants would move in, very often confiscating lands from the present inhabitants. She explained how the Ukraine was once owned and ruled by wealthy noblemen from Poland who were absentee landlords who never even visited their property. Rather, they had managers who were very hard on the peasants, and this situation created a climate for both hatred and rebellion. At the time my grandfather was there, Lwów was part of the Austrian Empire. Austrian immigrants also moved into the Ukraine, creating further animosity. Since my grandfather and Mr. Zigmund were from two opposing groups, their bitterness had its roots in this complex web of European conflicts. Both were probably peasants and were treated very poorly by the opposition.

So even though the Pole and the "Cossack" were both living in a new land, and the children of both families were thoroughly American, they still continued to live in the old world they had left, and would most likely do so until their deaths.

In the summer of 1943, my mother, stepfather, grandfather, aunt, brother and I all lived together in a very small three-bedroom apartment on Park Row. We always referred to the house as Kobcsenski's house, as Mrs. Kobscenski was the owner. My brother and I slept in an unheated attic that was entered by way of a trapdoor in one of the bedrooms. In the winter, the attic was the outside temperature. In the summer it would collect heat, and temperatures of 100 degrees were not unusual. Ventilation was through one small window. We never had a fan.

The room where the trapdoor was located was my grandfather's bedroom. Hanging on the wall next to the ladder leading to the trapdoor was a picture of a Polish general, General Pilsudski, astride a white horse, leading the Polish cavalry. Growing up in a Polish area, I had heard many discussions about him and knew he was considered quite a Polish hero, as he had apparently saved Poland from the

Russian invaders around 1920.

For some reason, my mother hated this picture. My grandfather frequently complained to my mother that my brother and I were always knocking his picture off the wall when we climbed the very steep steps to our attic bedroom. One day a pretty heated argument broke out and she told him to move the damn thing to another wall. Having some well-developed Polish characteristics, he refused.

The next day she decided to take action. While he was away on one of his almost-daily walks to Pulaski Park in Passiac, where he would meet his old friends from Fourth Streeet, she decided to burn the picture. She hoped that he would not notice it was gone, and even if he did there was not much he could do—or so she thought. She had a lot to learn about her own father.

It was a Saturday, perhaps 9:30 A.M., when he noticed that his precious picture was missing. He immediately confronted my brother and me, thinking we had taken it. He was in an absolute rage and we didn't know what was going on, as he couldn't speak English and we didn't understand Polish.

Finally, my mother stepped in and a heated argument in Polish broke out between them. It wasn't long before my mother was crying, as she watched her father begin throwing all her clothes out the second-story window. Apparently he was evicting her, even though it was she who supplied him with a home.

At some point, she made a deal with him to get him another picture. She went downstairs and began retrieving her clothes. After getting all her clothes back into the apartment, she informed my brother and me that she was going to Passaic to buy a picture of Pilsudski and that she would be back in a little while.

My brother and I decided to steer clear of our grandfather, so we left the apartment. We were playing on the stoop, pitching pennies, when we saw my mother walking back from Passaic. She had been gone at least four or five hours, and it was now about 3 P.M. She was weeping and looking very dejected, and she was not carrying a picture of Pilsudski.

We entered the apartment together and there was my grandfather sitting in his rocker, smoking his pipe, waiting for her to return. There was a short discussion in Polish. At the end, my mother took out five dollars, which was a lot of money back then, and handed it to him. He immediately left the house in search of a picture of Pilsudski. He returned an hour later . . . and yes, he had a picture of Pilsudski, as well as a bottle of Rock & Rye whiskey.

That night before we went to our attic bedroom, my mother warned us: "You be careful when you climb the ladder. I don't want any more trouble over that goddam picture."

And so, just as in his great victory over the Russians at the battle of the Niemen River, Pilsudski would triumph again on the wall of my grandfather's bedroom, much to the displeasure of my mother.

A very important Polish tradition was the preparing of the table with traditional foods to be blessed by the local priest at Easter.

The table would be covered with ham, kielbasa, decorated hard-boiled eggs, and other favorite foods, such as homemade cheese, horseradish, and a bread known as babka. Sometimes pictures or objects would also be placed on the table to receive blessings and perhaps even good luck. After much preparation, the requirement was to put a five dollar bill under the tablecloth to pay the priest for blessing the table. The priest would also write something in chalk above one of the doorways, although I never did know what it meant.

One Easter, the priest arrived sometime around 11 a.m, all dressed in his regalia, and after a short discussion with my mother began the process of bestowing his blessings upon the food. My brother and I, being somewhat fascinated by the procedure, watched from the doorway to the living room

Everything appeared to be going along pretty normally. Very subtly, while conversing with my mother, the priest's fingers began to probe under the tablecloth behind him in search of the five-dollar bill my mother had placed there. He kept going back and forth, meanwhile engaging in conversation, until in a moment of frustration he simply turned around, picked up the tablecloth, and looked for the money.

My mother was extremely upset and the priest was equally embarrassed when they both realized there was no five-dollar bill hidden beneath the tablecloth. To complicate conditions, my mother did not have any money on hand to give to the priest. She apologized, and in her state of confusion apologized again and again. The priest finally left when my mother promised him she would deliver the money to him by the end of the day.

As soon as he left, my mother confronted my brother and me about the missing money. It was soon obvious to her that we had nothing to do with its disappearance. She next headed towards the room of her father, who at the time of this incident was 84 years old. Considering the time of day, the door to his room should have been open, but it wasn't. In the past, she would always knock on his door and wait for an answer before entering—but not this time.

She opened the door and there he was, sitting in his rocking chair, obviously very drunk. A quick search of his dresser drawers revealed a hidden bottle of Rock & Rye whiskey, which was half empty. To my mother, the mysterious disappearance of the five dollars was now solved.

She was swearing in Polish as she dumped the remaining contents into the sink. My mother had no love for alcohol or those who drank it.

She ended up borrowing five dollars from our neighbor. After putting it into an envelope with another apology, she had me and my brother deliver it to the rectory where the priest lived. He was delighted to see us with the money, and after a brief chat he broached the subject of me and my brother becoming altar boys. With that, we quickly left—as we were both aware that we were not altar boy material, despite what others may have thought.

Grandpa

THE FIREHOUSE

Across the street from Sura's back yard stood the old wooden firehouse. The ground floor held one fire engine and a round table for card games. The upstairs was a large empty hall that was used for meetings, dances, the firehouse picnic, and any other events that required a large room. It also had a basement to hold all of the stuff connected to a firehouse, including all of the apparatus needed for cooking.

The firecall was a very loud siren reminiscent of a London air raid. I'm sure it must have shortened the life of some people living close to the firehouse by giving them premature heart attacks. It was also used to inform the local population when it was 12 o'clock noon.

The annual firehouse picnic was a major event, looked forward to by the local residents. The picnic offered foods that were not ordinarily available to the area people. At this time, people did not generally own automobiles; for us, supermarkets did not exist and we did not eat out. Our world of food was Belski's grocery store on the corner of Park Row and Adamson Avenue, although we did occasionally get to Boruta's Bakery (now Banas's), the Wallington Potato King, or over to Adams Market to pick up our smoked kielbasa for the Christmas or Easter holidays.

It was at one of the firehouse picnics that I discovered the taste of raw clams and hot sauce. However, I couldn't really indulge myself as the price was beyond my means. They wanted twenty cents for a dozen clams on the half shell. To buy anything at the picnic you had to first purchase tickets, which cost ten cents each. Since I had no money I had to wait until my mother showed up. When she finally arrived I asked her if we could have some tickets. Her first question was, "Whaddya going to buy?"

Not thinking, I told her I wanted a dozen clams.

"What the hell do you want those damn things for? You get yourself something good to eat."

"Okay, Ma."

She handed me two tickets and then reminded me that I had only four tickets left for the rest of the picnic.

I waited until she was out of sight then took off for the clam bar. The clam bar was located outside, next to the firehouse building. I ordered my dozen clams and covered them with cocktail sauce (horseradish and ketchup). When the man behind the table took my tickets, I noticed that he placed them in a can on the window sill of the firehouse.

Taking my clams, I went over to the fire truck, which was parked in the empty lot between the firehouse and Kobscenski's house to make room inside the firehouse for the tables selling food. I took a comfortable seat on the back bumper and began my feast. I was eating the clams very slowly to savor the flavor as long as possible. I was about halfway through when my friend Louie came over. I gave him a couple of my clams, and never having eaten one before he showed an attachment for them similar to mine.

We had finished the clams and were discussing how to go about getting another dozen when I remembered the can of tickets sitting on the window sill. We took a walk over to find out what was on the other side of the window. We discovered that there was a stand set up to sell roast beef sandwiches and that it was being run by the two Grigliok sisters, Mary and Anka. We left and quickly developed a plan to get that can of tickets.

The two Grigliok sisters had never married and were the nicest people you could meet. They loved kids and would even allow us to climb their pear trees for the hard winter pears. My family lived next door to them in Kobscenski's house after we moved from Sura's house. During the season, we always had a supply of pear pies that they baked for my mother.

Our plan was based on timing. There must be no customers at the stand. Louie went over to the far end of the stand, away from the window. He did not order anything, just simply engaged them in conversation. The Griglioks loved to talk to kids and soon they were both preoccupied with Louie. While they were talking, I began the crawl under the tables toward the window with the ticket can on the sill. From under the table I could see their legs, and when they were both facing Louie I reached up and took the can of tickets. I then crawled back toward safety.

I met Louie back by the fire truck and we proceeded to split the tickets. We quickly ditched the can beneath the fire truck as we were both very much afraid. He hung around for half an hour and then we split up. I returned to the clam bar feeling very guilty, as if I had robbed a bank. I instantly noticed a new can, which was not on the windowsill but in a very secure location.

I ordered three dozen clams on the half shell. The man gave me a strange look, and it was then that I realized I had made a mistake in ordering so many.

"That's a lot of clams for a little kid," he commented.

I told him I was buying them for my uncle who was busy at the numbers game.

"Who's your uncle?" he asked

"Jinx," I replied.

A smile crossed his face. "Yeah, I know Jinx. He helps out in Kobscenski's gas station." He placed the clams on the table. "Your uncle's quite a character."

I nodded and left. I returned to the fire truck and renewed the process of self-indulgence. Unfortunately, I dropped a dozen clams in the back of the fire truck. Things were not going well. Also, I was concerned about the man knowing my Uncle Jinx.

I waited a while and then decided to take the risk of ordering more clams. It seemed to me you could eat these things all day long and not get enough. Seeing me approaching the stand, the man yelled out, in a loud voice that made me uncomfortable, "Your uncle wants more clams, huh?"

Without really looking at him I replied, "Yeah, three dozen."

He took my tickets and placed them in the can and returned to the counter with three plates piled on top of each other. I had to separate them to be able to cover all the clams with hot sauce. He was watching me as I applied the sauce. I picked up the plates and was getting ready to leave when he spoke.

"Hey, kid, you eat too many of those things and you're gonna get sick."

Returning to the fire truck I placed the clams on the bumper. I began eating, but I did not have the same enthusiasm as before. Partly into the second plate my stomach began to get a little queasy. Living only two hundred feet from the firehouse, I decided to leave the remaining clams on the bumper and go home to take the stomach cure.

Arriving home, I poured a large glass of buttermilk and began drinking it. Within seconds I made a dash for the toilet to throw up. In the agony of throwing up, as the violent convulsions rocked my body, his words kept coming back to me: "Hey, kid, you eat too many of those things and you're gonna get sick." But I knew I'd have been all right if I hadn't drunk that damn buttermilk.

THE SAILOR

It was a pleasant Sunday as we walked from Park Row in Wallington to Fourth Street in Passaic to visit my Aunt Annie, who still lived there. My brother and I enjoyed visiting her as she always roasted a chicken and made the best coleslaw around. There was an additional reason why we liked to visit. We could now fully appreciate living in Wallington with all the more interesting things to do, but Wallington didn't have a Market Street or a Palace Theater.

My Aunt Annie was plain—wholesome, but plain. When we lived together on Fourth Street I can't recall her ever having a boyfriend or going on a date. This evening after supper I noticed a picture on the living room wall that I had never seen before. It was a picture of a ship and also a sailor. I asked her about the pictures and she proudly informed me that the sailor was her boyfriend and that they would be getting married when he came home from his tour of duty in the Pacific. I asked her what type of a ship he was on.

"I don't know," she replied, "but it's very big and has a lot of big guns on it."

"What's its name?" I asked

She walked over to the picture of the ship and, looking at, it finally announced, "The USS Pennsylvania."

"Aunt Anne, what does USS stand for?" I asked

"How the hell do I know, I work in a cigar factory."

The summer and fall would go by very quickly. War clouds were gathering everywhere. Adults were always discussing the possibilities of war and we kids knew pretty much about what was going on as we also listened to the radio—and to their conversations.

And then it happened, December 7, 1941, the attack by the Japanese on the American Pacific Fleet at Pearl Harbor.

Several weeks after the attack my aunt unexpectedly showed up at our apartment in Sura's house on Park Row. It was immediately apparent that something was wrong. My mother told my brother and me to go outside and play or to go into the attic, where we also played in winter time. After an hour or so we heard my aunt leave and quickly returned to the apartment to find out what was going on. On entering the apartment we saw my mother wiping tears from her eyes.

"What's wrong, Ma?" we enquired.

"Annie's boyfriend was serving aboard the USS Pennsylvania, and he was killed at Pearl Harbor."

On the right, Annie's boyfriend

WORLD WAR II

My first memory of World War II is of a Saturday in September of 1939, while we were living on Fourth Street in Passaic. It was my job to take out the garbage and to deposit it in the garbage can shed behind the apartment house. There was an alleyway between our building and the one next to us that I had to pass through to deposit the garbage. Upon entering the alleyway I heard a radio sitting on the windowsill make the following announcement: Fifty German tanks have broken through the Polish lines.

Over the next several weeks I heard isolated comments about the war, but to me at eight years old it did not carry any sense of importance, although the Polish people were always discussing it, as many of them were recent immigrants and almost all had relatives in Poland.

It was only after the Germans defeated France in 1940 that the war began to take on a new and serious perspective. And it was the air battle over Britain that finally awoke the consciousness of the American people to the dangers facing our country.

On December 7, 1941, our family was visiting relatives who lived on Hope Street in Passaic. It was a Sunday, and my brother and I were outside in the street throwing a ball with my stepfather when a window opened in the second floor apartment. My mother was at the window and she was very excited. "Steve," she yelled. "Quickly, come upstairs with the kids. We're at war, the damn Japs have bombed Pearl Harbor."

We went upstairs and we all sat around the radio waiting for more information. It got to be the same repetitious statement with no news forthcoming that hadn't already been heard. It wasn't long before the radio was turned off as it was time to settle down for the noon meal. At the meal the grown-ups began discussing the Japanese attack on Pearl Harbor. The discussion began with "Where the hell is Pearl Harbor?" They came to the conclusion that it was somewhere in the Pacific.

War activity now began in earnest and it could be seen everywhere you went. It was at this time that the radio took on a new value, as it was our only real means of finding out what was going on in the world. We were, as many others were, still suffering from the Depression, and money would not be squandered on purchasing newspapers. Although the factories in Passaic began humming with activity and the Depression was coming to an end, it would continue to be a part of most people's psyche for many more years to come.

The year 1942 saw many young men in Wallington volunteer for military service. Soon there would be a draft and many more would be called. Everyone knew who was in the service, as a flag in the window showed a blue star for every person in the household who was in the military. As a youngster during this period it seemed to me as if every household had someone in the service. Across the street the three Szymanski boys were in the Navy. There were several Kopecs and Kudlaciks in the service. The Kobscenskis also provided several servicemen.

The flags became very prominent when they had a gold star, which meant that someone had been killed serving the country. Mothers who lost their sons were known as "Gold Star Mothers." There were quite a few Gold Star families in my neighborhood, including Byra and Miskuff from Kossuth Street, Poloniak from Park Row, and Maciag and Shaira from Stein Avenue.

In the summer of 1942 a few of us kids were playing in Krug's woods when our complacent children's world came to an abrupt end. Next to the Pandorf house on Willow Avenue was an old dirt access road that led to a large field and Krug's woods (today's Jacob Street). We saw large army trucks pull in at the edge of the woods and unload their cargo of soldiers. There must have been fifty soldiers in those trucks. They broke into various groups and immediately went to work, some erecting large army tents, others with axes and saws clearing trees and brush.

Approaching the group of soldiers that were engaged in clearing the land, we asked if we could help. They put us to work dragging brush and treetops to a clearing where it was to be burned. After an hour or so of this kind of work we got pretty thirsty and decided to go down to the spring that was located near the police pistol range and get a drink of cold spring water (today a street nearby is called Spring Street).

When we returned, we told the soldiers about the spring and they quickly rounded up a dozen canteens for us to fill. The drinking water they were using was brought in by truck in five gallon tins and was pretty warm by the time they got to drink it. Our main chore from then on was to supply them with nice, cold spring water.

Although soldiers were working on clearing large areas the entire length of Showhank Hill, we were only familiar with those working in the vicinity of Krug's woods. There were other army units doing the same things south of Alden Street but we had no contact with them, although we heard some stories about the large snakes that they killed in this area while clearing brush for their barracks, most likely black snakes, which can get to be six feet long.

That afternoon they worked until about 4:30 P.M. The tents were now up and they began cleaning themselves off and settling into their new quarters. There was a special tent, different from the ones that they used for sleeping, which was square and had sides that could be rolled up. There were tables inside the tent as well as in front and it was all set up to serve food, although there was no stove.

A short time after the men had cleaned up, an army truck pulled up to the tent with the tables and began unloading what looked like large garbage cans. These were brought into the tent and the contents removed and placed on the table. The strange cans actually held trays of hot food, which were for the soldiers' meal. Soon a line formed and soldiers holding funny looking trays and canteen cups slowly walked by the tables as other soldiers served them food and drink. One of the soldiers in the tent was some kind of boss, and he told the servers to feed us since we were helping with the clearing. He then spoke to a group of soldiers, telling them that when they were through eating they should let us borrow their mess kits. The soldiers, when finished eating, would wash their mess kits in a large barrel of soapy water then dip them in a barrel of clean water to rinse them off. How proud we felt when the soldiers came over to us, handed us their mess kits, and told us to get some food. Slowly walking past the tables, we received a piece of chicken, mashed potatoes, green beans, and some kind of pink drink. After we ate, we tried mimicking the soldiers' behavior by washing the mess kits as they did. However, in the process of washing my mess kit I dropped it in the barrel and could not reach it in the bottom—I couldn't even see it in the dirty water. It was embarrassing to have to ask the owner to reach in and retrieve it.

For the next several days we continued to bring them cold spring water in canteens. Once the area was cleared, very large army trucks came to the encampment and began unloading prefabricated army barracks. In three days the barracks were all erected and the tents were then taken down. However, the canvas food tent remained, and three times a day a truck would arrive with hot food. If the weather was nice, the soldiers would sit on the ground outside and eat; if the weather was poor they would eat in the barracks.

The soldiers ate food that was far different from our normal fare, as we were still feeling the effects of the Depression and now food rationing had been added. One morning in particular was a real puzzle for us, as the cooks served us breakfast (we ate there regularly).

They put a blackened piece of toast on our trays then covered it with a loose type of hamburger meat mixed with sauce. We ate this with relish, then tried to find out what its name was so we could tell our mothers to make it. Even though I enquired, no one seemed to know. Finally one soldier yelled to another, "Tell the kids the only name we know it by is 'shit on a shingle'." I wasn't about to tell my mother *that* name.

One day we were in a part of Krug's woods where the soldiers had never been before. Suddenly, ten or fifteen of them arrived with axes and shovels, ready to work. Scattered through the area were large old tree stumps from another era, some three feet in diameter, probably old chestnut tree stumps. They carefully chose an area on a hillside with no large stumps and some of them began digging. Others cut down the taller cherry trees and cut logs about twelve feet long. When the large excavation was complete they covered it with the cherry logs, which were then covered with boards and two to three feet of soil. The entrance to this bunker was at a steep angle and it was covered by a very heavy tarpaulin. It was at this time that we learned what the soldiers were here for, as this was an ammunition bunker.

A few days later, as we returned from our spring water run, we were greeted by a sight which thrilled us and made us proud that we were part of the effort to create this army camp. Trucks began rolling in, each one towing a two-barreled anti-aircraft gun. This particular unit had about four to six guns scattered around the camp. And this was only one camp of many scattered along the hill. Soon after, they began stringing barbed wire to enclose the area. The guns and the ammunition depot were now ringed by barbed wire and patrolled by armed soldiers.

There was still no water available in the encampment. It all had to be trucked in, and usually it was warm. We kids were the water carriers, always providing the soldiers with cold spring water, which they really appreciated. They knew us so well that we had complete freedom to hang around the barracks. Even in the evenings we would go into the barracks to talk to them, and by their strange accents we knew they were from the South. They always seemed to be playing music on guitars, but there was one fellow who was very popular and he could really get his fellow soldiers stomping their feet and singing. I was familiar with guitars but this was the first time I ever heard a banjo.

One day I will never forget was the time when several of us kids were watching them practice on their anti-aircraft guns. The area was pretty busy with airplane traffic, especially coming from Bendix (now Teterboro) Airport. When a plane was sighted the three-man crew would traverse the gun until the plane was in its sights. It would then track the plane. One soldier operated a wheel that moved the guns vertically, while another moved the guns horizontally. There was also an ammunition loader. After they were through, one of them called out to us, standing fifty feet away, "Hey, kids, wanna try the guns?"

We just about fell over ourselves taking a seat on the anti-aircraft gun. We fooled around with the wheels that controlled the gun's direction for a while until we were told it was time to get down. Getting down from the guns and seeing the smiles on the soldiers' faces, we all felt ten feet tall.

That evening at supper I told my mother about the soldiers' allowing us to play with the anti-aircraft gun. Her face showed some concern.

"Were there any bullets in it?" she asked.

We got to know those soldiers so well that they were regular guests at many houses for Sunday dinner during the entire time they were stationed in Wallington. It was early in 1943 that the soldiers were withdrawn. It happened so fast that the whole camp was gone in a week, and hardly a sign remained. The only trace of their presence lasted for years, and that was the ammunition bunker in Krug's woods.

It was at Jefferson School that World War II would affect us on a daily basis, and it was expected that everyone attending would help in the war effort. Each day during the war began the same. After the class assembled, we would march into the main hallway and the entire hallway full of pupils would salute the flag and say the Pledge of Allegiance, the first, second, third, and fourth grades in the downstairs hallway and the fifth, sixth, seventh, and eighth upstairs. After we returned to class, the teacher would take attendance. When this was finished she would ask the class if anyone had money to purchase war bond stamps. If you wished to purchase a stamp at ten cents or a quarter you gave the teacher the money and she would give you a stamp. This you would paste in your war bond book, and when the book was full you traded it in for a war bond that cost $16.75. At maturity the bond was worth $25.

After this process was completed she would ask who had brought cans to school. She kept a record book of how many tin cans each pupil brought to school. If you brought in a certain number, usually in the hundreds, you would receive a chevron to sew on your shirt sleeve to show your rank. The ranks were the same as in the military: corporal, sergeant, etc. It showed how much you contributed to the war effort. One girl in the sixth grade became a general, she brought in so many cans. I believe her name was Audrey Vandervliet, and her father owned a restaurant.

Another item that we were supposed to collect was aluminum. Aluminum was not a popular item during this period, as most pots and pans were made from steel covered with porcelain. The only real sources of aluminum were cigarette packs and chewing gum wrappers, and it had to be carefully separated from the paper. As you collected these small pieces of aluminum you would add them to a ball being made from your collection efforts. When it was large enough, you brought it to school where they had a bin to collect stuff.

One day the teacher announced a new item that she wanted us to collect. It was milkweed. We knew what the government wanted iron and aluminum for, but no one could figure out what you could possibly want with milkweed. We eventually found out that it had to do with making synthetic rubber for tires and tubes. It really didn't matter, as it gave us an opportunity to comb the fields below Jefferson School as far as the railroad tracks to find our quarry. The pods contained a milky substance that was very sticky and very difficult to remove if it got on your hands. We would usually wipe our hands on our pants, to the displeasure of our mothers, who did the washing with an old-fashioned washboard. (Washing machines were scarce items during the war; although a few people had the wringer-type machine, this was still the age of washboards and iceboxes.)

Several times a week during the entire war we would have to suffer through mock air raid drills. The procedure was as follows: upon the ringing of a bell each class would line up and be marched into the long hallway separating the classrooms. We would have to kneel down and cover our heads with our hands. The purpose of this procedure was to get us away from the large glass windows that all the classrooms had. At the beginning of the war these drills were taken quite seriously, but after the removal of the anti-aircraft guns from the hill even the kids knew it was all a sham. We used to kid around that all the anti-aircraft guns on the hill were there to protect Jefferson School.

All through Jefferson School were buckets of sand placed in important locations, to be used in case the school was hit by incendiary bombs that might have missed their targets. We would receive lectures about these incendiary bombs and one of the main points was never to put water on them as it only made the fire worse. Did they expect us to fight fires? What we really learned was that the bombs contained magnesium and were even at times referred to as magnesium bombs. By 1943 we had our own supply of magnesium, as one of the factories nearby was dumping it at Van Kruiningen's dump.

The hallways of Jefferson School also held a good many posters about helping the nation during the war. Posters were everywhere, showing the enemy—the Japs and Huns, as they were commonly called—in the most unflattering of caricatures. One in particular I remember very well was a Jap pilot with large buck teeth and Coke-bottle eyeglasses, an obvious reference to their physical inferiority.

The posters of Germans would often show them as Neanderthals with low foreheads and large eyebrows, carrying a gun with an over-size bayonet, usually bloody. (I've often wondered what kind of posters they had in Japan and Germany depicting us. Also, how come there were no posters showing Italians?)

Sometime around early 1944, someone placed a destroyed German tank next to the factory known as Tube Reducing, which was on Main Street in Wallington (across the street from Jasontown). It was another symbol to remind us who the enemy was. People going to their strategic jobs at Curtiss-Wright and Tube Reducing would be constantly reminded of the war as they went to work. To us kids it was an object to play on, and a reminder of how superior we were compared to our enemies, just like the posters at school taught us.

Those posters did wonders to remind us that we were at war and that we should keep up our efforts to defeat the enemy, which we did. We kept those tin cans, gum wrappers, and anything else we could find coming in to school.

Once a week at Jefferson School there was a general assembly. I believe it was on a Thursday. This was in two sections, as the older kids were upstairs and the younger downstairs, and the largest room could not contain the entire student population. During the war there was quite naturally a war theme most of the time. When the weather was nice we would assemble on the flat field at the east side of the school facing Wood-Ridge. A Victrola would play marches and we would parade to the sounds of John Phillip Sousa. At other times we would sing patriotic songs in the assembly, and some pupils would even participate in plays which they put together. In one assembly, I sang a song with a friend of mine. It was a rewrite of an old army song. I can only remember the first stanza:

"Over hill, over dale, we are on Hitler's trail

"As the caissons go rolling along," etc.

All the assemblies had some variety, which encompassed not only the war but also poetry and music. Most of us kids during the war years had little interest in poetry but this did not prevent the teachers at Jefferson School from trying to interest us in it. One even required us to memorize a poem. It began "Abu Ben Adam, may his tribe increase/ Awoke one night from a deep dream of peace." The entire class had to recite the whole poem during assembly.

Poetry was bad enough but sing-alongs were worse. One particular song used to grate on me when the teacher played it on the piano. It had something to do with a worm. Brightworm, or lightworm, or glowworm, whatever its name it set back my interest in music by years.

Lectures on incendiary bombs and guest speakers were far more interesting. One guest speaker that really stands out in my mind was a native of Wallington who had moved to Alaska. His name was Miskuff, and I heard later that he was a bush pilot. He showed us all kinds of Eskimo clothes and the tools that they used. It was the harpoons that attracted the most attention.

There was also an assembly in which movies were shown concerning Jefferson School kids playing around the railroad tracks below the school. Most of us were well aware that boxcars were being opened and that kids were doing some damage along the tracks. Hidden cameras would take movie films of kids along the tracks and these would be shown in school to discourage the kids from hanging around the tracks. This did not work out too well, as when someone in the assembly was recognized general laughter would break out. At times someone would say out loud, "Look, there's . . . ." At one particular assembly, at least half a dozen kids from the Morrissey Avenue section were filmed along the railroad tracks.

Jefferson School had no lunch program, so if you wished lunch you brought your own. Lunches were eaten in the basement and seating was on long wooden benches. You could buy a half pint of milk for two cents or drink water from the fountain. On nice days many of the kids chose to eat outside. However, there were no benches so most would just lean up against the school building while they ate. The only lavatory for the entire student body was in the basement.

During the war years, usually about 10 o'clock in the morning but sometimes in the afternoon, we would get a short break and everyone would receive a box of raisins. Sometimes we would receive a half pint of milk also, at no charge. I could only conclude that too many grapes were being produced or the government expected a long war and was trying to get its future soldiers healthy.

Whatever programs were going on at Jefferson School, such programs were also taking place in schools all over America to contribute to the war effort. However, in our minds it was Jefferson School and the Wallington servicemen that won World War II.

Jefferson School, unchanged in 2003

THE BUS

It was February of 1944 when tragedy struck. I was in the seventh grade and the teacher/principal was Miss Rymarcik. It was a very cold day and snow was lightly falling as we began the walk to Jefferson School. We rarely had a day off from school due to the weather. There were no radio programs that announced a school closing. Since no one was bused to school, at times we would walk to school to find out that the teachers couldn't make it and that school was closed. When there was snow the teachers would not try to climb the Park Row hill but would go the long way via the Paterson Plank Road to Mount Pleasant Avenue.

That morning about 10 A.M. we had just finished our arithmetic lesson when the teacher was called to the door by someone who wished to speak to her. As usual whenever the teacher was distracted, this provided us with an opportunity to engage in our personal conversations. We were in a gay mood as it was anticipated that we would be let out of school early, and for us boys that meant sled riding down Park Row hill. And if conditions were really good we would go higher and begin at the top of Willow Avenue. Starting way at the top was sometimes a little risky, as the sled would build up too much speed and it would be very difficult to make the curve at the bottom of Park Row. Very often you would hit the snow embankment and end up in Dolack's yard.

The teacher returned to the front of the class and stood there in silence as if debating how to go about addressing us. She was acting very strangely and her behavior clearly indicated that she had gotten information that was very disturbing to her. Sensing the uncomfortable situation the class became very quiet in anticipation of some very bad news. At this time our lives were very much dominated by the events of World War II, and I assumed that any bad news she would tell us was somehow war related.

"Children, it is very difficult for me to convey this news to you," she began. "However, I've just been informed that this morning one of the buses that goes through Wallington to Passaic has had an accident and has gone off the Market Street bridge into the Passaic River."

There was a stunned silence as each pupil tried to gauge his personal relationship to this event. Slowly hands began to rise as the pupils sought answers to put this tragedy into perspective.

"Was it an Olympic or Comfort bus?" one pupil asked.

"I do not know," the teacher replied.

"Was it going to Passaic or coming back?" another asked.

Again the teacher replied that she didn't know.

"What time did the accident occur?" someone asked.

"I have no information to add," responded the teacher.

She allowed the students to converse, as it was quite impossible to continue the lesson. She knew we were very concerned because many of our parents took either the Olympic or Comfort buses to their jobs in Passaic. Both bus lines used the Market Street bridge.

Very little was accomplished the rest of the day and we were not let out of school early as we had hoped. The school system was always somewhat reluctant to permit early dismissals as most of the pupils' parents were working in defense plants in Passaic and the younger ones might not have anyone to care for them.

Finally 3:15 arrived. The last instructions from the teacher were, "I want you all to go directly home and don't tarry at any of your friends' houses." By this time we all knew why—our parents might have been on that bus.

On our walk home all we talked about was the bus in the river and whether our parents were on it. I arrived home (Kobscenski's house) and found my grandfather sitting in the kitchen at the porcelain table playing with his dominoes. He did not seem to be aware of what had happened, and anyway his command of English was very poor, making the transfer of information impossible. I would have to wait until the usual time that my parents came home to learn the extent of what had happened and to whom.

I was really very worried and imagined the worst, but there was nothing I could do. Sitting in the rocker and looking out the window, I began to doze off. I was sharply awakened by the sound of the downstairs door closing and footsteps beginning to ascend the stairs to our apartment. I recognized my mother's footsteps immediately. I quickly picked up a comic book to show an attitude of unconcern. It was not manly to exhibit one's emotions. Entering the apartment, my mother removed her coat and shoes before speaking to me.

"Did you hear about the bus going into the river?" she asked.

In the most nonchalant way, so as not to reveal my concern, I replied, "Yeah, Ma, I heard about it. What's for supper?"

The bus that plunged off the Market Street bridge was actually returning to Wallington when it skidded on the ice and crashed through the guardrail into the Passaic River. At the time the tide was high and the river was coated with ice. Several very brave men who were working at U.S. Rubber went into the frigid waters to save some people. However, not that many survived and I believe about twenty-two passengers drowned.

POISON IVY

Moving from the city environment to a small town with a large expanse of woods and fields radically changed my life. I was a young boy with a whole new world to explore and one of the beautiful things about this new world was that it was relatively free of adults—at least the uninhabited area, which was only visited by a few hunters and the hobos who hung around the railroad track. I took to this wooded area like a duck to water, spending as much time there as possible.

However, in all new exciting worlds nothing is ever perfect and no solution simple. What I discovered here was a plant that caused blisters and itched like crazy, called poison ivy. This plant seemed to have a special attachment for me, for when spring came I was always plagued by its most intense symptom, those annoying itchy blisters.

One day at about 4:00 P.M. our neighbor, Mr. Bednarz, was sitting on his bench reading the newspaper. Back then all of the older men had their own wooden benches, and they would sit by their houses or sometimes get together and talk or play dominoes. Mr. Bednarz called me over to ask me a question, and seeing my hands in my pockets and constantly scratching asked me what was wrong. I told him I had poison ivy, and explained to him that my treatment was to scratch the blisters open then to swab the area with rubbing alcohol, this to be followed, if available, by a coating of Octagon soap, a dark soap used for laundry and anything else you could think of.

I didn't dare tell him that my pants pockets were completely holed out and didn't even exist as pockets. Actually, my legs and genitals were completely covered by poison ivy and when my hands were in my pockets I was scratching my private parts.

He thought for a moment, then walked over to some bushes and began picking leaves. He returned with a large handful and explained how this would help cure the poison ivy. He said I should cover the poison ivy with the leaves and hold them in place with some bandages. Back then we had a great deal of respect for older people and I figured he was some kind of sage, as he seemed to know a lot and could speak not only Polish but Russian. I also knew from hearing my mother talk to other women that the Polish people were big on home remedies. I gladly took the leaves and thanked him for providing me with a solution to my problem.

The next day before leaving for school I decided to apply the leaves to my private parts, as this was the area that itched the most. I was having a great deal of difficulty trying to hold these leaves in place in an area that did not lend itself well to bandages. The problem was solved by simply stuffing the leaves into my underwear. Off to school I went with the confidence that I would soon be free of this pestilence.

The teacher that I had in the eighth grade was the most disliked teacher in the school by unanimous agreement of the older boys. Her whole demeanor was one of belligerence towards the boys in her class, and she never passed up an opportunity to humiliate or chastise us. To illustrate the effect she had upon us, one day a group of us boys met after school at our special hangout in the woods to decide how to get even with her. After much discussion, and over the objections of the timid, a course of action was agreed upon. In the morning before she arrived in class we would place a copperhead snake in the upper drawer of her desk where she kept her attendance book. (We really wanted to use a rattlesnake, but none of us had ever seen a rattlesnake in the area.) We never carried out the scheme because the weather became too cool for us to find a copperhead.

This was the class I was to enter that day, and I was carrying an unusual burden: my underwear stuffed with strange leaves that were supposed to cure me of poison ivy.

Everything was pretty normal, at least as the word normal applied to this classroom. It was about 10:00 A.M. when the teacher called my name to go up to the blackboard and solve an arithmetic problem. To me there was nothing more distasteful than doing things at the blackboard before the entire class. All the girls knew who the dummies were and when you were called to go to the blackboard you had to run the gauntlet of sly comments and looks, knowing you were a form of entertainment for others. At this particular age the girls performed in class much better than the boys, which helped explain their behavior.

I arose from my seat and approached the dreaded blackboard with resentment. This always fed the feeling that the teacher was picking on me. I removed a piece of chalk from the tray and began studying the problem to be solved. My thought process was interrupted by the teacher, who asked in a rather threatening tone, "What have you got in your pockets? You're making a mess on the floor."

It was then that I realized that leaves were apparently escaping from my underwear and falling down my pants legs to the floor. I shook my head and shrugged my shoulders, portraying an "I don't know anything" attitude. Being very aggressive, she insisted that I empty my pants pockets right then and there. Placing my hands in my pockets, I turned them inside out revealing two gaping holes which obviously indicated that they were not capable of holding anything.

She stood there staring at me, as if waiting for her brain to kick in with a new approach to humiliating me. The strain that this episode placed on me resulted in an intense desire to use the bathroom. I raised my hand, breaking the spell, and asked her if I could go to the boys' room. Without a word, she simply handed me the small wooden pass.

As I was leaving the room I could now feel the crumbly leaves falling down my pants legs to the floor. Arriving at the boys' room,

I quickly dropped my pants and removed what was left of the now-dried leaves from my underwear. I was quite surprised how few were left.

I returned to the classroom, and as soon as I entered, the teacher called out my name.

"William, before returning to your seat, pick up the leaves that you dropped on the floor on the way to the boys' room."

Again I had to suffer the humiliation of going before the class and picking up all the fallen leaves. While returning to my seat I noticed that the room was extremely quiet, and that all the other students were staring at me with puzzled looks on their faces, as if mesmerized by the mystery of the leaves.

As I took my seat and tried to compose myself, random thoughts began to enter my head. The most dominant one was to somehow, someway, get that copperhead into her desk.

THE FOURTH OF JULY

It was getting close to the Fourth of July and I was hatching a scheme that I hoped would make me some money, which was always in short supply. My plan was to get a supply of "punks" (brown cigar-shaped tops of the cattail plant) and a large bottle of citronella oil, both of which I would sell to the people being pestered by mosquitoes during the fireworks display. The punks would be lit with a match and they would smolder, giving off a smoke that kept mosquitoes away. The citronella would be rubbed on the skin and also served to repel mosquitoes.

On the hill just above Park Row was a large open field that extended to Jefferson School. On the evening of the Fourth of July, hundreds of people would congregate here to watch the fireworks display taking place at the Passaic Stadium. Behind Jefferson School, paralleling the railroad tracks, was a swampy area that extended almost to the Paterson Plank Road. This was the breeding ground for the mosquitoes that would plague people during the evening when the fireworks were being displayed. These were the conditions that would create the climate for my first business adventure, at the age of fourteen. This would be my introduction into the world of capitalism and another world I was only dimly aware of.

My first challenge was to find a source for punks. Although they were plentiful in the wet areas alongside the tracks, it was too early in the season for new ones and so I had to search for some of last year's punks that had not deteriorated from the weather. I did manage to find a good supply at the Pump House, the lake that supplied water to the Hammersly waxpaper mill.

Next, I needed fifty cents to buy a large bottle of citronella. I decided to ask my mother.

"Ma, can I borrow fifty cents? I'll pay you back next week."

She looked at me suspiciously. "You want money, go earn it."

I tried explaining to her my scheme to make a lot of money on the Fourth of July. Her answer was the same: "You want money, go earn it."

I offered to do extra jobs around the house to earn the money. She gave me a cold stare; this was followed by the comment, "You eat here for nothing, you work here for nothing." Damn, she was tough!

I had to approach getting fifty cents another way. It was then that I remembered that some of the older kids used to go to Van Kruiningen's to pick copper wire and other stuff. At this time they were filling in the sandpits located behind his house with refuse.

I spent a lot of time around the dump waiting for trucks to come in and unload. The competition was fierce, but eventually I got quite a bit of copper wiring. Next came the rotten job of burning off the insulation. The wire had to be repeatedly turned over to make sure it all burned off. It was then necessary to hit it with a stick to get the encrusted insulation to fall off. The dealers would not buy the wire unless it was clean. Last of all was taking the copper to a dealer that was located on the Passaic River across the street from Passaic Stadium. At this time, copper was selling for about six cents a pound. I ended up getting about sixty-seven cents for all my efforts. A lot of work, but at least I could buy that bottle of citronella. A walk to Market Street in Passaic to make my purchase, and all was now ready.

It was the morning of the Fourth of July when I realized that I needed a sign to advertise my wares. I quickly made up a sign that read

Beat the Mosquitoes
Punks 5c
Citronella Rub 10c

That day after supper I informed my mother that I was going to the hill to watch the fireworks. In my excitement, I arrived much too early, as the fireworks did not begin until dark. However, I occupied my time watching people flying their kites. The hill at this time was a favorite place for kite flyers and almost all the kids participated in this sport. The competition was in who could get his kite the highest and with the longest tail. Some kites were quite colorful, especially when they used old neckties for the tail.

Before I knew it, people were beginning to assemble on the hill to watch the fireworks. Most carried blankets to sit on, as lightweight folding chairs did not yet exist. I began to circulate among the people, constantly flashing my sign to attract their attention to my wares. I did manage to sell some punks but it seemed I always had to explain how to use them, as most people didn't know what they were for. I'd just assumed everyone knew about burning punks to repel mosquitoes.

As it got darker, the mosquitoes began to arrive and soon became a nuisance. Some of the older people that knew about citronella even paid ten cents to rub their faces and arms with the stuff. Things were going pretty well and I was about two dollars ahead of my investment when the fireworks began, very slowly at first. I knew once they started in earnest my sales would be pretty much over.

I was just about to end my sales when I was called over by two attractive females I judged to be about seventeen or eighteen who were sitting on a blanket.

Walking towards them, I continued to announce my wares: "Punks, five cents. Citronella, ten cents a rub."

"Young man," one of them called out, "we'll take two citronella rubs."

I was elated that I should make a sale just before quitting. I walked over, and one of the girls handed me two dimes from her sitting position. I held out the bottle of citronella for her to take, but she refused, saying she had paid for a citronella rub, as my sign had indicated. I tried to explain that a rub meant that you rubbed yourself. She thought for a moment, as her girlfriend tried to control her giggles. She then offered me an extra ten cents for each of them if I would apply the citronella. She explained that her hands were chapped and that they shouldn't be wet. Being gullible and greedy, I accepted her offer.

Since they were both sitting on a blanket and it was already getting dark, I had to kneel next to them to apply the mosquito lotion. The girl extended one of her arms and I started at the wrist and began rubbing the oil into her skin, working my way towards her shoulder. After I finished both arms, she raised the long blonde hair that extended down her back and instructed me to rub her neck—which I did. Even to me, their faces began to reveal that something was going on and it had nothing to do with fireworks.

Finishing her neck I moved into position next to the other girl to give her a rub. It was at this time that the first girl said, "You're not through yet. You have to do my legs."

I was beginning to get uneasy, but what the hell, I thought, money is money. I began at her ankles and massaged the citronella up to her knees. I then turned to the second girl to begin. But before I could start, the first girl tugged on my shirt to get my attention. Turning towards her, I was informed that I had not finished the job. Now I was having second thoughts about what was going on, especially as her girlfriend was controlling herself with difficulty. She obviously knew something I didn't know.

I asked the first girl what was wrong, and she proceeded to inform me that mosquitoes don't stop at the knees. Looking down at her legs, I could see that her dress was now eight inches above her knees. I began to sweat and get very uneasy. Powerful forces were at work and I felt like a pawn being manipulated—but for what?

Reluctantly, I put some oil into the palms of my hands and, taking a kneeling position between her legs, began to massage her thighs. I did not fail to notice the smiles being exchanged between the two girls. It was when I saw that she was slowly pulling her dress up higher that I panicked and jumped up. Quickly I took a dime from my pants pocket and threw it on the blanket next to the second girl.

"Here's your dime," I announced. "No more rubs. I'm out of business."

I would always remember this Fourth of July. This holiday is a remembrance of America's baptism into the world of nations. However, this one was my baptism into the world of women, and it is only appropriate that it was accompanied by fireworks.

THE FACTORY

Located across the railroad tracks from Wallington was the town of Wood-Ridge. On both sides of the tracks were woods, overgrown fields, and swamps. Wallington and Wood-Ridge each had a hill and the railroad tracks ran between the two hills. Located in Wood-Ridge was a factory that processed movie films. The back side of the factory was in a heavily wooded area but there was also a clear area where they burned their garbage, which was primarily waste film.

I don't know who came up with the ideas for how to use this film, but it wasn't long before I became pretty adept at handling the stuff. As kids we were always trading things like marbles and baseball cards; however, if you had a roll of film you could trade off pieces of it for just about anything. It was a high-demand item.

It was usually quite easy to get the film, as the discarded film was thrown into fifty-five gallon drums. These drums would not be burned until they were full, so a trip to the woods behind the factory would almost always yield us some rolls of film. Sometimes the rolls would be quite large, reaching a foot or more in diameter.

Film at this time contained a very high amount of oxygen, high enough so that even if there was no outside supply of air it would continue to burn. It was this property that led us to find many ways to utilize this product.

Although some kids, including myself, did make bottle bombs, they were even by our low standards much too dangerous to fool with. Besides, we never really had any reason to make them, although I did see them being used around the Horseshoe Pond to stun fish near the surface.

One time I was showing one of the kids in the Star Homes section how to make a bottle bomb. We were at the end of Crescent Road just behind Posluszny's house, which was on Kossuth Street. He was sitting on an old wooden milk crate while I gave him instructions.

"It is most important," I explained, "that the twist-on cap be very tight and that you immediately throw the bottle away. After throwing the bottle turn your face away from the direction that the bottle was thrown in, as they sometimes burst too early."

Next I took a jar and stuffed it with pieces of film. I then took an eight-inch piece of film and placed it in the jar, leaving about two inches sticking out. This was to serve as the fuse and would quickly ignite the film in the jar. All was now ready for the demonstration. Holding the jar in one hand and the lid in my mouth, I struck a match and lit the film protruding from the jar. It rapidly burned into the jar and I waited until the inside film caught fire. Then I took the metal cap from my mouth and tried to put it on the jar. For some unknown reason I could not get the cap to lock on. Finally it caught, but I knew from experience that this one was dangerous and I would not have time to throw it, so I simply dropped the bottle and turned away. It exploded on contact with the ground and it did not have much force, I suspect as a result of breaking when it struck the ground.

I immediately checked my legs to see if I had been hit by any flying glass. I was in luck: a piece of glass had sliced my pants leg and that was it. Relieved, I now looked up at my friend. He was still sitting on the crate but he had an astonished look on his face as blood seeped from a wound in his forehead. I could see a jagged piece of glass, which was the bottom of the jar, still stuck in his forehead. It was easy to remove and the several cuts it made weren't very deep, but they did bleed a great deal. I cleaned up the wounds as best I could with a handkerchief and a little spit, and he was on his way home.

We were very lucky and I knew it. After this experience I would never make another bomb.

Another use we made of the film would usually occur around Halloween. There were quite a number of large grassy fields on the hill in the area of Jefferson School. The grass was straw-like and about a foot and a half tall, and grass fires were not unusual. When it was dark we would select a field to burn. Then several of us kids would walk the field, crisscrossing it while unrolling the film. The pattern we laid down with the film was such that when we lit it in one place the fire would quickly branch out and in minutes the whole field would be ablaze. People living in local houses would be very fearful and the fire department would be called. At the sound of the siren we would take off. Since grass burns very quickly, by the time the engine arrived the fire would be pretty much burned out. We did make an error once when we failed to see that someone was dumping hedge trimmings and tree branches in one of the fields behind his house. The timely arrival of the fire truck saved his fence and his coop full of chickens.

Most of the film was reserved for the making of stink bombs (or, as some kids called them, smoke bombs). The amount of smoke that could be produced by a two-foot length of film was amazing. To make a smoke bomb was relatively easy. A two foot length of film would be rolled up slightly off center so that it would be about three inches long. It would then be wrapped in paper. The best paper was from brown paper bags, as newspaper tended to burn too fast. Both ends of the paper would be twisted so that they extended about two inches from the film. One end would then be lit and the stink bomb placed on the ground. When the burning paper reached the film, a jet of flame would shoot out. Now was the time to step on it and make the fire go out. The film would not burn now, but it would give off an incredible amount of white smoke until all the film was consumed. If you were going to throw the smoke bomb you had better be careful, for sometimes they would burst back into flames from a hotspot on the paper.

Four of us boys were sitting alongside Belski's grocery store on the corner of Park Row and Adamson Avenue when a flatbed truck turned in to Adamson Avenue from Kossuth Street, which was a dead-end street. The flatbed was loaded with boxes of fruit and vegetables. The back of the flatbed had been raised in the center so that the contents of the boxes could be examined easily. The driver had parked the truck and was attending to some customers when we decided to play a trick on him. One boy went to the opposite side of the truck where he couldn't be seen, lit a smoke bomb, and threw it under the truck. Smoke began pouring out from under the truck and between the boxes of fruits and vegetables. Seeing the smoke, the driver assumed the truck was on fire. He bent down to look underneath but couldn't see anything because of the heavy smoke. With the help of two customers, he hurriedly began removing the boxes to save his fruits and vegetables. About a quarter of the truck was unloaded when suddenly all the smoke dissipated. Looking around for an explanation he could not help but notice us four kids sitting there laughing our sides off. He finally reached the conclusion that we had something to do with all that smoke. He and the customers reloaded the truck, and when they finished he removed four apples and walked over to us. In his heavy Italian accent he said to us, "You no more joke, not nice." He handed each of us an apple. "You gotta no do that, be nice boys."

Even though we were young pranksters and not prone to sensitivity, we all felt somewhat humiliated by his kind understanding. There was no anger in him, something we were not used to seeing in adults.

It was a summer day when Cassey Kudlacik and I decided to head over to the film factory and pick up some film. We took the long way across Kossuth Street to Krug's woods then down to the railroad tracks by the Curtiss-Wright plant. There was a large round boulder near to the tracks and flowing from beneath was a clear spring. After a cool drink we followed the tracks to a path that went through the woods to the back of the film factory, where there were usually several fifty-five gallon drums containing film waiting to be burned. Today there were none. We decided to be brave and go to the front of the factory and look around. We saw several barrels, and sure enough they contained discarded film. We each took several large rolls and headed home in a leisurely fashion. Going back we took the short way, which was to cross the tracks and head up the hill towards Jefferson School. From here we would drop down the hill to Park Row.

After crossing the tracks I happened to glance back and saw two men obviously coming after us. We threw our load of film into the bushes and took off running for the steep climb to Jefferson School and safety—we hoped. At the bottom of the steep hill on the right were rows of very large overgrown hedges perhaps fifteen feet high. There was sufficient room between the rows to make your way through. The rapidly approaching men forced us to try to get away by going into the hedges rather than climbing the steep hill. It was at this time that I learned how fast Cassey could run. I lost sight of him in the hedges and opted to leave them and head for an open field. Leaving the hedges I ran smack into a heavy clump of briar bushes and I could not force my way though. I lay down in the briar bushes, and by being very quiet I hoped that the men would not notice me. I was startled when I heard one of them say, "I got him. He's over here." His next words were, "Okay, kid, come on get up." I was caught.

We began the walk back towards the factory and I was feeling somewhat numb, as I had no idea what was going to happen to me. They brought me into the main office and told me to be seated. It wasn't long before a Wood-Ridge police officer arrived. He ordered me to follow him to his police car then drove me to the Wood-Ridge police station. When we arrived at the station the officer in charge told me to empty my pockets on the table. I placed my pocket knife on the table first. He picked it up and examined the blade.

"Your mother know you carry this around?" he asked.

"Sure," I responded. "All the kids carry pocket knives."

"What else have you got in your pockets?"

I placed a very dirty blood-stained handkerchief, six cents, and a book of matches on the table.

Looking at me with disgust, he asked, "Is that it?"

I simply nodded. At this time I was beginning to get worried. What if my mother finds out, or worse, what if they pick her up at work and bring her here?

After finding out where I lived, the officer picked up the telephone and called the Wallington police. He explained to them what had happened and requested that they pick me up. About twenty minutes later a Wallington police officer entered the police station. It was OK Sura. I had mixed emotions about seeing OK. I didn't know whether to be happy or not.

"Get your stuff, Billy," OK announced. "I'm taking you home."

The Wood-Ridge officer handed me a paper bag with my stuff inside. OK drove me back to Wallington, to Kobscenski's house where I lived. On the way there he asked me who the other kid was that was with me. I told him that it was Cassey Kudlacik.

"You have any film at home?" he asked.

I told him that I had several rolls. Parking in front of the house, he told me to go get them and to bring them to the police car. Upstairs in the apartment I was relieved to see that no one was home. I climbed the ladder to my bedroom and finding only one roll of film I returned to the police car. I was surprised when OK told me to get inside. He then drove up to the Kudlacik house, which was only four houses away. Cassey was sitting on the front porch with his mother and father when the police car pulled up. Seeing the police car and me sitting in the back he instantly jumped the railing, ran through the garden, and in a flash was over the back fence and gone. Damn, he was fast.

OK never spoke to Cassey's mother or father, he simply turned the car around and took me home. As I was leaving, his final words were, "Billy, one of these days your mother is going to get wise to your behavior."

I nodded and left. Another close call. I went upstairs with the paper bag containing my stuff. Opening the bag I found that my pocket knife was missing. I cursed the cop in silence for stealing my pocket knife.

Kudlacik's parents never found out about this incident and neither did my parents. OK Sura knew we were just kids and needed time to grow up.

One day a group of us kids were playing at the Horseshoe Pond. Most were from the Star Homes on Crescent Road. We were all involved in making smoke bombs as part of the entertainment. It was a common practice to keep a small roll of film in your pocket and to leave the end of it sticking out several inches. Whenever you wanted a piece of film you simply pulled on the strip and it would unroll in your pocket. You would then tear off a piece, continuing to leave a strip hanging out of your pocket.

Nunnu Sudol was one of the kids playing at the Horseshoe Pond that afternoon. Just like everyone else, he was making smoke bombs and had a roll of film in his pocket with the end hanging out. Somehow the strip hanging from his pocket caught fire (it was suspected that someone lit it when he wasn't looking). The fire burned into his pants pocket, igniting the roll of film. He began screaming and beating at the fire to put it out. This was impossible as there was no way you could extinguish a film fire by beating at it. Things became very confused at this time but he ended up in the Horseshoe Pond, which put the fire out. His clothes in the area were completely burned away and his skin was charred black.

In great pain he made his way home, which was very close, and soon an ambulance arrived to take him to the hospital. He had received third degree burns and was in the hospital quite a long time before he recovered.

Between the film factory making sure that the discarded film would no longer reach the hands of kids and Nunnu Sudol's bad burns, the era of smoke bombs came to an end.

THE RAILROAD TRACKS

It seems to me that as a young boy growing up there was always an attraction between me and the railroad tracks. Did it represent in my mind a means of escape or perhaps an unconscious desire to change my world and follow a new path? Maybe it was the seclusion of the woods and fields that usually bordered the tracks, as no people lived along the tracks in Wallington and Wood-Ridge.

Tracks represented a world where imagination was king, but all too often they would trigger events that as young kids we could not foresee. To be sure we were reckless and in many cases irresponsible, but this was the world we were learning to grow up in, without adult supervision. We did not live in a world of store-bought entertainment—we created our own. The railroad tracks were a natural playground for a boy growing up in the 1940s, especially in a town like Wallington.

It was Sunday and I had no love for this day, as it rudely interrupted my normal pattern of living, which did not include going to church. The church that we attended was in Garfield just off Monroe Street near the old Ritz Theater. For kids, the real challenge always occurred after church, when we were required to attend catechism classes taught by the nuns. The trick was to escape, and it was not easy.

It was a bitter cold day in February, probably around 1943. My mother got us ready, and my brother and I were off to church by 7:30 as we had to attend the 8 o'clock mass, which was primarily for children (although some adults did attend).

I always had trouble understanding how so many of the kids that came to church were so well prepared for catechism classes and didn't seem to mind attending. As for me, the most important thing on my mind was to escape going to the basement where classes were held. I had a simple plan that usually worked. First, I would arrive at church about ten minutes late (if you came early the ushers would have you sit up front). Adults that came stayed at the back of the church, which was actually quite small, and very often there were people standing in the rear. The idea was to get close to a woman and when she left you stayed by her side as if you were with her. Occasionally you had to make a dash and run the gauntlet.

This day, my brother and I had no desire to attend church or catechism. As we walked towards the church, the weather was wicked. There was a light snow, the wind was blowing at a good clip, and the temperature was bitter. Despite these uncomfortable conditions we made it as far as Monroe Street where the railroad tracks cross. We decided to skip church and began following the tracks back towards Wallington. We planned on going over to the Horseshoe Pond and building a fire to stay warm.

We walked on the ties between the rails, as there was less snow on the ground there. We got as far as the Pump House when we saw a train coming towards us on another track. This was a double set of tracks so we continued walking on our tracks, not paying any mind to the approaching train. At this point the tracks made a sweeping turn to the south, going between Wallington and Wood-Ridge.

We continued walking along the tracks, our hats pulled over our ears and our collars turned up to protect us from the biting wind, which was worse on the exposed railroad bed. The train on the other track was now passing us and the noise was deafening. We were oblivious to everything else around us.

My brother and I were walking side-by-side when for some reason I turned and looked backwards. With our hats pulled over our ears and the noise from the train on the other track we never heard the train that was approaching from behind us on our track. I instantly grabbed my brother by the arm (his hands were in his pockets) and jerked him off the tracks as I jumped out of the way. The approaching train never saw us and was perhaps a hundred feet behind us when we both cleared the track.

We stood beside the track as the train went on by. We were both quiet for a while, trying to digest the ramifications of this event. All became very calm, the noise ended, even the wind died down.

"Bill?"

"Yeah, Joe?"

"I think maybe we should go back to church."

"Let's go. If we hurry we won't be too late."

We headed back towards St. Joseph's Church but instead of following the tracks we took the road, which was quicker. We arrived about fifteen minutes late and entered the church. It felt good to get warm again and although I disliked organ music, even the organ music sounded good. It wasn't long before the basket was passed for donations. I placed my nickel in the basket plus an extra nickel I had in my pocket.

I was a firm believer in the old adage: One good deed deserves another.

There were times when the trains would not be moving and boxcars would be standing idle on the tracks. Boxcars contained things, and kids are always interested in things. There was only a simple object between our curiosity and what the boxcar contained. It was a thin metal seal and it was easily broken.

I believe it was the month of August when Stan Posluszny and I attended the Ritz Theater in Garfield for an afternoon show. We exited the movie and began the trek back to Wallington. Upon leaving the railroad overpass at Monroe Street we noticed a few boxcars a short distance away. A couple of kids were removing watermelons. They had apparently broken the boxcar seal and were helping themselves. Stan and I decided to go over and get a couple of melons. Seeing us approach, the kids ran off, burdened by a watermelon under each arm.

We entered the boxcar to get some melons, and a few minutes later several adults appeared at the boxcar door. They asked us to hand them some melons, which we did. Shortly after, more adults showed up and asked us to hand them melons. We really didn't have much choice, as we were trapped in the boxcar. We were now getting pretty nervous, as we had a healthy fear of the railroad dicks (detectives). Finally, we set a few melons by the door, jumped out of the boxcar, took the melons, and began walking down the tracks towards Wallington. We had gone only a hundred yards when a police car pulled up to the boxcar. We knew we were safe then, and without any hurry headed towards the Pump House.

Arriving at the Pump House we made our way over to where we had a swimming place, which was where we planned on eating a melon. I took out my pocket knife and began cutting a melon in two. We both noticed a car approaching us from Main Street (where the skating rink is today) down the dirt road to where we were. Feeling very guilty and scared, we assumed it was the police. Abandoning our melons, we headed for a brushy area between the Saddle River and the Horseshoe Pond. We got away, and it wasn't the police after all.

Fear of the police, teachers, priests, and especially our mothers was a powerful force that kept us from going too far astray. They were very powerful in modifying our behavior.

This was the last time we would enter a boxcar. The forces of fear had won again.

Sometime around 1946 I became aware of what trapping was all about when I came across some traps that were set at the Horseshoe Pond. I knew a lot of muskrats lived there as I could see their trails, tunnels, and the large grass houses that they built in swampy areas along the shoreline. What I did not know was that you could sell a muskrat pelt for up to two dollars. That was a lot of money back then, so I decided to become a trapper and cut into this moneymaking trade. Alex Bednarz and Duley Sumnick were trapping the area, so I had to search around and find a new area to trap. I also needed traps. Thoroughly searching the area, I found that some Garfield kids (one had the nickname of Foxy) were trapping along the Saddle River where it flows behind the Catholic Orphanage. I did not experience any guilt in helping myself to their traps.

One area I decided to check out as a place to trap was along the railroad bed about where the Wright aircraft engine plant ended near the tracks. The swamp was pretty small and I noticed it was being drained by a culvert which carried excess water away from the swamp. The culvert was made of concrete and measured about three feet by three feet and went underneath the railroad bed. It occurred to me that if I partially blocked the culvert I could raise the water level of the swamp and greatly increase its size, which would help increase the muskrat population and also my net worth, which was always just a few cents above personal poverty. With all the money I planned on making I could get rid of my single-shot .22 caliber Springfield and get me a Winchester pump, what we usually called a "carnival" gun, as they were pretty popular at shooting galleries.

Searching around I found a flat piece of board which would serve very well as a shovel. From around the railroad ties I began removing the crushed stone and shoveling it into the culvert. It was a slow process and I was completely absorbed in the filling of the culvert, oblivious to the world around me.

I never saw the handcar approach down the railroad tracks. I became suddenly aware of it when two large men got off just a few feet from me. I could tell I was in for a hard time, as all of us kids knew about the dreaded railroad dicks.

"What the fuck are you doing, kid?" one of the men asked. The tone of his voice was very threatening. His choice of swear words scared the hell out of me, as that word was generally not used around kids.

"I'm not doing any harm," I explained. "I'm only partially filling in this culvert to raise the water level so more muskrats can live in the swamp."

"Fuck your muskrats."

Pow! This two-hundred-pound guy threw a roundhouse punch right into the side of my jaw. It lifted me off of my feet, and although I didn't go down I was seeing stars for a few seconds. After regaining my senses I could feel some chips of teeth in my mouth and the familiar taste of blood. Not wanting to spit and show him the damage, I mixed the chips and blood with saliva and swallowed. Next he grabbed me and threw me into the culvert.

"Here's your fucking board, you clean that shit out of there."

I quickly shoveled the stones into the swamp and climbed out of the culvert, not knowing what was going to happen next.

"You get your fucking ass out of here," he said. "If I ever see you here again I'm not going to let you off so easy—understand?"

I nodded, turned away, and began walking towards Krug's woods on the hill. I kept looking back until I saw them climb back onto the handcar and head down the tracks.

My first stop was at a spring to refresh myself and calm down. I then climbed the hill to Krug's woods and found a nice place beneath some chokecherry trees to sit down and assess the situation that had just occurred. The more I thought about that big guy punching me the madder I got. As my fear subsided I began to get angry. A slow rage began to turn into the desire for some kind of revenge—but what and how?

As I continued on my walk home, my brain poring over different ways to get revenge, I finally settled on a plan, a way to strike back at the railroad.

I went directly to the basement of Kobscenski's house, the large house that held our apartment. I removed the model airplane box from its hiding place. This box held my 22 caliber Springfield rifle, which by removing a bolt could be taken apart into two pieces. In another spot, hidden under a pile of coal, was a cigar box containing several boxes of 22 caliber ammunition, 50 bullets in each. I put one box in my pocket, and taking the model airplane box I left the basement and headed for Krug's woods—and revenge.

Arriving in the woods, I removed the gun from the box and bolted it together. Next I hid the box beneath a pile of brush, then started the downhill walk towards the culvert and the railroad tracks. When I arrived at the tracks I crossed to the Wood-Ridge side, as it was on that side that the poles carrying the electrical wires were located, with the insulators that held the wires to the pole and kept them from being shorted. Also, this side of the tracks was more heavily wooded and I could remain hidden as I went about my business of getting revenge.

From my hiding place I easily shot the ceramic insulators holding the wires to the nearest pole so that they shattered, leaving the wires floating freely. I then carefully sneaked through the woods to the next pole and from a hidden position repeated the process until no insulators were left. Sometimes it took several shots to knock an insulator off if the angle was not good, as the bullets were easily deflected by the round insulators. I continued this process until I had used up all 50 bullets and was out of ammunition. I now felt considerably better, although my jaw still hurt.

Damn. I suddenly realized that to get my gun box I would have to go back through the area where I did all the shooting. I didn't want to take a chance, so I took a shortcut up the hill past Jefferson School then down to Park Row. Arriving at the school I took the gun apart and stuck the two halves down my pants leg, holding them in place by tightening my belt. I made it home without incident, and went to the basement to hide my rifle.

At the supper table that evening my mother noticed the bruise on my face.

"What happened to the side of your face? It's all bruised."

"Aw, it's nothing, Ma," I said. "I was helping Posluszny move some lumber and when he swung around a board hit me in the side of the face."

"You're always helping other people," she replied. "You should spend more time helping out around here."

THE CHICKEN

One day several of us kids were at the Pump House, swimming and generally enjoying ourselves and the new diving board we had just erected, when we saw two men get off a slowly-moving train on the other side of the Pump House. They set up a makeshift camp on a piece of land that jutted out into the lake. After swimming was over most of the kids went home, but my friend and I decided to go over and visit with them. Hobos were always glad to chat and would fascinate us with their stories.

We were there only a short time when they indicated to us that they were hungry and one of them asked if we knew of any chicken coops that were close by. Innocently, I told him that the closest coop was Posluszny's but that it was quite a distance away. He kept reminding us about how hungry they were and asked if we could get them a chicken. I explained that I had never stolen a chicken before and that I had no idea how to go about it. Besides, I added, they make too much noise.

"It's easy, kid," he said. "I'll tell you how to get one."

I listened carefully as he described how to go about stealing a chicken, although I felt somewhat uncomfortable at the thought of stealing a Posluszny chicken since Stanley (Moose) and I were in the same class and the best of friends. It was their hunger that was the motivating force.

"Kid, just go into the coop quietly and don't get them rattled.

They should be sleeping anyway. Now, they sleep with their heads turned around and tucked into their feathers. So what you do is select the chicken you want and if he he's asleep you tap him lightly to wake him up, then when he raises his head you grab him around the neck and quickly leave before all the chickens make a ruckus. Got it?"

"Yeah," I replied, "but what if the owner comes out, what do I do then?"

"Why, kid, you run like hell. But don't come back here."

It was now dark, and my friend and I approached Posluszny's chicken coop. We had come by way of Crescent Road, as this was the fastest and it ended near where the chicken coop was located. We climbed over the back fence and went directly to the chicken coop. Slowly opening the door, we both entered the coop. Some of the chickens were already awake but they weren't making much noise, and being somewhat fearful I disregarded all instructions and simply grabbed the closest chicken by the neck and headed for the door. The chicken began flapping his wings like crazy and pretty soon all the chickens were scattering to get away from us. The place was bedlam.

We quickly got out of the chicken house, but trying to get over the fence holding this chicken by the neck was a real challenge. I somehow managed to get over the fence and we both took off running for Krug's cow pasture. We exited the cow pasture near Van Kruiningen's house on Main Street, went down to the old sandpits, and took a trail to the Pump House and the two hobos. We delivered the still-live chicken to them and since it was getting late my friend and I left.

The next afternoon we returned to find them still there and the remains of the chicken scattered around. I never realized a chicken had so many feathers. The place was a mess.

"Hey, kid," one of the men said to me. "Here's a dime [it may have been a quarter], go to town and buy me a small can of Red Devil paint remover."

I took the coin and the two of us left for the closest hardware store, which was on Locust Avenue at the corner of Hathaway Street. While walking there we had a discussion about what he could possibly want paint remover for. Maybe he would use it to start fires, or perhaps he was sick and paint remover was some sort of home remedy. Or maybe they used it to kill lice on themselves.

Coming back from the store we took our time, even chatting with some kids we knew, questioning them to see if they had heard about someone stealing chickens. They hadn't heard anything.

When we returned to the Pump House about an hour later, I gave the hobo the can of paint remover and watched with fascination as he poured it into an old tin can. Next he took an orange and sliced it up and put that in the can. Taking a stick, he ground up the orange in the can, adding a small amount of pond water.

"Here's to you, kid," he said, raising the can, and he then began to drink the stuff.

All of a sudden everything clicked into place in my mind. My mother's words came back to me.

"Goddam bums, they're lazy good-for-nothings and drunks to boot."

These weren't hobos, they were bums.

We left, disgusted and ashamed over what we had done. The last thing we saw was the white chicken feathers covering the ground.

ICE SKATING

When winter finally arrived and the temperature dropped low enough to create ice, the Horseshoe Pond became the main center of activity, as it was usually the first place to freeze over. The lake we called the Pump House would become more popular when it finally froze, as it was much larger and better suited to playing hockey, which was very popular among the neighborhood kids.

The Horseshoe Pond, being very shallow, was the safest place to ice skate. Knowing this, we would all too often venture onto the ice when it was very thin and not really suitable for use. As the day wore on the ice would soften, and it would bend and undulate with the movement of the water beneath it. We always referred to this ice as "pompy" ice. Also, the ice would have a tendency to melt away from the shoreline, making it a risky venture to return to dry land without getting a soaker (getting your feet wet).

Very often ice skating or just playing on thin ice was an adventure in itself, as we tried to avoid holes where other kids had broken through or new cracks that had formed. All in all, playing under these conditions was a very wet proposition. There was always a fire burning somewhere on shore with clothes and socks hanging on sticks to dry out, or a kid wearing wet socks sitting on a crate drying out his socks or warming his feet by the fire.

When it became cold enough for the ice to thicken to about four inches, much of the ice skating was transferred to the Pump House.

There were areas on the Pump House that had to be avoided because of the numerous springs that kept the ice very thin and dangerous. After a while you would learn to recognize these areas by the color of the ice and the amount of air bubbles in the ice. Sometimes markers would be placed over these spots so that in the excitement of a hockey game you would be aware of the danger.

The big game on the ice was hockey, with skates on or even with just shoes, although this resulted in a lot of bruises as falls on the ice were very common while wearing shoes. Since most of the kids couldn't afford hockey sticks we made our own from tree branches. A four-foot or smaller branch with a six-inch side branch was the usual hockey stick; and if it broke, a pocket knife could easily cut a new stick and you were back in the game. Normally, a tin can served as a puck.

However, there were several kids who took the game very seriously and were equipped with real hockey sticks and a rubber puck. Walt and Eddie Wodecki were both well equipped and very good at hockey (in fact, they were good at all sports). During one game I was a goalie, and unfortunately I was not on their side. I was guarding the goal posts when Eddie broke loose from the pack and approached me at high speed. I was getting ready to block the puck with my homemade stick when he suddenly stopped twenty-five feet from me. He swung his hockey stick at the puck and the damn thing left the ice, rose about four feet above the surface, and went sailing past my head. The only thing between me and that flying rubber puck was a wool hat. There really was no reason for a shot like that, as the goal posts were usually a couple of tin cans or rocks and we had no net to catch the puck, which sailed past me for another fifty yards and ended up in a pile of cattails. I found out later this was called lifting the puck and he was just practicing. I vowed to get me a real hockey stick someday so that I could do that, too.

On weekend evenings, quite a few adults would show up to ice skate, especially at the Horseshoe Pond. There was always a large bonfire burning and five gallon cans or wooden crates to sit on. At times the adults would bring hot dogs and cook them over the fire. We kids never had hot dogs, but we would bring potatoes with us and cook them in the hot coals. Sometimes we could swap a hot potato for a hot dog. There never were rolls with the hot dogs—you ate them right off the stick. One time one of the kids was given a raw hot dog, so he cut himself a long stick to cook it on. He inserted the stick at one end and pushed it through the hot dog to the other end, where it stuck out a little. When he cooked the hot dog over the fire, the end of the stick burned off and left a hot glowing point just inside the end of the hot dog. Unfortunately for him, this was where he took his first bite.

It was a day off of school when I arrived quite early at the Horseshoe Pond for a day of ice skating. The ice was not too thick and there was already an indication that it would turn out to be a warm day for this time of year. The first thing I did upon arriving was go over to a dump behind the Hammersly paper mill and search for some tar to build a fire with. I found a large barrel turned on its side, its contents of tar dried out and frozen on the ground. I began to chip away at the tar with a pipe that I also found on the dump. I found an empty five-gallon can and filled it with chips of tar until it was half full. Returning to the pond I built a fire and placed the can next to it to melt the tar.

As I was waiting for the tar to melt, a kid I knew from the Star Homes came down to the pond for a day of skating. After getting our skates on and spending a few minutes checking out the condition of the pond, we returned to shore and the fire. We now ignited the tar, as this would burn for a long time and we would not have to keep constantly searching for wood, which was getting in short supply due to the number of fires. We returned to our hockey game, which was really just practice as one person played the goalie and the other tried to get the puck (a tin can) past him.

After a while we noticed that the ice was melting quite quickly where we were playing, so we decided to move to the other side of the pond where there was more shade to protect the ice.

We skated back to the burning bucket of tar and decided to move it to the other side of the pond where we would be skating. The idea we developed to do this was quite simple. We put the fire out by covering the top of the can, just to be safe. Next we slid an eight-foot pole beneath the metal handle of the large can. My friend would take the front of the pole and I would take the rear and follow him. We would skate to our new location on the other side of the pond and then restart the fire in the can. We always had a small roll of film somewhere and this was the perfect material for starting fires.

All was now ready and we began our journey to the other side of the Horseshoe Pond, the bucket of hot tar swinging back and forth on the pole in rhythm with the motion of our ice skates. We did not get very far, however, before my friend's skate broke through a hole that was covered by a thin layer of newly frozen ice. Down he went to one knee, taking the pole with him. Before I could react, the bucket of hot tar slid forward, striking him on the shoulder. The contents of the can poured out over part of his head, neck, and shoulder, the tar running down the side of his face and over his ear.

We quickly returned to shore to assess the extent of the damage. We were very lucky that the tar was not hot enough to cause serious burns. My friend was very frightened, more concerned about the reaction of his mother than about any physical damage he might have. A brief examination showed that in the cold air the tar was hardening fast and since he was afraid of going home we decided to go to my house on Park Row to see if we could get him cleaned up.

I knew no one was home at my house except possibly my grandfather, but when we arrived even he wasn't there. I realized that removing the tar from my friend's clothing was an impossible task so I concentrated on cleaning his hair and skin. By this time a great deal of tar was on my hands and I had to get them cleaned up first. The first thing that I tried was brown laundry soap but it only made soapy tar. The next thing I tried was rubbing alcohol—no results. The only thing left under the sink besides cleanser was a jug of kerosene, which was sometimes used to start fires in the coal stove when the wood was wet.

I went to the rag box to get some rags for applying the kerosene. I cleaned my hands and then began peeling the tar off the side of my friend's face. Although the tar hadn't burned him, it left a nasty looking red welt wherever it was pulled off. The kerosene-soaked rag would not remove the heavy covering of tar on his head and neck, just turning it into a thick liquid that turned everything else black. Getting a pair of hair cutters, I began removing the hair on one side of his head and neck as this was the only way to get rid of the large clumps of tar.

Finally, nothing more could be done—we had reached the limits of our ability to return my friend to a normal condition. Frankly, he was a mess. His face was covered with red blotches from pulling the tar off. He was missing all the hair on part of his head and neck. His scalp was dirty black and there were still pieces of tar in his hair. His jacket was covered with tar. The time had come to admit defeat, so I sent him home. Besides, it wasn't my fault. I didn't fall on the ice. With tears in his eyes he reluctantly started for home and the inevitable confrontation with his mother.

I cleaned up the area in the pantry as best I could, given the mess I had made there. Everything I touched had stains from the kerosene-tar mixture and an odor to boot. I knew I had to do a good job or my hawkeyed mother would quickly notice things and ask questions. My last act was burning all the soiled rags from the cleanup process by throwing them into the stove.

Several days went by without any word concerning the condition of my friend. Then one day at supper my mother asked me, "What happened to your friend, the kid that you were ice skating with?"

I played dumb. "What kid?" I asked.

"The one that got covered with tar."

"Oh, him." I was caught by surprise. How did she find out and how much did she know? I relied on the old strategy of half truths when dealing with my mother.

"You see, Ma, we had this fire burning to keep warm and it melted some tar that was nearby. We didn't know that tar was there and he tripped and got some tar on his clothes."

"How did it get into this hair?" she asked.

"I don't know. I left to continue skating."

The next day my mother was getting ready to do some cleaning when I heard her call out, "What the hell happened to all the rags that were here?"

THE ATTACK

I t was January or February of 1945. There were three of us boys, all in the eighth grade, all about fourteen years old. We were just beginning to be affected by the presence of girls, and the realization that they could provide a superior form of entertainment beyond sports. This new information and these new feelings primarily served to stimulate the imagination. Frankly, we didn't know how to relate to the feelings, the information, or the imagination, as nature subtly began the process of changing us into adults. For kids like us, on a long leash, this period of transformation was fertile soil for trouble.

The three of us were ice skating one evening at the Horseshoe Pond. The fire had burned down to a large pile of hot coals, and it gave off a great deal of heat. After removing our skates, we sat on a couple of old wooden milk crates and began eating the potatoes we had cooked in the fire. We had left them in the fire too long and the outsides were a half inch layer of black carbon. We ate what we could—ice skating and cold air made you awfully hungry. We were all alone in our own world, as everyone else had already left.

We were in no particular hurry to go home and as we sat around talking the conversation drifted in the direction of one particular girl from the Star Homes who was a frequent skater at the pond.

This girl was a grade behind us (although she was our own age, 14) yet she was the focus of our stimulation. There were many more attractive girls at Jefferson School, especially in my eighth grade class; however, this girl had something none of the other girls possessed—a reputation. She had an older sister with a great many boy friends, who was always being picked up by guys with cars (a very rare commodity then), and this was probably how the stories about her began. In our fertile imaginations these stories were true, and from these stories a sinister plot developed that would eventually pit imagination against reality.

Sitting around the fire, we discussed how nice it would be to kiss her. That's it! All we wanted in our wild, wild imaginations was to kiss a girl. The talk slowly began to mold itself into a plan of action. It would take place next Saturday night—that is, if she showed up to skate at the pond The chances were very good that she would be there as she was an avid skater and there was not much else to do on a Saturday night.

The Horseshoe Pond had the shape of a giant horseshoe, hence its name. However, there were a few little coves along its sides that were too small to skate in but would make a perfect hiding place for three young boys waiting to spring an ambush. People skating on the pond usually circled the entire pond, the large burning fire reflecting off the ice providing enough light to see pretty well except at the ends of the horseshoe. It was here that one of the small coves was located.

Our plan, stimulated by the twin devils of imagination and desire, was quite simple. Towards the end of an evening of skating the three of us would hide in the secluded cove and prepare the ambush. Then when the girl skated by we would rush out, grab her, and pull her into the cove. We would take turns kissing her, after which we would let her go. The whole premise was that she would be very cooperative, as according to the stories she was a girl who liked to tease and was considered wild.

Saturday night finally arrived, and everything proceeded according to plan. The evening was dark, a large wood fire was burning, and sure enough she arrived just after dark. I went over to the fire to move the potatoes cooking in the coals. This also gave me a chance to converse with her, as I knew her quite well, and I used this as an opportunity to find out how long she would be skating. She told me she would be there the whole evening.

By about 9 P.M. many people had left, and she was still skating around the pond. The time had come to make our move. The three of us headed towards our hiding place in the cove. One stood near the front to serve as a lookout and to let us know when she was coming.

"Here she comes," the lookout announced several minutes later. "Shit, she's got her older sister with her."

We would just have to be patient and wait until she was alone. We were getting cold hidden in the cove. We weren't wearing heavy jackets as those were normally too warm when you were skating.

"Here she comes," whispered the lookout.

"Is she alone?" I asked

"Yeah."

We all moved up to the entrance of the cove. We were like three leopards waiting to spring out at a helpless victim. Only this victim was supposed to respond to our interest in a positive manner, or so the stories we had heard suggested.

She never knew what hit her. Down she went onto the ice. The script began to change drastically as she struggled while being dragged into the small bushy cove. She wasn't supposed to behave like this. According to all those stories, she was supposed to be enjoying the attention we gave her. In the ensuing struggle we all managed to get our kisses in, but I doubt if we knew what the hell we were kissing. We had expected that she would be cooperative. Unknown to me at the time, one of the guys with a better imagination than mine and likely a bigger supply of testosterone began to explore with his hands an area that was never covered in our discussions of what we were supposed to do. After receiving our reward for all this intricate planning we let go of her and hurriedly skated away, leaving her in the cove. We were all operating under the illusion that she didn't know who we were. After she composed herself by the fire and talked to her sister, they both left.

Sunday was a very quiet day, but by early afternoon we began to hear stories about what had happened at the Horseshoe Pond last night. How did they already know the names of the three of us that were involved? It was then that I realized she must have recognized us. I began to take a ribbing from some of the kids living on Crescent Road who lived very near to her. One of them thought that this would be a good time to play a joke on me.

"Hey, Billy, the cops are looking for you."

"For what?"

"For raping that girl at the Horseshoe Pond."

"Hell, all we did was kiss her."

"That's not what she told me," he said, with a big smile on his face. He was obviously enjoying the situation.

I left soon afterwards, walking home through the back fields and jumping a few fences to avoid the police. I spent the rest of the day worrying about the police and more important about what would happen if my mother found out. I couldn't believe all the fuss over kissing a damn girl. Besides, from what we had heard she was no angel either. I felt relived when Sunday came to an end and nothing had happened.

Arriving at Jefferson School on Monday morning was another story. Rumors were rampant among the seventh and eighth grade classes about what had occurred that Saturday night at the Horseshoe Pond. The stories were getting more and more elaborate. I began to get strange looks and glances from some of the girls in the class, which really unsettled me. I simply could not grasp what all the fuss was about.

Sometime in the early afternoon Margaret Destefanko, who was acting as a messenger that day (Jefferson School had no intercom system), came into the eighth grade class and spoke to the teacher, Miss Huptick. Miss Huptick then called out the name of one of us three who were at the attack and instructed him to report to the office of the principal, Miss Rymarcik. It now became apparent that what had occurred at the Horseshoe Pond on Saturday night had been reported to the principal of Jefferson School.

As he left the class on his way to the principal's office, my friend's face clearly showed two things: one, he was confused about all the fuss; and two, he had just begun to hear about all the strange stories that were circulating. He and the other kid were both from the hill section near Morrissey Avenue and had not heard anything until arriving at school on Monday. As he left, the attention of the other kids in class now began to focus on me and my fellow attacker. There was something strange about the girls, who were always so straitlaced. They seemed to be enjoying this whole episode as if they had been awakened from some giant slumber.

I couldn't believe the direction things were taking over a couple of kids kissing a girl. We thought girls wanted to be kissed. A few weeks earlier Miss Huptick read us a story about a box—Pandora's Box. On first hearing it I thought it was a great story. Now I had a first-hand acquaintance with it.

After twenty minutes or so Margaret Destefanko returned with attacker number one. She spoke to the teacher, who called out the name of attacker number two and told him to report to the office. I could feel the concentration of attention on me, attacker number three. Again, after a short interval attacker number two returned to class, but not escorted by Margaret Destefanko. He took his seat, obviously embarrassed by his discussion of events with Miss Rymarcik, the principal.

Although I was uncomfortable for the rest of the day, I was never called to the principal's office.

It didn't take long to find out why the girl didn't report me. She was from the Star Homes and most of the kids I was friendly with were also from the Star Homes. In fact, we had a gang that operated out of Krug's woods called the "Robin Hood Gang." Many of the kids from the gang were her neighbors and I also knew her. It seems she didn't want me to get into any trouble because of my close contacts with all the kids she knew from her neighborhood. However, the other two kids were from the hill and since she didn't know them she felt no remorse about reporting them as her attackers. In Wallington in the early and mid 1940s, the Mt. Pleasant Avenue and Morrissey Avenue kids were from another section of town and this girl's loyalties lay with the kids she knew and the Star Homes.

THE DUMP

Van Kruiningen's dump was located just off Main Street, where Nelkin Road is today in the apartment complex known as Jasontown.

Before becoming a dump it was a large lake always referred to as the Sandpits. The Van Kruiningen family at one time owned this land and it was heavily mined for the fine sand it contained. At some point in the sand removal process springs were encountered which eventually flooded the pit, turning it into a lake. In the early 1940s this lake was a very popular recreation area for both kids and adults. Swimming, fishing, and ice skating were all popular activities at that time.

Sometime around 1943 a new use was found for these beautiful sandpits which were so well-used by the locals. World War II had increased the production of war materiel all through the area and new dumping grounds for waste products were needed. It was at this time that the Sandpits were transformed into Van Kruiningen's Dump.

This was no ordinary garbage dump for household refuse. Rather, it catered only to waste material from factories. This waste was the major attraction that brought many local kids to the dump.

At this time, if a kid wanted money he would have to go out and earn it. There was no such concept as a weekly allowance for spending money. The general rule was, "You want money, go earn it." You could ask your parents for a quarter or so, but they would almost always ask, "What do you want the money for?" And too often you wouldn't want to say.

Van Kruiningen's dump became a bonanza for many local kids, as this was the place where a kid could make some good money—at least by our standards at the time. In fact, a few would hit the proverbial jackpot.

There were the usual moneymakers such as copper wiring, chunks of lead, and other metals that could be cleaned up and sold. However, this was not the main attraction that brought so many kids to this dump and that constantly flirted with their imagination—it was cash (coins) or perhaps some gold, mostly in objects such as rings, jewelry, eyeglass frames, pins, and even gold fountain pens. For many kids the rainbow ended at Van Kruiningen's dump.

One of the factories that used the dump, Clifton Paper Board Company, processed old clothing and rags. They used the material in making high-quality paper. These were the loads we waited for. You had to be at the dump when a truck loaded with rag wastes arrived, because whatever value it contained would be quickly removed.

The rags were in large bales about four feet by six feet. Steam would usually be coming off of the bales, as in the factory the rags were somehow cooked to sterilize them. Part of the process was also to strip all buttons from the clothes. These buttons and all items that were left in pockets were separated from the boiled rags.

When a truck arrived and parked to drop its load, kids would jockey for a position near the tailgate. The driver would then begin raising the dump body to deposit the load. As the dump body got higher the first thing to exit would be thousands of buttons and other items, and in this mixture would be our treasure, the stuff people left in their pockets. Finally, out would tumble the large hot bales of rags. At this time a mad scramble would begin to get near to the pile of buttons. At times the buttons would be covered by the bales and these would have to be pushed away, although we sometimes had to wait until the hot bales cooled off.

On this particular day very few trucks were arriving with their loads of hot rags and buttons. Finally, when one did arrive, it was surrounded by a bunch of kids eager to get at the load of buttons and their imagined treasures. I was one of them. Luckily, I was able to get a very good position next to the pile of buttons. The way the bales fell very few kids had access to the buttons, as there were more kids than places for them to look for the treasure. Using a flattened stick and squatting next to the pile, I began sifting through the buttons and pushing the ones I had gone through behind me, between my legs. I was picking up a few coins here and there but nothing spectacular.

It was then that I heard a loud yell just behind me. Alex Bednarz hadn't found a place next to the buttons, so he was looking through the pile I had already gone through. My carelessness paid off for him, and he found the pot of gold at the end of our rainbow. He showed me the ring he had found in the material I had discarded, and my heart almost stopped beating. It was a large gold man's ring with a circle of ten diamonds on top. He never sold the ring and as we grew up together over the years I would always see him wearing it, a constant reminder of that old adage, "Haste makes waste."

THE RADIO

During the 1930s and 1940s, one object in the house that was truly venerated was the radio. It was the only real source of entertainment that most families had. It seems that no matter how poor a family was there was always a large radio sitting in the living room. It was the most treasured possession and people treated it as such. Generally speaking, children were not allowed to play with the radio. You would have to wait patiently for the time your program was being aired then inform one of your parents, who would turn the radio on and dial to the correct station. Radios were considered too expensive and important to allow young children to touch them.

Most families had only one radio, typically a three-foot-high console model made by RCA or Philco. There were other popular brands but in my world RCA was king. Over time, as economic conditions improved in the early 1940s, a small table model radio would be added. If there were young children this would always be placed on top of the icebox or on a closet shelf where it couldn't be reached and damaged.

Since the radio was so important to the children it also served as a means of punishment. For those who misbehaved, disobeyed, fibbed, or committed other infractions against expected behavior, hearing the words "No supper for you tonight" was bad enough. But when the words "and no radio" were added, this was about the worst punishment you could inflict on a child.

Our radio provided various forms of entertainment and news. The most important to the adults and some of the older kids were comedy programs. "Amos 'n' Andy," with their friend the Kingfish, rates as one of the most listened-to programs by adults. It came on at 7:30 P.M. and it never failed to draw an audience, as it was a welcomed relief from the drudgery of most people's lives during this era.

Jack Benny and his violin was another favorite, as his miserliness and penny-pinching resonated well with people during the Depression. Surprisingly, the entertainers were never negative but were always upbeat about America and its people. It's a good thing I learned about the Depression when I grew older, as I never knew we were in one at that time. To me and most other kids, this was just the way life was and radio rarely dwelt upon the condition.

Favorite programs for the women were played around noontime and some women were so attached to them that they scheduled their chores around these soap operas. A common phrase heard at this time was, "Be quiet, I'm listening to the radio." One popular program was "Our Gal Sunday," the story of an orphan from Colorado who marries a British aristocrat. However, the favorite was "The Romance of Helen Trent," which the announcer said "set out to prove that romance can live in life at 35 and after." From what I could gather, Helen Trent was having difficulties proving that to be true.

Radio programs for kids usually consisted of dramas with a plot that was based on a good guy getting the best of a bad guy. By far the most popular of these programs was about the "Lone Ranger" and his Indian friend Tonto. In these episodes good always triumphed over evil, kindness was always rewarded, and the law was always enforced regardless of circumstances.

"The Shadow" has to rank as one of the most entertaining series on the radio for kids. These programs were very scary and usually involved sadistic criminals. They were also very heavy on human psychology, always illustrating the depths of human depravity that people can so easily be led into. The introduction to every program was the same—a deeply resonating voice (originally Orson Welles) slowly delivered the following message: "Who knows what evil lurks in the hearts of men? The Shadow knows." This was followed by laughter that was enough to make a young boy cringe, as it was not a laughter of joy or happiness but rather a mockery of the human condition. We were subtly getting doses of reality that we would not appreciate until we were much older.

Another program which fascinated young people was a series called "The Inner Sanctum." These were complicated murder mysteries or stories involving ghosts or other strange phenomena. Unusual science topics or mysteries were also covered. There were heavy doses of speculation which were guaranteed to excite and frighten any youngster. As most of us young kids had a healthy fear of ghosts and such, it did not take much to frighten us. The program always began with the opening of a door that would squeak in a sinister manner, like the heavy oak door leading to a dungeon or someplace that was to be feared.

Radio was also used for listening to music, although this was at the very bottom of the list in importance. Music listening rarely occurred during the week as people were pretty much occupied until the evenings, at which time we would listen to serials. On weekends when the women in our neighborhood were busy ironing and cleaning house they would sometimes listen to music on the radio. Needless to say the most popular stations that they listened to played polkas.

The only competition the radio had in our house was from an old Victrola with a hand crank that had to be wound up every few minutes. The quality of the sound was at best poor and the steel needles constantly wore out. However, my grandfather had it in his bedroom and he would spend hours playing records with songs from Poland, as he always remained deeply attached to his mother country.

The last and in many ways the most important use of the radio was as a source of news. It was our only real contact with the world outside of our immediate area. Radio became especially important to our family and to many Polish families in the Passaic area as World

War II began with the invasion of Poland, and many families had relatives in what they would always refer to as the "old country." After the German invasion all contact with Poland was cut off and the only real source of information was the radio.

During the war years, people would gather around the radio every evening at 7:00 P.M. and listen to the news, with reports by Edward R. Murrow and other reporters overseas. Through the 1930s and 1940s the most important broadcasts were by President Roosevelt, which were always referred to as "fireside chats." He was a very popular president and people put their faith and trust in him as they listened to him talk about the Great Depression and then World War II.

Children had to remain very quiet during radio broadcasts, whether Roosevelt's fireside chats or just plain news. Any fooling around or noise was not tolerated, and punishment for breaking the rules was usually severe. Listening to the radio was a way of life for most families and this would not end until televisions became popular in the mid-1950s.

THE GREAT FIRE

t was a warm summer evening around 1944 or perhaps 1945. I left the house on Park Row and headed for Zampacota's candy store at the corner of Kossuth Street and Main Street. Finding no one there that I usually associated with, I figured they might be over at the Horseshoe Pond. Sure enough, there was a football game going on when I arrived. We usually played in an empty field above the pond and across the street from the Gulf gas station (where the Seven-Eleven store is now). We played touch football until it began to get dark, which was about 8:30 P.M.

After we rested for a while several of the older kids began rolling a large fifty-five gallon drum into the middle of the field. There was no top on the drum so they sort of rolled it on the bottom edge. After the drum was in place we all congregated around it to find out what was going on. The drum was filled with shiny metal shavings. I knew the shavings were magnesium, and that they must have come from the Curtiss-Wright factory or from Van Kruiningen's dump, but I had never seen them in this quantity before. Some of the kids were very excited, as they apparently knew what was about to take place, or should I say they had expectations of what would take place.

Finally it became dark—time to fire up the magnesium. A small wooden fire was built on top of the shavings but it did not have the necessary heat to ignite the magnesium. One kid left the group, saying he was going behind the Gulf station to get something to light the magnesium with. He returned with a can full of an oil-gasoline mixture and proceeded to pour it on the contents of the barrel. A match was thrown into the barrel and although it burned furiously, as gasoline usually does, the magnesium again failed to ignite.

Another kid volunteered to try, informing us that he was going home and would be right back. He returned with a partially-burned railroad flare. He ignited the flare with a match and it readily lit up with a bright flame. By now it was very dark, and the burning flare threw an eerie light on the faces of the kids circling the barrel. After waiting to be sure the flare was as hot as possible, he shoved it into the magnesium shavings.

We waited in anticipation. Three seconds, four seconds. Then the magnesium caught fire. A blinding white light began to emanate from the barrel—we couldn't even look at it. It began to get larger, and everyone started to back away from the barrel. The fire continued to get brighter and brighter, and suddenly everyone took off running to get out of there. We had unleashed a monster.

I ran for home. As I passed in front of the Gulf station it was like daylight outside. I couldn't help noticing as I ran that I could see my shadow on the clouds. Turning my head to the right to look back, I was startled to be able to see the large water tower on the other side of the Passaic River. I could even read the writing on the tank. Damn, now I was scared. I headed up Kossuth Street, then turned in to Adamson Avenue and stopped before reaching Park Row. My mother and the neighbors were standing in front of the house wondering what the hell was happening. I heard the siren go off, and Company No. 3's lone fire engine took off for the fire. I hoped the magnesium fire would go out before they put water on it.

After everything settled down I went upstairs to our apartment in Kobscenski's house. When I walked in, I tried to put on an air of nonchalance and ignorance.

"Where the hell have you been?" my mother demanded.

"I was at the Passaic Boys Club." This was my regular alibi.

"Well, thank God you're home," she said. "The damn Germans are up to something."

TIPPY

Phil Kobscenski owned a very small gas station where the Eighth Street bridge meets Main Avenue in Wallington. The building was so small that all grease jobs, oil changes, and tire repairs were done outside in all kinds of weather. The small building was really only an office and a storage shed for tires and tools. The entire family worked very hard to make ends meet. As my mother would later say, "I knew Liz Kobscenski when she had only one dress."

After World War II began their fortunes rapidly improved, as rationing of tires and gasoline created an economic condition that favored them in many ways. Sometime in the early 1940s they built a new home on the corner of Main Street and Stein Avenue. My Aunt Annie and my grandfather moved from Fourth Street in Passaic to the vacated Kobscenski apartment on Park Row. This house was always referred to as Kobscenski's house as it was still in the family. During this time period when you were a renter and you wished to convey to someone where you lived you would give the name of the landlord and the street the house was on.

My Aunt Annie hated dogs. She considered them only slightly better than pigeons, which to her were the bottom of the totem pole. Her attitude towards dogs was simple.

"What are they good for?" she would say. "All they do is eat, sleep, and shit where people can step in it."

When the Kobscenskis left the apartment on Park Row to move to their new house they owned a white spitz dog by the name of Tippy. Tippy did not like his new home on Stein Avenue and kept returning to Park Row and my dog-hating aunt. My aunt would at times bring Tippy back, or one of the Kobscenskis would come over to get him. However, at the first opportunity he would return. Against my aunt's best interests, Liz Kobscenski finally convinced my aunt that she should keep Tippy. Of course my aunt realized that she was renting an apartment from the Kobscenskis, and just recently getting it did not want to create any bad feelings with the landlord.

Tippy was totally unaware of my aunt's feelings toward dogs. Had he known, he probably would have tried harder to accustom himself to his new home on Stein Avenue. My aunt was single at the time that Tippy came to live with her and his being treated as a dog was to come to an abrupt end. My aunt always saw him as a dirty little boy—and Saturday was bath day for dirty little boys.

Several months after Tippy became a resident with my aunt she received another setback. My mother was informed by OK Sura that we would have to vacate our apartment so his now-married daughter could occupy it. My mother could not find another apartment in the area, so my mother, my stepfather, and my brother and I moved in with my aunt. In several months she had acquired a dog and two kids. Saturday bath day was getting complicated.

Somehow Tippy always knew when Saturday had arrived. As soon as my aunt got up he would look for a place to hide, and he would remain hidden until finally located and brought to the bathtub. The most difficult place to get at him was when he was found hiding under a bed. A broom was usually required to dislodge him.

I suspect taking a bath was a very humiliating process for him, as his fur was pure white and stood out from his body giving him a regal look. Once placed in the tub and completely soaked, however, he looked like a half-drowned opossum. His eyes would reflect his embarrassment at his degraded condition.

Perhaps six months had passed when a married couple my aunt knew stopped by for a visit. They had never seen Tippy before and admired him for his clean healthy look (he had had his Saturday bath). My aunt, sensing a possible opportunity to foist Tippy on someone else, began to extol his virtues as a dog. My clever aunt then informed them that due to the crowed conditions of the apartment Tippy was going to have to be put away unless someone gave him a home. (Of course, she really had no intention of putting him away.) The emotions of this childless couple began to soar. My aunt, sensing victory, continued to lavish praise on Tippy as a wonderful companion and watchdog. She added five dollars to cover whatever costs they might incur, and the couple left with a reluctant Tippy.

The last words of my gleeful aunt to them were, "He doesn't like a bath on Saturday, so pick another day."

THE CARNIVAL

Sometime around the middle 1940s our area received a real treat, a form of entertainment we were only vaguely aware of and this only through films and stories. Even so, what we usually saw depicted was a circus, animals and all. What was coming to town was no circus. There were no animals and no big tent for performers, and what there was usually took your money from you if you were a fool—especially a male fool. This was a carnival.

I had found out about the carnival from Walt Bednarz, who always seemed to know what was going on in the area. He was vividly describing how he had sneaked under the tent into one of the girlie shows and was able to watch the girls strip down and do a dance on a small stage. After listening to him I knew I had to make a trip to the carnival and investigate this new form of entertainment. I made plans to go there the next night, which was a Friday.

The carnival was located in South Hackensack, across the street from where the Home Liquor store is today. In the 1940s, fields covered the area from the railroad tracks to the Saddle River, and up to the graveyard behind the orphanage (currently Felician College).

I arrived at the carnival in the afternoon to check things out. It was summer vacation and it would not get dark until 8:30 P.M., which would give me plenty of time to look around, go home for supper, and return later. As I began to wander around the carnival I became aware of how little money I had. Everything cost ten cents and the total amount of money in my pocket was around thirty-five cents.

I wasn't about to waste my precious money on rides and games, although the shooting gallery did tempt me with its metal ducks that moved along on a wire and flipped over if you hit them. The wire was suspended over a trough of water to create the illusion that the ducks were swimming.

Observing all the games that people were playing I formulated the concept in my mind that most adults were crazy. They were throwing pennies, nickels, or dimes into cups to win prizes, or they paid to throw hoops over pegs. Another game was to knock over milk bottles with a baseball. The thing I noticed was how few of them ever won anything, and if they did win they usually got some cheap stuffed animal. I could not comprehend why adults would throw away their money like that to try and win a useless stuffed animal. I was beginning to take an interest in human psychology.

It wasn't long before I found myself in front of a large tent with two full-size pictures of almost-nude girls. Their stance and their smiles were very suggestive and indicated a superior form of entertainment over what the rest of the carnival had to offer. So this was the tent that Walt Bednarz had gotten into. This was the much talked about "peep show," where you could see nude females dance. Further investigation revealed a sign with information that it cost fifty cents to see the show and you had to be twenty-one years old to get into the tent.

I began looking the tent over to see how to sneak under the canvas. This approach did not look too promising to me so I made my way between this tent and another to get a look at the back of the tent. I was surprised to find that the back of the tent was only fifty feet from the Saddle River. I knew the area quite well, as the Saddle River flowed from this location past the Pump House near to the Horseshoe Pond then turned behind the Hammersly factory before entering the Passaic River. I returned home following this route, but at the Horseshoe Pond I climbed a short steep hill that led to an empty field on Main Street (the "three corners") and headed home to Park Row.

After supper I told my mother I was going over to the carnival with some of my friends and that I would be back late. She took the opportunity to remind me to watch my money as carnivals were full of crooks. I wanted to get there by 7 P.M. when the first "girlie show" started, to look things over. There would be a show every hour after that until 11 P.M.

I arrived just about the time the girls were giving a demonstration in front of the tent. A barker with a fedora hat and a cane was working over the all-male audience by pointing to the girls' anatomy and extolling the beauty of the female body. There were perhaps thirty or forty men in front watching the demonstration, and when it was over most paid fifty cents to see the show.

It was much too light to attempt anything so I just wandered about the carnival waiting for darkness. Towards 8 pm, when the sun had already set, I slipped away from the carnival and made my way to where the Saddle River ran beneath the road. I then turned to the right to follow the river behind the girlie tent. Carefully making my way through the tall grass I reached the back of the tent and began looking for a way to see inside. I could hear two girls inside the tent laughing and giggling. I was not daring enough to do a Walt Bednarz and attempt to get in by crawling under the canvas where the spectators stood. I had to find another way.

The answer was right in my pocket. Opening my pocket knife, I slowly inserted the long thin blade of the three-bladed knife into the canvas and moved it downward to make a slit about two inches long. Next I inserted a small stick in the hole to slightly spread the canvas so I could see. I was nervous and my heart was beating overtime as I put my knife away and leaned towards the peephole I had just made.

Wow! Both girls were almost naked and they were only eight feet away. They were giggling and playing with several brightly colored balloons in a most suggestive manner, which at this stage of my life I could not comprehend although it was very stimulating. The show hadn't started yet and I guess they were warming up. The tent was divided in half by a moveable curtain. The back half where I was viewing them was actually a dressing room. The show so far was way beyond my expectations.

Pretty soon they got ready for their dance act, as a large crowd of older men was waiting to see them. Suddenly, the curtain was drawn back and the two girls climbed onto the stage and began their dance, which was really only squirming and gyrating to the sound of a Victrola. From my position I could see the backs of the girls very well, and even the front when they turned around and bent over so the audience could get a close-up look at their rear ends. The audience seemed to be dumbstruck by what they saw, as there was no clapping or noise of any kind. The men just looked mesmerized.

After about fifteen minutes of this show the curtain was suddenly closed and the girls once more retreated into their private area. With my little slit in the tent, however, it was not so private any more. From the other side of the curtains I could hear the barker telling the audience that if they paid one dollar more they would be able to stay and watch the girls peel off what little they had on. There was some grumbling as the men now realized they had been taken; however, about half elected to pay a buck to see the next part of the show.

About this time I was getting as carried away as the audience, and removing my pocket knife I decided to enlarge the slit in the tent. Inserting two fingers, one from each hand, I was able to slightly spread the canvas and get my eye closer to the hole, as there would be no stick in the way now. Hearing the barker and the two girls talking, I knew that they came from somewhere in the south. I had become very familiar with the southern drawl as in the early part of World War II a half dozen or more anti-aircraft units from the south had been set up on the hill in Wallington. The south must be a hell of a place to live, I thought to myself as I watched these girls get ready for Act II

The curtain came apart—Act II had begun. The stage the girls climbed up on was about three feet high and the men in the front row were standing only a foot or two away. The girls slowly removed their remaining clothes as the music played. When a girl was completely nude, she would approach a male and gyrate practically in his face. She would then offer him a purse and if he dropped a couple of coins inside she would continue her act and a little more. Some big guys connected with the show made sure no one touched the girls.

Finally the show ended, the curtain was closed, and the girls were once more alone—that is, except for me. I watched as they put some clothes on and then began to count the money deposited in their purses.

It was time to go home, and as I made my way past the Pump House and the Horseshoe Pond I kept thinking about the strange exciting world I had just witnessed.

The next day was Saturday and it wasn't long before I was meeting most of my friends from the Star Homes. Needless to say, the main topic of conversation was the carnival and my graphic description of what I had seen and how I managed to pull it off. I even described how I got to the back of the tent by following the bank of the Saddle River. Not left out was my use of the pocket knife to cut the tent. They asked a lot of questions about the girls, who I described in a way that would do justice to a fifteen-year-old with a good imagination.

The darkness of Saturday night was rapidly approaching as I made my way back towards the carnival. I was anticipating another evening of pure pleasure, only this time I would have company, as a friend of mine who desperately wanted to see the show would be along. It was just approaching dark when we rounded the final bend in the Saddle River before reaching the tent. Apparently my vivid descriptions of the girlie show had made the rounds of most of the local kids and I was shocked by what I saw. The back side of the tent was covered with kids and one of them was even using my peep hole. I was completely shut out from the show.

It was then that I noticed that where the side of the tent met the roof there was a scalloped overhang overlapping the side by six inches. Perhaps it covered an opening, or why else would it be there? The tent was held in place by ropes extending from the roofline to large stakes driven into the ground. Being nimble, I decided to check it out. I shinnied my way up the rope to the scalloped overhang. As I climbed the rope the tent shook a little, but the girls were already on stage and no one noticed. Grasping the roof with both hands and wrapping my feet around the rope I felt secure enough to use one hand to lift the flap. Eureka! There was a narrow gap I could see through.

I was watching the show when suddenly I became aware of something going wrong. I felt myself begin to bounce on my perch, and I was horrified to see other kids climbing the other ropes that held the back part of the tent. They must have gotten the idea from seeing me up there, looking beneath the flap. The back of the tent became very unstable, and it wasn't long before one of the pegs pulled out of the ground, to be followed by another. The back of the tent collapsed and as I hit the ground I was already headed for the safety of the banks of the Saddle River. Looking back as I ran, the last I saw of my dream world was a lot of kids running, and flashlights behind the tent looking for those who had caused this debacle. I tripped and fell a few times in my exodus from the field and did not rest until I reached the Pump House.

As I slowly made my way home I realized that I was the cause of what happened. If only I had kept my mouth shut.

THE NELKINS

A well-known name in Wallington is Nelkin. In the not-too-distant past a park in Wallington was named the Samuel Nelkin Park. At the time that I was growing up this park did not exist; rather, the area was heavily wooded, the woods extending over the hill all the way to Mount Pleasant Avenue and in some places down to the railroad tracks which separated Wallington from Wood-Ridge.

In the 1930s and 1940s the name Nelkin was always associated with the Comfort and Olympic bus companies which were located on Main Street in Wallington near to where the Pulaski statue is today. (Or, if you are old enough to remember, about where Butch Kopec drove his car into the Passaic River.)

I did not have any contact with Sam Nelkin, as his world was very remote from mine. I would occasionally see him around the bus company, and I remember him as a very natty dresser. He really stood out by the fine clothes he always wore. This was a time and a town where fine clothes stood out like a sore thumb.

This story is not about Sam Nelkin but about his brother Abe Nelkin. There are no memorials to Abe or parks that we will remember him by, but many of the kids growing up in Wallington have only fond recollections of him. I do not know whether Abe was a part owner of the bus company or if he was just an employee of his brother Sam. However, the contrast between the two was like night and day.

In the 1940s, when Wallington did not have a high school, some kids from town attended Bloomfield Vocational and Technical High School. I was one of these, along with about twenty other boys and about six girls. No matter where you lived in town, the ten-mile trip to school began on Main Street in front of the bus company. Some kids had a very long walk, as they would come all the way from Morrissey Avenue. Regardless of weather, temperature, or distance we met there for our ride on the bus, which left about 7:15 A.M.

This was where most of us would have our first contact with Abe Nelkin, who worked in the bus garage. Abe wore work clothes or dirty coveralls, as he was always working to keep dozens of buses running. When we arrived about 7:00 A.M. Abe was always there, and it was apparent that he had been working for some time.

Abe would always come out and chat with us if he wasn't overloaded with work fixing buses. He was a pleasant man and loved to kid around, even sharing funny jokes with us. He was a powerfully built man but this was not apparent unless he gave you a demonstration or showed you a trick of some kind. One of these tricks I tried unsuccessfully to duplicate for many years. He would take an ordinary glass milk bottle and place a dime inside. Next, he would spin the bottle with his wrist as rapidly as possible. Then he would instantly bring the bottle to a stop and the dime would exit right through the side of the bottle, leaving a hole the size of the dime. Some of the larger and stronger kids in our group tried it, always without success.

Some of the kids taking the bus would not bring a lunch but would eat in the school cafeteria. Other kids would sometimes forget to bring a lunch. You could always hit up Abe for twenty cents (the cost of lunch) by explaining that you had no money or that you forgot your lunch. Even though it was understood that you were to pay him back this did not happen very often. Abe never asked for the money you owed him; in fact, I still owe him eighty cents.

I understand that Abe has departed this world. Although he is no longer with us, he left a legacy behind that will endure. A hard-working man who didn't mind dirty jobs, a gentle and understanding man who loved kids, his monument exists in the hearts of those who knew him—especially those kids who took the bus to Bloomfield Tech.

WALT BEDNARZ

The family of Walt Bednarz moved to Wallington from Fourth Street in Passaic in the early 1940s. Fourth Street and its vicinity was a regular pipeline for Polish people moving to Wallington for a better life. The Bednarz family bought one of the first newly built homes in the development known as the Star Homes. The land for this development came from the sale of part of Krug's dairy farm.

Walt's first job was delivering the Passaic Herald News in his neighborhood when he was about ten or eleven years old. One day a representative of the Newark Star Ledger approached Walt about delivering that paper. Walt accepted, as it paid much more. However, the drawback was that he had to deliver the paper to the entire town of Wallington. Using his bicycle, he would deliver the paper from the Crescent Road area to the Eighth Street bridge before arriving at Jefferson School in the morning. After school he would do the rest of the town.

With the development of Van Kruiningen's dump, however, Walt and many other local kids could find a more lucrative way to get money. Hanging around Van Kruiningen's dump became a way of life for many kids, as jobs for kids were rare unless you wanted to work on a farm in the summer for ten cents an hour.

Sometime during this period Walt came upon an unusual material being deposited on the dump. He was able to recognize it and where it came from as we had seen it being stored in the fenced-in yard of the Curtiss-Wright factory in South Hackensack. World War II was in full progress and this aircraft engine plant was heavily guarded to prevent sabotage; however, the woods at the back of the plant allowed us to get close to the fence where we could see the storage barrels. It didn't take Walt long to figure out that the barrels were filled with magnesium shavings from machining pistons for aircraft engines. It was not unusual for Walt to display his expertise with magnesium on the Horseshoe Pond, especially during the winter when it was covered with ice. The magnesium would be ignited on the ice, usually with the stub of a railroad flare that had been picked up along the tracks. The heat would melt the ice and a spectacular fire would occur when the cold water came in contact with the magnesium. Everyone knew from our instructions at Jefferson School that we could be bombed with incendiary bombs, also called magnesium bombs, and that you should never put water on them. Testimony to this was the number of sand buckets throughout the school to be used in case of incendiary fires.

Walt and I both attended Bloomfield Tech and we both had the same attitude towards school, which was to play hooky as often as we could get away with. There were a few times that we would miss a week of school, preferring to hang around the Pump House or Van Kruiningen's dump checking things out—especially those loads from Clifton Paper Board Co.

This not going to school could be quite risky, as the town of Wallington had a truant officer by the name of Hettle. Mr. Hettle would walk around town looking for kids or informing their parents that they had missed school. Our parents rarely found out, as they were never home during the day. There was a candy store on the corner of Main Street and Kossuth Street which was owned by the Zampacotas, and it was a hangout for kids. Mr. Hettle could always be spotted at a great distance as he had only one arm, and we would immediately take off. However, there were times when we were caught by surprise and Emily Zampacota would hide us in the back room of the store. This store was especially popular during the warm summer months. The store had a pinball machine which cost a nickel to play. The machine would often have to be changed as some kids were always drilling holes in the side so they could insert a piece of a coat hanger and rack up free games.

When we did take the bus to school, that did not necessarily mean we would go into the school. There were some interesting diversions in the surrounding area of Bloomfield. Our favorite pastime lay in the city of Newark, a few miles away. We would take the trolley from Bloomfield to Newark and after wandering around Newark for a while we would head for the burlesque show. Even though you were supposed to be eighteen to enter, if you had the money you could always figure on getting in. The problem lay in getting home afterward, as we would miss the school bus and have to walk back to Wallington—a two hour or longer walk to get home.

No one scouted the area surrounding Wallington more efficiently than Walt Bednarz and his friend Buddy Richards. Sometime during the latter part of World War II they ended up along the banks of the Passaic River behind Tidewater Iron and Steel Company, which was across the street from the Passaic Stadium.

This area was a dumping ground for salvaged war materiel brought back by ships as ballast. The first item that attracted their attention was a German tank lying on its side with the machine gun still in place. There were piles of junk war materiel lying everywhere waiting to be processed. Much of the stuff was in bad condition but they managed to find some small guns in pretty good condition, including a "burp" gun (a .45 caliber handheld machine gun). Returning a few days later they took home a German light machine gun in very good condition. They were showing the gun to quite a few people and an older person advised them to get rid of it as it was against the law to own a machine gun and they could be arrested. Walt and Buddy became a little concerned, so after wrapping the gun in an old tablecloth they buried it between Walt's house and the Gulf gas station, which was located at the three corners.

On one of these excursions to their own private arms depot they noticed a large flat barge tied up at the dock with part of a ship on it. This aroused their curiosity so they boarded the barge to investigate. Only one item attracted their attention: it was the ship's bell, which was still attached to the wreck. Try as they might they could not free the bell, which they badly wanted. Returning the next evening with a hacksaw they managed to cut through the steel bolt holding the bell. With great difficulty, but with big smiles, they managed to lug the heavy brass or bronze bell back to Park Row where Buddy Richards' aunt lived.

There was a factory in Rutherford that Walt took me to—another find on his scouting expeditions. It went under the name of B-D, for Becton-Dickinson, and they manufactured syringes of all sizes for the medical profession. Behind the factory was a dump filled with broken and rejected syringes. Whenever we were overcome by boredom we would make a trip to the dump in search of syringes, which we used as squirt guns. We would usually bring back enough to supply the whole neighborhood with our brand of water pistols. Being glass they did not last long, as—to put it mildly—we were very careless. This type of entertainment was very low on our list of interesting things to do, as our area provided much more interesting opportunities for young boys to run amok.

One afternoon I bumped into Walt at the Horseshoe Pond and I noticed he had a most unusual looking pistol in his hand.

"What kind of pistol is that?" I asked.

"It's a flare pistol," he replied. "It shoots 12 gauge shotgun shells."

"I never heard of a shotgun pistol, can I have a look?"

He handed me the gun. "Be careful. Don't cock it, it's loaded with a shotgun shell." He then explained that the gun was made to shoot flares into the sky and that the flare was the same size as a 12 gauge shell.

"Boy," I replied, "that would make some rabbit gun. Where'd you get it from?"

"I got it from one of the airplanes at Bendix Airport."

"How do I go about getting one?" I asked

"Why don't you do what we did, go down to the airport when it's dark and sneak into one of those two-engine patrol planes and find where they stash the 'ditch kit.' It usually contains a rubber raft, water, a flare pistol, and flares, plus food in cans and other stuff—help yourself."

Several days passed by before I found two other kids willing to take the chance on entering these planes. We walked from Wallington to Hasbrouck Heights. From the Heights we could see Bendix Ariport stretching below us paralleling Route 17. We decided to walk to Route 6 (46) as it was near to the end of the runway. It was just about dark when we arrived at the runway, so we decided to walk right down the runway to where we could barely make out some parked planes at the other end. One side of the airport had a road the whole distance, with airplane hangars, workshops, and all kinds of small buildings needed for operating an airport. During World War II this was a pretty busy place. The other side of the airport was nothing but a swamp with eight-foot-tall cattails its whole length.

We were perhaps a third of the way down the runway when suddenly we heard engines and turned around to see a two-engine plane coming in for a landing. Just about this time the pilot turned on his landing lights. The entire landing strip lit up and the control tower could now see three boys standing on the airfield. In panic, both of my friends took off running for the side of the air strip that held the swamp and safety. I elected to drop flat on the runway, hoping the plane would miss me. It did, passing ten feet over my head. Instantly sirens went off and Jeeps could be seen driving onto the runway. Recovering, I now headed for the swamp alongside the runway and the security of the tall grass. It took a while before my friends and I could locate each other and make our way through the tall cattails and back to Route 6.

We made our way to Hasbrouck Heights, hoping to be able to get a ride on the Olympic bus back to Wallington. It was probably the last bus of the evening that pulled up, as it was now near 11:00 P.M.

The driver stopped, opened the door, and in the light that went on saw three dirty, mud-covered kids standing there waiting for a ride. I don't know what went through his mind but he promptly closed the door and drove off, leaving us standing there.

My parents were not awake when I arrived at home, as they both went to bed very early, since they were usually up at 5:00 A.M. Being very quiet so as not to awaken them I climbed the ladder that led to the trapdoor and my attic bedroom. My brother woke up when I climbed over him to reach my side of the bed, which was against the wall.

"Where have you been so late?" he asked. "Ma asked me where you were before she went to bed."

"What did you tell her?"

"The usual. I told her you went to the Passaic Boys Club."

"Thanks, Joe." With that we went to sleep.

When Walt Bednarz and I were a little older, but still somewhat reckless in our pursuit of amusement, he introduced me into one of the most bizarre forms of entertainment imaginable. Meeting me one day, he asked, "Michalski, you wanna come shooting rats with us tonight?"

"Sure," I replied, "But where are we going to do the shooting?"

"We're going to the pig farms in Secaucus," he said.

His reply surprised me as I had never heard of shooting rats there, although I was familiar with the name and the smell of the town.

"And bring plenty of .22 caliber ammunition," he added. "If you can get .22 caliber birdshot all the better."

That evening he drove up with his friend Buddy Richards and we proceeded to drive the six miles to the pig farms of Secaucus. During the 1940s and later this area near the Meadowlands was well known for its pig farms and the stench that emanated from them. At one time they even tried using perfume but nothing could stop the foul odor that this area produced. Part of the problem was that the pigs were fed garbage collected from the surrounding institutions. There were mounds of rotting garbage that the pigs would wander over in search of food.

When we drove into one of the pig farms, the car's headlights revealed piles of garbage with hundreds of rats feeding off the refuse. Walt drove a little farther on with the lights off and parked twenty-five feet from a pig barn. He then gave me instructions: "You and Buddy stand in front of the car but to the side of the headlights. There's a large hole in the side of the barn and when I put the headlights on the rats will come pouring out of the hole. Aim at the hole and when I switch on the headlights start shooting at the hole and don't stop until your gun is empty. Don't try to aim at individual rats, just shoot at the hole." He turned on the headlights and the rifles began to bark, continuing until they were empty. About fifteen rats lay dead or wounded near the hole.

"Walt," I asked, "what do we do with the wounded ones?"

He laughed. "When the pigs are let out in the morning, that'll be their breakfast, the fresher the better."

We next took our flashlights and entered one of the large buildings housing the pigs in pens which were very overcrowded. Rats could be seen running over the backs of the pigs. Rats were everywhere, walking along the rails in the pens, even in the wooden rafters. The pigs began to get very excited, as they were familiar with people and guns and knew their party was about to begin. Using birdshot, we began shooting the rats from the rafters and on the wooden rails that formed the pens. Rats struck with birdshot would only be wounded, and when they fell into the pens the pigs would get hysterical trying to catch them. When you stopped shooting you could hear the sounds of pigs crunching on rats, the breaking of bones and the squealing of the rats creating a surreal atmosphere.

On the way home from shooting rats we would always stop at an all-night diner on Route 46. After spending the evening the way we had, I never understood how Walt Bednarz could order what he did at the diner. It was always the same: bacon and eggs.

Secaucus will always be remembered as a small town that raised thousands of pigs. One of its favorite sons, a Polish pig farmer named Henry Krajewski, ran for president of the United States. His campaign poster showed a picture of himself dressed in his farmer's clothes with a small pig under his arm.

Walt quit school at Bloomfield Tech when he was seventeen. His first job was with the Rayco company, where he learned how to make car seat covers. He became very good at this trade, which was in popular demand. Back in the forties and fifties almost everyone who purchased a new car would have seat covers installed to protect the seats. This was also true of living room furniture. A couple would spend weeks looking for a beautiful fabric only to have it covered, never to be seen again. (It was during the fifties that a solution to the problem was found. People would buy clear plastic covers which allowed you to see the beautiful fabric. However, there were several drawbacks to this solution. One was that the plastic usually turned a dull yellow. The second was that sitting on plastic made you sweat through your clothes.)

In 1952 Walt purchased the Gulf station on the "three corners," which was next to where he lived with his mother, father, and three brothers. Here he learned how to be a first class mechanic, and quite naturally the back room held a Singer sewing machine where he also made seat covers.

Recently I visited Walt, who now resides in Pennsylvania. As he showed me around his beautiful home, I was reminded very much of how he lived in Wallington. His garage reminded me of Bednarz's Gulf Station, with cars being worked on inside and several cars on the outside waiting to be fixed. He took me upstairs to a large room above the garage, and just as in Wallington it was filled with radio controlled airplanes, some in the process of being built, others being repaired. I noticed that the planes were much larger now and instead of using small airplane engines his planes were now powered by chainsaw engines. The last part of the tour was the basement, which turned out to be a machine shop with two lathes and a milling machine. Walt was better equipped now in his retirement than when he was in business. The only thing missing was an old Singer sewing machine.

As we sat in the living room of his immaculate house, I asked Walt some questions concerning past escapades. Walt never knew about the troubles my friends and I had trying to get a flare pistol from the airplanes at Bendix Airport, and until my visit I didn't know about the time that he and Buddy Richards were rummaging around a twin engine plane and as a lark decided to try and start it. Walt knew enough to first walk the propeller to clean out the radial engine. Inside the cockpit they began fooling with the dials and switches until the engines turned over and began running. As soon as the engines were running they both decided it was time for them to start running, and they headed for the security of the cattail swamp.

I asked Walt about the ship's bell he and Buddy Richards took. With a proud look on his face, he told me that even though it was more than fifty years ago, he could even remember the name on the bell. It was from the U.S.S. Alcoa Pointer. (An internet search revealed that this was a freighter built in 1943 and finally scrapped in 1966.)

"Where's the bell now?" I asked

"The last I saw of it was quite a few years ago at Buddy Richards's house. Buddy died five years ago, but I'll contact his wife and see if she still has the bell and if she would send me a picture."

"Walt," I asked, "when you were getting guns from Tidewater how did you get over the fence? I went there a few times but could not find a way over the wired fence."

He smiled. "Michalski, you had to go there when the tide was low. Then you could walk right around the fence where it ended at high tide."

I asked him what ever happened to the German light machine gun. He told me that after he bought the Gulf station he looked for the gun that was buried between his parents house and the gas station, but that he was never able to locate it. Today Walt's Gulf station is gone, having been replaced by a Seven-Eleven store.

HOT DOG NIGHT

For me and for many other children growing up in the 1930s and 1940s in Passaic and the surrounding area, Saturday night was a very special night. We always referred to it as Hot Dog Night. This event was sponsored by the Passaic Boys Club and was open to any kid who could get there. The club was located on Third Street in Passaic next to the Reid Library.

Kids would begin arriving at 6 P.M. even though the program would not begin until 7, so that they could get a seat up front, as we often sat on the gym floor. Depending on the weather and time of year you could almost always count on the gym being full.

The program would usually begin with the club director introducing things going on at the club and any changes occurring. At this time the club director was Ken Reynolds. This would be followed by movies that were always of a comic nature, with Laurel and Hardy being the favorite. Other popular comics were Abbott and Costello and the Three Stooges.

After the movies would come the treat we were all waiting for—a hot dog with mustard and sauerkraut. If attendance was poor due to the weather we would at times even get two hot dogs. To us this was heaven. I recall seeing kids wrapping up the second hot dog in their handkerchiefs to bring home and share with their younger brothers or sisters. During this time period, of all the foods we ate the hot dog was king. I realize that today the hot dog is not considered a treat but we always compared it with our standard fare, which was mainly soup and bread with butter.

After we had eaten, the stage would be prepared for the final event of the evening—boxing matches. Many kids during this period were very good at boxing as it was a very popular sport, especially at the Passaic Boys Club where boxing instruction was part of an ongoing program. Virtually all grudges between kids were settled with boxing gloves at the Boys Club, although this did not apply when you were on your home turf, when it would be bare knuckles.

To select two boxers one of the program directors standing on the stage would call out, "Who wants to box?" Usually, dozens of hands would rise and the director would randomly pick two. However, since everyone was sitting on the gym floor it was difficult for him to pick opponents evenly matched in height and weight. No corrections were made, and you simply did the best you could, although if the match was very unequal it would be quickly stopped.

Several times I was chosen to box on the stage but I remember only one time, as it taught me a very valuable lesson. I was matched with another kid from Wallington who I didn't know, as he was from the southern part of town. His name was Popec or Popeck. I was somewhat cocky when it came to fighting, but after three rounds with him and barely managing to pull out a draw I learned never to underestimate anyone.

Actually, my learning how to box was the result of an incident that occurred while we lived on Fourth Street in Passaic. Some of the older kids in the neighborhood had developed what can best be described as a juvenile protection racket to obtain money for themselves. First, they would rough up some young kids, which included my brother and me. Next they would approach the kids' parents for a handout of a quarter or fifty cents to leave them alone. My mother, being the lone parent and helpless, usually gave them something. I remember her throwing coins to them from our second story apartment.

That Sunday my uncle Jinx, who was well known in the area, paid us a visit. Everyone knew when he was visiting as he had a car, which was a very rare sight on Fourth Street in the late 1930s. Seeing me with a black eye he asked me what happened. I told him about the older kids hitting us and demanding money. He asked my mother if this was true, that she was paying those kids money for not beating on us.

"What could I do?" she responded.

My uncle asked me who the ringleader was and I told him it was a kid named Eddie. He got very angry and told me to come with him. My mother was petrified about what might happen because she knew her brother's explosive nature very well.

Apparently he knew this tough kid, as he led me to an apartment house a few buildings away. We walked up several flights of stairs to where Eddie lived, and without even knocking Jinx opened the door and walked in.

The family was sitting around the kitchen table having a traditional Sunday chicken dinner. They instantly stopped eating on seeing my uncle. I would find out later he had quite a reputation for being tough. Seeing Eddie sitting there, he went over to him and jerked him out of his chair. He said something to him, which I do not recall, and followed this with a punch that sent poor, poor Eddie to the floor. No one at the table got up to confront my uncle nor did anyone say a word.

We went back to our apartment and my uncle informed my mother that my brother and I would no longer be bothered. The next day after work he returned to our apartment and without even asking my mother he went into the living room and began screwing a punching bag into the ceiling. Even though my mother objected, he dismissed her by simply ignoring her. After installing the punching bag he opened a box containing a new set of boxing gloves, and I received my first instruction in this sport.

Over the following months he would continue to drill me in just two aspects of boxing until I had them down perfect:

1. Always throw your punches straight and with a snap, and
2. Always throw them in combinations, left jabs to be followed

by rights.

Needless to say, he was unmerciful as an instructor and thought nothing of knocking me down if I didn't box properly. I remember so well my mother's great sigh of relief when one day he came over for a visit and took the punching bag down.

Uncle Jinx

CHARLEY THE CROW

It was April of 1945 when Dicky Miscuff told me about four young crows that he was raising. He had removed them from their nest, which was located in a large oak tree near the Wallington Police pistol range. He kept the young crows in an old chicken coop across the street from his house on the corner of Chestnut Street and Pine Street.

I wanted to see the young crows so we both headed for the coop. As we entered they began to make a racket. He explained that whenever they saw him they expected to be fed. I waited while he returned to the house to get some food for them. He brought back a small bowl of milk and some white bread. After dipping the bread into the milk he had to drop it into their wide open beaks, as they could not feed themselves but simply raised their heads waiting to be fed.

At this time I knew that I had to have one of those crows as a pet.

"Dick, you got four crows, how about selling me one?" I asked

He thought for a moment, not about selling me a crow but about what he thought he could get for one.

"How about three bucks?"

"Dick, there's no way I can get three dollars," I replied. "How's about a dollar?"

He had me and he knew it. "Okay, one dollar and your pocket knife."

"C'mon, Dick," I pleaded. "I can't part with my pocket knife."

"Okay, how about two boxes of .22 caliber long rifles. Peter's High Velocity," he added.

"You got a deal," I replied.

We shook hands, and I was now the owner of a crow.

"Dick, can I leave him here until he gets older? Then I'll take him home."

He agreed, so for the next month, three times a day, I would visit the coop to feed the crows. At first it made no sense to choose one, as I couldn't tell one crow from another. However, the time came when one of the young crows became more dominant and I was able to recognize him by his aggressive behavior. I arranged with Dick to remove him to a separate part of the coop and we agreed that I would feed only my own crow.

It was now time to give my crow a name. He wasn't a dog, but he would be my pet—so I named him Charley.

I took very good care of Charley, slowly changing his diet to meat. On my way to Jefferson School in the morning I would stop to feed Charley. Usually I would remove some of the cold cuts from my sandwich to feed him. At lunch time I would return to the coop, which was only a hundred yards from the school, and feed him the rest of the lunchmeat from my sandwich. My lunch usually consisted of two slices of bread with some mustard. Returning home after school I would stop at the coop, usually bringing a few kids with me. I would work out a deal: I'll show you my crow after school if you bring him some of the cold cuts from your lunch. No peanut butter and jelly.

It was quite a moment when I took Charley from the coop and threw him into the air for his first real flight. It was obvious even to me that this was a training flight and that Charley had a lot to learn about being a crow. He was very insecure and would never venture too far from me, always keeping me in sight. He would quickly return to my arm when other birds began harassing him. Apparently crows were not very popular with other birds.

For some reason, probably diet, all three of Dicky's crows died and only Charley remained. He was now big enough to bring home, but there were some serious problems I would have to deal with. First and foremost was: how would my mother respond? Second, where would I keep him? Third, would my mother buy cold cuts for a crow?

I had to be somewhat clever in bringing Charley to his new home and introducing him to my mother, for if I could not get her to accept him it would be goodbye, Charley. I knew my mother well enough that I could not just walk in the house with a crow on my arm. I developed a plan based upon what I learned about crows when Charley was learning to fly. I knew that they were attracted to shiny objects and if I threw a shiny coin a few feet away Charley would fly from my arm, pick it up, and return to my arm.

I chose a Saturday afternoon for the encounter, as my mother would be hanging the laundry on the line to dry. My strategy was simple: I would be in the back yard playing with Charley when she came out with the laundry and hopefully her curiosity would be aroused enough that in this temporary state she might be more accepting of him.

Saturday finally arrived. I spent most of the morning in Krug's woods with Charley practicing picking up coins in preparation for the meeting with my mother. Then it was time to go home, and we slowly made our way to Park Row and the back yard where the encounter would take place. It wasn't long before my mother came outside with a reed basket carrying the laundry to be dried on the line.

She didn't notice me sitting on a wooden crate with Charley on my arm and almost tripped over us. Dropping the basket of clothes she suddenly drew back, as she was startled to see me sitting there with a large black bird on my arm.

"What the hell kind of chicken is that?" she asked, her voice carrying the sound of fear.

"Ma, it's not a chicken," I responded. "It's a crow."

"It looks like a skinny chicken," she said. "Besides, what is a crow good for?"

"Ma," I said, "Charley is good at finding money."

Her attention and curiosity immediately picked up upon hearing the word "money."

I took a new dime from my pocket and threw it twenty feet away in the grass. Instantly, Charley flew from my arm to where the coin had landed, found it, and returned to my arm.

My mother was impressed. She asked me for the dime, which she also threw about twenty feet away. Charley flew down to the spot where it landed and quickly found the coin, but on returning tried to land on my mother's shoulder.

She panicked, and wildly flailing her arms kept yelling, "Get that goddam thing away from me!"

After a few minutes she settled down. "What else can that damn thing find besides money?"

"Ma," I replied, "he can find anything that's shiny, like earrings, rings, or keys."

Suddenly my mother's look changed.

"Can I touch him?" she asked

"Sure, Ma," I said.

We had won, and Charley was now a member of the family.

Charley was to share the bedroom in the attic of Kobscenski's house with my brother and me. All we had to do was keep the window open and he would come and go as he pleased. Charley would be up with the first light of dawn and usually wanted to be fed at this time. Charley loved cold cuts, especially salami, so in the evening when he was asleep I would put some on the windowsill so he would have something to eat when he awoke. However, there were times when I would forget, and then Charley would come over to where I was sleeping and very gently take my eyelashes in his beak and open my eyes. I would then usually get him something to eat and return to bed.

I began hearing some complaints from the neighborhood involving Charley, as apparently he was a suspect in the disappearance of some garage keys. People had a habit of hanging the keys on a nail outside the garage. One morning I found some keys on the window sill, so I knew Charley was the culprit. However, there was nothing I could do so I simply ignored all that I had heard.

Charley and I became inseparable companions, and wherever I went Charley would follow me, usually flying from rooftop to rooftop.

Sundays turned out to be a real problem, as Charley would always follow me to church when I went—which was really not very often, although my mother was operating under the assumption that every Sunday morning when I left the house I would be going to church. Charley would fly from roof to roof as I headed towards the church. Upon arriving, he would sit on the cross until I came out. All during the time I was inside, however, he would make a racket, cawing constantly. The priest found it annoying and asked me not to return to church with my crow. I was more than happy to oblige and never returned to church.

That summer I took Charley to Camp Ocawasin with me, and to say the least he caused quite a stir. Then, sometime in late September or October, our area was hit by a hurricane. For three days Charley was missing, and despite my searching the neighborhood I could not find him. I suspected foul play, as he had never missed a night on his window sill.

Finally one day, returning home from school, I found him in the hallway. Someone had to have put him there, as the door was closed—but who? I never found out.

It really didn't matter, as I was overjoyed to see him. I took him upstairs and cut up some cold cuts for him. I was surprised when he wouldn't eat—this was not the way he usually behaved when it came to cold cuts. He seemed very lethargic, but I didn't care as I was so glad to see him. However, I became concerned after several hours when he still would not eat. Going to bed that evening, I placed Charley on the windowsill and kept the window open. I also left some cold cuts on the windowsill should he decide to eat.

The next morning I found Charley on the floor. He had died some time during the night.

I was heartbroken at his death as only a young boy can be. I could not comprehend why this had happened. I had never experienced grief before and I didn't know how to deal with it.

I buried Charley in the back yard. I even made a small stone monument for him so that I would have a place to go to remember him. Charley is now only a memory, yet to me he is as alive today as he was back in 1945.

CAMP OCAWASIN

I was living on Fourth Street in Passaic when I first heard a strange word that I could not understand: Ocawasin.

My mother and my uncle Jinx were discussing how to get me into a camp called Ocawasin. My brother, being a year and a half older, made the requirements but I was too young by half a year. Apparently my uncle had some connections and he assured my mother that he would be able to work things out. Several weeks went by before he returned with the news that both my brother and I would be accepted provided that we had a physical exam and that we remained together in the same cabin so he could watch over me.

Shortly after receiving the news that we were accepted we were on our way for a physical from Dr. Weinert, who had an office on the corner of Market Street and Mercer Street in Passaic. After the exam he handed us an envelope to give to the director of the Passaic Boys Club. The envelope was not sealed so we decided to take a peek to see the results of our examinations. We stood in the lobby of the Palace Theater while we did our best to decipher Dr. Weinert's handwriting. We had a very difficult time trying to read what he had written, except that one word stood out: malnutrition. We did not know what the word meant and I waited a week before I asked my mother the meaning, I didn't want to arouse any suspicions about us looking at the contents of the envelope.

"Ma, I heard this word 'malnutrition.' What does it mean?" I asked.

She thought for a moment, but it was very obvious that she was not sure what the meaning was.

"It has something to do with people that have nothing to eat," she replied.

Well, I thought, it has nothing to do with me and my brother. Why, we had all the cabbage soup and bread and butter we wanted.

It was late in June of 1939 when the day finally arrived for us to leave on our two-week vacation to Camp Ocawasin. In preparation for our stay, the Passaic Boys Club gave us a list of things to bring to camp. Several days before we left, my mother went scrambling around to stores and our neighbors trying to get the needed items. She somehow managed to get everything that was needed by borrowing some woolen blankets and finding a store on Market Street that sold large four-inch blanket pins. We were all set to leave, although we had to pack most of our gear in pillowcases as she could only borrow one small suitcase.

We walked from Fourth Street to Third Street carrying all our gear, and when we arrived at the Passaic Boys Club instead of a bus waiting to take us to Camp Ocawasin there was a large old stake-body truck with rows of wooden benches in the back. When all was ready we handed up the containers holding our clothes. There were a few suitcases but most of the kids had canvas bags, cardboard boxes, burlap bags, and of course old pillowcases. The last thing handed up was the assorted collection of rolled-up blankets. Finally, we were told to climb aboard and take a seat on the benches. The old truck with its load of happy kids left the curb and headed for Monroe Street and, hopefully, Camp Ocawasin.

When the truck turned onto Monroe Street benches began falling over. It soon became apparent that the benches were very unstable. After almost every turn the benches would have to be picked up, and by the time we got to Route 46 the benches had been pushed to one side and the kids were sitting on the floor or on top of the piled luggage and blankets.

It wasn't long before a slight drizzle began, and since we had no protection we simply sat there and got wet. The open-bed truck was now moving quite fast down Route 46 and arriving at a circle it turned up Route 23. The air was much cooler here, and blowing over wet kids mostly wearing t-shirts it felt downright cold. The ride took about an hour and we were all very glad when the truck turned off Macopin Road onto a dirt road that had a sign saying Camp Ocawasin. It stopped in a large field very near to the mess hall and we were told to get off the truck.

After we left the truck, all the baggage was taken off and placed in a pile. One of the leaders told us to get our gear and to find a bunk in one of the nine available cabins. The kids who found their stuff quickly went to the cabins closest to the swimming docks, which were cabins 3, 4, and 5. These kids knew the ropes, as the best place to wash yourself was off the docks. There were nine cabins, each holding eight kids. My brother and I ended up in cabin number 9.

The cabin leaders were all in the cabins when we arrived and after helping us get squared away they marched us, by cabin, back to the large field where the Ford truck was still parked.

At the field, we were lined up by cabin. Ken Reynolds, the camp director, informed us that cabins 1 through 5 would be representing the Pioneers and cabins 6 through 9 would be representing the Indians. He next informed us that all cooking of food was done with wood and that we had to bring in a two-week supply of wood—now!

"You will make separate piles," he continued. "One pile will be made by the Pioneers and the other pile will be made by the Indians. Whoever brings in the most wood will get dessert for supper."

The Indians would gather wood north of the field, where the dirt road came down from Macopin Road. The Pioneers would get their wood from the west of the field. The time allotted for bringing in wood was two hours. The cabin leaders had some saws and axes, the kids would be the coolies. There was a great deal of activity as both sides went to work with enthusiasm, and soon the piles began to grow as kids shuttled back and forth lugging their burdens. At a signal, everything stopped and all the kids assembled around the piles to see who had won dessert.

Ken Reynolds came over to examine the piles. Carefully looking them over, he announced that the Indians had won dessert. A great roar arose from the Indians while the Pioneers were very quiet. He then told the leaders to take us back to the cabins and have us get cleaned up for supper. Naturally, we marched back by cabin number.

Back at the cabin the leader told us to get cleaned up, put on clean clothes, and get ready for supper. I went to my pillow case and removed a towel, a toothbrush, and the bar of soap my mother had wrapped in waxed paper. However, I didn't know where to wash so I decided to ask the cabin leader.

"Where are the sinks to wash in?" I asked.

He gave me a funny look as if to say, Welcome to Camp Ocawasin—your new life begins here.

"You'll be using the lake for everything," he informed me. "You'll wash in the lake, brush your teeth in the lake, wash your clothes in the lake and swim in the lake.

"And," he added with a sarcastic smile, "many of the kids when they're swimming even piss in the lake."

I took my cleaning gear and headed for the lake. A few kids were already at the water's edge washing themselves. Cabin 9 had the worst access to the lake for washing, as the shoreline was mostly cattails with a small area of free water. It was very shallow and the water was covered with algae. Finding a place next to the other kids, I ran my washrag through the water, then rubbed some soap into it. My mother, in her haste, instead of giving me a bar of Ivory soap had given me a bar of brown laundry soap. As I was trying to get clean I could see some bluegills circling a few feet away. There was a constant croaking of frogs from the nearby cattails. It was at this time that I began to question the reason I was sent here. I never did anything bad enough to deserve this place. When I finished washing I thought I had done a pretty good job of getting clean, until I used my clean white towel to dry myself off. However, I dismissed the stains as being from the brown soap.

The large bell rang, and it was time to march to the mess hall and take our designated places for dinner. A short prayer was said asking for God's blessings, then one person from each table went to pick up the food while another was assigned to supply the drinks and to keep the water jugs full. At the end of the meal those two were responsible for cleaning up the table.

After the meal was over and the tables cleaned, Mr. Reynolds got up from his separate table and told the Indian side to go pick up their dessert for having won the wood-gathering contest. There was much rejoicing on the Indian side as platters of sliced watermelon were brought to the tables. Then Mr. Reynolds announced that each of the Indian tables had an extra tray of watermelon slices, and that we could eat it or we could share it with the Pioneers, who had no dessert. A loud roar went up to share the watermelon slices with the Pioneers—winners and losers would both have dessert. It was beginning to dawn on us that Camp Ocawasin was no ordinary camp.

That evening our cabin leader explained the regulations and gave us complete instructions on how we were supposed to function at Camp Ocawasin. He began by showing us how to fold our blankets together and secure them with blanket pins so that they formed a sleeping bag. Each cabin had four double bunks which consisted of a piece of canvas suspended between two rails. The cabin leader had a metal cot with springs and a mattress. We were informed that inspection would be held each morning, and that bunks not properly made would result in the blankets being thrown outside regardless of the weather.

Reveille would be the sound of a bugle at 7:00 A.M., he continued. "Get out of your bunk quickly, get dressed, and get down to the lake quickly and wash up. When you're through make your bunk up, sweep the floors, and police the outside of the cabin."

It was now just turning dark and all of the kids climbed into their bunks for a night's rest from the rigors of the first day at Camp Ocawasin. Then, at dark, came one of the most beautiful sounds imaginable, one we had never heard before and one we would never forget: a bugler playing taps, the sound reverberating off the hills surrounding Camp Ocawasin.

The first night was strange, as we listened to all the sounds around us, sounds that we never heard on Fourth Street. The frogs were constantly croaking, but especially loud were the bullfrogs. I must admit to being somewhat frightened, as I could hear noises in the woods outside the cabin.

I had a very difficult time sleeping as I had no pillow and was not used to sleeping without one. Besides that, my blankets kept separating, allowing my feet to get cold.

I was glad when I heard the bugle sound that it was time to get up. It was cold as I began to get dressed. The cabin was in a constant state of activity as kids were quickly getting dressed so as to be the first to go down to the lake to wash. It wasn't long before everyone had washed, made their bunks, and policed the area around the cabin. We heard the bell ring and lined up before the cabin for our march to the field where we would attend the raising of the flag. Arriving at the field we lined up by cabins. The bugler played his song and we all saluted as the American flag was slowly raised.

After the ceremony was over personal inspection was held, and each kid was quickly examined to see if he was clean, the neck and ears getting the most attention. Several cabin leaders did the inspecting and they were referred to as the "goon squad." Several boys were withdrawn from the ranks and made to stand apart from the group, which was very embarrassing as everyone knew why. Since this was the first real day at camp they were given a warning. However, the entire camp was informed that beginning the next day all kids found to be excessively dirty would be marched down to the dock and thrown into the lake.

The next day I found out that this place meant business and the rules were not to be trifled with as three kids were taken away to the dock and pushed into Lake Hird.

THE KNIFE

The summer of 1942 was fast approaching and my brother and I were preparing for our trip to Camp Ocawasin. We both wanted to take knives with us, but neither of us had one. Next to the Palace Theatre on Market Street was a hardware store that displayed all kinds of knives in their window. My brother and I collected what money we could and headed to the store to buy ourselves a couple of knives. After we entered the store, the owner showed us a large display of all kinds of knives that we didn't know existed. My brother, having more money, chose a sheath knife with a six-inch blade, which cost him about a dollar and a half. I would have liked to get something like that but I had only seventy five cents, so I settled on buying a pocket knife.

As soon as we left the store, my brother attached the sheath knife to his belt and proudly wore it home. We were sitting in the kitchen listening to the radio when my mother walked in, having just returned from work. Old Hawkeye instantly saw the large knife hanging from my brother's belt.

"Where the hell did you get that goddam thing from?" she asked. Not even waiting for a reply she continued, "You take that damn thing off and give it to me right now."

As my brother was removing the knife from his belt he tried explaining why he needed a knife. "Ma, we're going to Camp Ocawasin soon and all the kids carry knives that go there."

My mother was adamant. "They feed you there, you don't have to kill what you eat. Now, where did you get this thing from?"

With tears in his eyes my brother handed over his three-hour-old knife. "I got it at the hardware store next to the Palace," he told her. He knew full well he would never see his sheath knife again.

My mother then turned to me. "You got a knife like this?" she asked.

"No, Ma, I don't have anything that looks like that," I replied, and I was being quite truthful, for you can't compare a sheath knife to a pocket knife.

"Both of you wait here until I get back, you hear me?"

My mother then left to begin the trek from Park Row to Market Street and the hardware store. While she was gone I congratulated myself on my wisdom in buying a pocket knife which couldn't be seen, completely forgetting that the pocket knife had been selected only for a lack of funds.

Well over an hour later my mother returned carrying a bag, not a sheath knife. Opening the bag in front of my bother and me, she removed a large coil of clothesline rope. She informed my brother that she had traded in his knife for the rope.

The matter was ended. Not only did he lose his sheath knife, but he lost his dollar and fifty cents. When he began to protest the loss of his money, my mother cut him short. "Your clothes also hang on the line."

Lining up for a hike at Camp Ocawasin, 1943

LIFE AT CAMP OCAWASIN

Programs

At Camp Ocawasin, most programs began at 9 A.M. They were usually divided in such a way as to take advantage of the fact that the camp was split into two sides, Pioneers and Indians. For example, when the Pioneers swam in the morning the Indians would swim in the afternoon. If nature classes were held in the morning for the Indians they would be held in the afternoon for the Pioneers. Most of the programs and some of the facilities simply could not handle the entire camp at one time.

Some of the programs had to be broken up into smaller groups. Nature walks would often be in smaller groups. One group might be studying along Hird Lake, another would be collecting leaves, while the third would be preparing for Explorer or Trailblazer badges.

Some programs dominated every camper's day and it was required that you become reasonably proficient in that program. First and foremost was swimming. Every kid had to learn how to swim. There was a time to play but you were always being checked on your progress in becoming a better swimmer. Going along with swimming was boating. There were three or four wooden rowboats and two canvas canoes. These were mainly used for instruction, but were also used by good swimmers for other purposes such a fishing or just paddling around the lake.

The nature programs, although not occurring every day, were major activities at Camp Ocawasin. "Pop" Mills was one of the mainstays of the nature program when I was there. I believe he was a forester who donated his time during the summers to help the camp out. There were several years when his two sons attended Camp Ocawasin. Pop Mills would take us on nature walks and explain all kinds of things to us. On one such walk we came upon an area with many dead trees, and he explained that they were chestnut trees that had been killed by a disease and that very few were left.

A small log building across from the mess hall was always referred to as the nature cabin. It held many exhibits and things that any kid might collect, such as birds' nests, snake skins, and animal skulls, as well as cages for a few animals that had been caught. One such cage had a large black snake, another held several bats, and there was also a glass aquarium that held newts and frogs. Outside the cabin was an area enclosed by heavy wire, which was reserved for turtles.

One of the turtles was a snapper and his shell was the size of a bushel basket. I remember when he was caught in Hird Lake. One of the cabin leaders had seen him hanging around the boat dock where kids used to fish for bluegills. Because the kids would throw the fish back into the lake, many of the fish in that area were injured, which would explain why this large snapper was hanging around. That day, the cabin leader baited a large treble hook with a dead frog and, using a gallon jug as a float, placed it near the boat dock. Several hours later, his jug could be seen bobbing under water and moving around the area.

He and another cabin leader went out in a rowboat to retrieve their catch. They could not get the turtle into the rowboat and considering its size they didn't try too hard. They returned to shore to get help and extra equipment. By this time everyone in camp was watching along the shoreline to see how they would get this monster turtle on shore.

The leaders returned with a volleyball net and, taking a rowboat, went back after the turtle—which was easy to find, as the jug was still bouncing on the surface. They finally got the turtle tangled in the volleyball net and began rowing back towards shore, towing the turtle. Arriving at the shore they pulled the turtle onto land. The powerful turtle, now on land, began to shred the net with his claws. The leaders continued to wrap him in the net, and when he was good and tangled dragged him off to the fenced-in pen at the nature cabin.

He was a big attraction, as the kids would poke sticks into the cage to watch him bite them in half. Then one day he was gone, having ripped through the rusted wire fence and, I presume, made his way back to Hird Lake. After this, many kids had no desire to swim in the lake, and even when washing and brushing their teeth in the morning would keep a sharp eye on the water for that gigantic snapping turtle.

Fishing, although not a program, was a favorite pastime of many kids. You could really only fish between activities, which allowed a kid several hours a day to pursue other interests, although it was mandatory that every day after lunch you take a nap from one to two o'clock. A fishing trophy was given during each two-week camp session for the largest fish caught. I wanted the trophy badly and one year I was in the lead, having caught a fifteen-inch bass. Then Tom Pirog, a friend of mine from Wallington who was in cabin 9, came up with a twenty-two inch bass. However, he was disqualified from getting the trophy as he had caught the fish by stunning it with an oar from the rowboat while it was spawning. On top of that, he had snuck out during the one-hour rest period—a major offense at Camp Ocawasin.

Whenever a large bass was caught it would be given to the camp cook, Mr. Robinson. He would prepare the fish, and at supper that evening you would get a part of your catch and Mr. Robinson would get the rest. He loved baked bass. Mr. Robinson, a black man, was always there to do the cooking. For all the years that I attended Camp Ocawasin (1939-1946), he was more than just a cook—he was an inspiration to all the kids who knew him. When Mr. Robinson was not cooking he could always be found playing his favorite game, horseshoes.

Another program that kids were required to attend was riflery. The rifle range was located in the woods behind cabin 1. We were instructed in the safe handling of firearms and taught the fundamentals of shooting. The guns used were .22 caliber single-shot Springfields. The final test was to get three out of five shots into the bull's-eye from a prone position. You would continue to practice until you could get it. Camp Ocawasin was not a half-way camp.

Archery was another popular sport, but it was not mandatory. There were times when you were given the option to choose what you would like to do. You could elect to have a volleyball game or practice archery. Another option was the horseshoe pits. There were very few baseball games, and I never saw a football or basketball game at Camp Ocawasin. There were times when you could spend two weeks there and never see a ball.

Competition was the essence of Camp Ocawasin. There were always contests of some sort going on. Foot races, the fifty yard dash, the standing broad jump, the running long jump, Indian hand wrestling and foot wrestling, and the most popular of all, boxing matches. The competition even extended onto Hird Lake. There were swimming contests and boat races and even jousting with boxing gloves at the end of poles. You had to knock the other kid out of the canoe.

When it rained at Camp Ocawasin and outdoor activities had to be cancelled, everything would move into the mess hall. Tables would be moved to accommodate the competition, which centered around individuals pitted against other individuals, boxing being the most popular form of entertainment. The cabin leaders were usually very innovative in putting on short plays or in storytelling, the theme usually something scary.

Another major program was hiking. Sometimes these would be day hikes as long as five miles, at other times they would be overnight camping trips with a walk of ten miles each way. Camp Ocawasin at this time had a horse and wagon which would accompany us and carry all our equipment for cooking and sleeping, enough stuff for seventy-two kids and ten adults. Where we camped was a steep hill that had to be climbed and the horse could not pull the wagon up the hill, so the kids now helped the horse by pulling the wagon. We camped in a beautiful area that had a large unused log cabin (in what is now the Norvin Green State Forest). We found out that the land and cabin were once owned by a German organization, and it was referred to as the German Bund Camp. It was closed with the outbreak of World War II.

Council fire

Anyone who has ever been to Camp Ocawasin will never forget evenings at the council fire. This was held outside every evening except when it rained, when we would meet in the mess hall. However, the basic format would be the same.

The council fire was held in a heavily wooded area about fifty yards from cabin 1. There was a small building that had a stage and adjoining storage area and a dressing room. Logs about twelve feet long and ten inches high, but flattened on both sides, were the seats. They were arranged in a semicircle, each cabin having its own place to sit.

At 7:00 P.M., upon hearing a bell, each cabin would line up for the march to the council fire area. You would enter the area in sequence, cabin 9 being first, followed by cabin 8, etc., until all were seated, always in the same place. The council fire would then be lit. Sometimes we would get a lecture on camp conditions but more often on behavior problems. This would usually be followed by games of competition such as Indian hand wrestling or foot wrestling—boxing matches were never held here. Very often the cabin leaders would put on skits or short plays to entertain us. Then there would be the singing of songs, some of which I remember:

> *It's gonna be a long winter*
> *And what will de boidies do den, de poor tings?*
> *Dey fly to the south with woims in dere mouth*
> *And tuck dere heads under dere wings, de poor tings.*

Dere was a little chicken couldn't lay an egg
Rubbed hot water up and down his leg
De little chicken cried, de little chicken begged
De little chicken laid a hard-boiled egg
Boom boom, ain't it great to be crazy
Boom boom, ain't it great to be crazy

Horse and a flea and three blind mice
Sitting on the curb, shooting dice
Horse slipped, fell on the flea
The flea said, "Whoops! There's a horse on me."
Boom boom, ain't it great to be crazy
Kiddy and foolish all day long
Boom boom ain't it great to be crazy

Old hambone and sweet, sweet bacon am good,
possum meat is very, very fine
But give me, please give me, I really wish you would,
That watermelon that hangs on the vine.
When I went to get that watermelon 'twas on a rainy night
And the stars had just begun to shine
The white folks they saw me and shot me through the fence
But I didn't leave that watermelon behind

Some time around 9:00 or 9:30 P.M. the council fire was allowed to die down, after which we were to return to our cabins and prepare for bed. Taps would then be played and each cabin leader was responsible for seeing that all of the kids in his cabin were in their bunks.

Quite often this would be the time that cabin leaders would leave the cabin to try and scare kids in other cabins. The stage would first be set at the council fire with the telling of a story. One story in particular was about a madman that lived in the woods near the camp.

This madman hated kids and would foam at the mouth when near them. After all the kids were sleeping, a cabin leader would quietly sneak up next to a nearby cabin. The sides of the cabins were half wood and half screen. The double bunks were next to the wall, so the kid in the lower bunk would face a wooden wall; however, the kid in the upper bunk would have a screen alongside his sleeping position. This made him most vulnerable. In preparation for scaring the kid, the cabin leader would cover his mouth with shaving cream to mimic the madman. He would hold a lighted flashlight below his chin, and scratch on the screen next to the kid's head to wake him up. A kid waking up this way would usually turn towards the sound, and seeing this face lit up by the flashlight and covered with foam would scream and bail out of his bunk in terror. Quickly, the leader would put the light out and disappear into the woods. The other kids would then try to convince the terrified camper that he had had a bad dream.

One of the cabin leaders tried this scary trick with unexpected results. One kid in my cabin was so afraid from hearing all the stories about madmen that he slept with his six-inch hunting knife next to him. One night the foam-covered ghost appeared next to his upper bunk. When he heard the scratching on the screen he took his hunting knife and plunged it right through the screen, very narrowly missing doing serious damage to the cabin leader playing madman. Now it was the madman's turn to be frightened, and he took off running. Cabin 1 was never bothered again after this incident.

Almost every kid at Camp Ocawasin had a knife. Some carried pocket knives but most carried sheath knives. There were no restrictions on knife carrying. It was not uncommon, when the leader of a cabin was not present, for the kids in the cabin to use the door for knife-throwing practice. A target would be placed on the door and knives would be thrown at the target. Only those that stuck in the door would be counted as a hit. Many thrown knives did not stick into the door but bounced off, making a lot of noise. One day Ken Reynolds, the camp director, heard the banging against the door and decided to investigate. He climbed the three steps to the door of cabin 1 and opened the door. At the instant the door was opened a thrown knife went sailing past Mr. Reynolds' head. He closed the door and left. Nothing was said, but later we were all informed by the cabin leaders that knife throwing in cabins was forbidden.

Punishments

Yes, kids at Camp Ocawasin were punished for bad behavior, uncleanliness, and breaking rules. Punishments were almost always administered by a cabin leader to kids in his own cabin. I remember only two real forms of punishments, although these had variations.

The first was known as walking the field. This punishment consisted of carrying a knapsack full of rocks around a field located across from the mess hall. Depending upon the severity of the infraction it could be from one to three hours. If it were for something really bad, such as stealing, you could be doing this at night. That was usually quite frightening, as most of us kids were thoroughly afraid of the dark because of the constant diet of scary stories we were always being told. A variation of this was having kids run around the field at night until they were exhausted. One year the kids in my friend Stanley Posluszny's cabin were made to run around the field at night until they couldn't run anymore. Stanley kept running and running long after all the other kids had dropped out. He was still running after three hours, and the other kids were sleeping in the grassy field waiting for him to quit. Finally the cabin leader gave up and ordered them back to the cabin. Never again did he impose this punishment on his cabin. Oh, and Stanley ran back to the cabin!

The second form of punishment was the canoe paddle. This punishment was usually directed against kids who wised off to cabin leaders and for those kids who were bullies and picked fights or perhaps beat up a smaller kid. (In addition, bullies of this sort were very often chosen to box with other kids who were excellent boxers.) A kid receiving the canoe paddle punishment was usually required to put on a bathing suit and then to enter the lake to get it wet. Next, he was required to bend over and touch his toes. Anywhere from one to five whacks would be administered across his buttocks, but usually by the second one most kids were in tears and the paddling would be stopped. This form of punishment provided what could best be called an electric shock to your bottom—believe me, I know.

Pets at Camp Ocawasin

Kids at camp were always looking for some kind of personal pet to own. Some kids collected small animals just to use for practical jokes to be played on other kids. The favorite animal, and the easiest to obtain, was the newt. Kids could always be seen looking for them, turning over rocks and logs, carrying a tin can to put them in. There were two different kinds of newts; one was all green and the other was spotted. The spotted ones were more in demand but they were far less prevalent.

Frogs were also very popular but they were very difficult for most kids to catch, as they could be found only along the shoreline of the lake and in the weeds. They weren't used as pets so much, but were mostly put into other kids' shoes or in their blankets. Many of the kids could not tell the difference between a frog and a toad. If you had a toad, the other kids would quickly begin to tease you. The most common tease was that if a toad pisses on your hands you're going to get warts all over.

Small snakes were also collected for practical jokes, and these could also be placed in boots and bedding but were most often placed in pants pockets. Most of these practical jokes would be discovered in the morning when kids were getting dressed. A loud scream or cursing would indicate that someone was a victim of a joke.

One year, several kids in their hunt for small snakes found exactly what they were after near the dam on Hird Lake. It was a nest of very small copperheads. Not knowing what kind of snakes they were, the kids brought them back to their cabin. The kids had them on the cabin floor when the leader walked in. Instantly recognizing what they were, he got a broom and swept them outside the cabin, after which they were killed. None of the kids were bitten. The cabin leader attributed this to the very cool morning, which had made the little copperheads very lethargic.

Charley at Camp Ocawasin

In the summer of 1945 I brought my pet crow Charley to Camp Ocawasin. Charley was very popular with everyone, but he took an exceptional liking to Mr. Robinson. It didn't take Charley very long to figure out that Mr. Robinson was the cook and that being friendly with him would guarantee him his favorite food—cold cuts.

At this time I was in cabin 1 and all of the kids tried feeding Charley so as to make friends with him. They would bring him small frogs, lizards, newts, and even locusts; however, Charley disdained this diet, as Mr. Robinson always provided him with his much-loved cold cuts.

Troubles developed for Charley when he discovered that there were other crows in the vicinity of Camp Ocawasin. One morning there was a great deal of commotion from a gang of crows that were hanging out in the woods near cabin 9, on the other side of Hird Lake from where Charley lived with me. Charley, hearing his relatives for the first time, flew across the lake to where the other crows had gathered, hoping to have a joyous reunion with his extended family. I was worried that when he met other crows he would never return, preferring a life with his own species. However, several crows immediately pounced on Charley and began pecking away at him and treating him as an intruder. He quickly flew back across the lake with three hostile crows in pursuit. Seeing me, he headed directly for my outstretched arm and the security it would provide. Charley never tried to associate with crows again; from here on his only companions would be people.

But strange things were beginning to happen around cabin 1, and even to a smaller extent around other cabins. There was a thief amongst the campers and despite being very watchful the leaders could not find out who it was. Almost nothing was safe, but apparently the crook preferred small shiny objects such as coins, crucifixes, marbles, small pocket knives, blanket pins, or any knives and forks that were left lying around. Since most of the material stolen was from cabin 1 it was assumed that the thief came from that cabin. But despite watching all the kids in the cabin and searching their luggage, no one had a clue as to who the thief was.

One day I was hanging my clothes out to dry behind cabin 1 when I noticed Charley go under the cabin. Despite my repeated calls to him he would not come out, which was very unusual, as he always responded to my first call. After hanging all my clothes on the line I went over to the crawl space beneath the cabin to see why Charley wouldn't come out. I could see him next to a mound of some material that I couldn't make out. I called him again but he refused to leave the mound. Crawling further under the cabin, I finally saw why he wouldn't come out. He was guarding his pile of stolen stuff—Charley was the thief.

Pioneer/Indian Wars

Anyone who went to Camp Ocawasin during the 1930s and 1940s will always remember the Pioneer and Indian Wars. The basic format for this contest went something like this: the Pioneer side of the lake (cabins 1-5) would wear blue armbands. The Indian side (cabins 6-9) would wear red armbands. These armbands could be tied on your arm with only one knot. Then either the Indians or the Pioneers would be led by their cabin leaders somewhere into the woods to hide and try to ambush the other side, which would be sent out to find them. When the two groups finally met, a gigantic wrestling match would begin.

This would involve a total of seventy-two kids. The object was to select an opponent and wrestle him to the ground and forcefully remove his armband. Nearby leaders would collect the armbands representing their side. After finishing off your opponent you would continue to look for another; however, as numbers dwindled two or three kids often ganged up on one. This would continue until all of the armbands on one side were captured. There was only one main rule that had to be followed: wrestling only, no punching. The reward for winning was dessert for supper, usually watermelon.

Yes, there were many bruised bodies as kids fell on rocks, stumps, and logs. Some kids might sprain an ankle or arm. There were cuts, bloody noses from the violent contact, and an endless array of torn shirts and pants. And no, there were no lawsuits.

The Trailblazer

The most coveted award at Camp Ocawasin was the badge of a Trailblazer. This badge would be sewn onto a shirt or jacket and was always worn with pride.

Before preparing to become a Trailblazer you had to pass a series of tests and first become an Explorer. There was one final test that had to be passed before receiving your coveted Trailblazer badge. Preparation for this event included a knowledge of map reading and the use of a compass, and the ability to find your way in the woods using both. You had to be proficient in the use of tools, mainly the axe, knife, and saw. There were tests in wood lore such as tree identification and the construction of shelters. It was also necessary to show the ability to make snares to capture small game.

The final test was a ten-mile overnight hike to the area now called the Norvin Green State Forest. This final test was done in pairs. You left early in the morning with all your gear and a map of where you were supposed to camp that night. In the evening someone would check on you to make sure you were in the right place, and he would also inspect the shelter that you constructed. You had no matches on this trip—you started your fire with flint and steel. You walked the ten miles back the next evening and if the leaders who were responsible for you agreed on your ability to take care of yourself in the woods, you were made a Trailblazer at a special ceremony.

Sometime around 1943 or perhaps 1944, two kids went on their ten-mile Trailblazer hike, but somewhere along the route they made a wrong turn and entered a restricted area of the Wanaque Reservoir.

This was World War II and the reservoir was heavily patrolled. The cabin leader sent out to check on them couldn't find them and reported them missing back at camp. A truck was sent out with more leaders joining the search, but they still could not locate them. However, early the next day the missing campers were brought to Camp Ocawasin by the guards that patrolled the Wanaque Reservoir. A patrol dog and guard had found them both up in a tree, where they had spent the night. It seems they knew they were lost, and being afraid of bears and wild dogs (many of the scary stories told at Camp Ocawasin involved wild dogs) had decided to spend the night in the tree. They did not make Trailblazer.

The Snake

Attendance at Camp Ocawasin was for a period of two weeks, although you could sign up for a longer period. One Sunday was set aside every two weeks for visits from parents and relatives.

It was a beautiful Sunday afternoon and many guests were walking along the lake shore. One of them spotted a large black snake in the cattails near cabin 1. I was bass fishing nearby when I saw the commotion, as the man began pointing the snake out to other guests. Going over to check things out, I saw a large black snake wrapped around some of the cattails. The snake was only partially visible but he was a big one; we were all familiar with such snakes, as they were common throughout the area. I informed one of the cabin leaders, and he and another leader decided to capture the snake. They planned to capture him from the lake rather than from the shore, and I followed them to where the rowboats were kept and asked if I could go along. One of them got in the front of the rowboat while the other sat in the middle and rowed. I had the seat at the back of the boat.

They had to row the boat far out into the lake to get around the floating dock and the roped-off swimming area. Slowly approaching the weeds so as not to frighten the snake, they eased the front of the rowboat very near to him. The twenty or thirty people on shore who were watching were perfectly quiet, mesmerized by the events taking place. Very slowly the leader reached down, and grasping the snake by the tail pulled him off the cattails. The size of the snake was now revealed: he was a good six-footer. A gasp went up from the people on shore. The leader had brought along a large forked stick, which he now used to hold the head of the snake against the outside of the rowboat.

The rower, anxious to get back, was putting a great deal of effort into the oars. We had just rounded the floating dock when somehow the black snake managed to free himself from the stick holding him against the boat. The leader who was hanging onto the tail, seeing the other end of the snake crawl over the side of the boat, jumped into the lake. The snake, now in the rowboat, headed in the direction of the rower in the center. Looking over his shoulder and seeing the snake coming towards him he panicked and also jumped into the lake.

There I was, sitting barefooted in the back of the rowboat, watching a six-foot snake making his way over the center seat towards me. I knew I didn't swim well enough to jump into the lake, so my instincts took over. I raised my feet off of the deck, and when the snake was just beneath me I smashed the heel of my right foot against his head, pinioning it against the floor of the rowboat. I was afraid to raise my foot even though I felt some of his teeth puncture my heel. Slowly the snake began to wrap himself around my leg, reaching up almost to my knee. Reaching over, I took one of the oars from the oar lock and—not taking my foot off the snake's head—began to paddle the rowboat towards shore. It was a painfully slow process and a large group of people were observing me from the shore; however, the sides of the rowboat kept them from seeing the snake wrapped around my leg. As soon as the rowboat scraped bottom I jumped out and started running towards my cabin, thinking the snake was still in the boat. Stopping to rest, I was shocked to find the snake still wrapped around my leg. In a state of absolute panic I began swinging my foot sideways, banging the snake against a tree until he finally came off. I was only mildly pleased to see the badly injured snake crawl away.

The next day I received a sharp reprimand from the camp director for the way that I handled the snake episode in front of all the parents and visitors. When I asked him what I was supposed to do with a six foot snake wrapped around my leg, he calmly replied, "You should have caught him and brought him to the museum."

I walked away thinking to myself, Museum, my ass. There's no way I'm picking up a six-foot snake for a museum.

A Ghost Story

Everything began normally. The bell rang, telling us it was time for all the cabins to begin heading towards the council fire area where we assembled every night.

This evening when we walked in, something was different. Between the stage and the logs where we sat, a fire would usually be burning. But tonight, instead of a fire, a large wooden coffin lay in the open area. Sitting behind the coffin was a hooded person covered with a long white robe (actually a bed sheet). The hood obscured his face and made him look very sinister. On top of the coffin were seven lighted candles. We all quietly took our seats and waited. The hooded figure remained silent, the flickering candles occasionally revealing a face that was completely white. The silence was almost unbearable; only the sounds of the frogs were familiar, but even these seemed out of place as we gazed at the coffin with the burning candles.

Suddenly, the hooded man began to speak. You could hear a pin drop; even the frogs seemed to go quiet. He began telling a short, frightening story. When he finished, he blew out one of the candles. He then began another ghost story which also was very short. This was also followed by the blowing out of a candle. He continued this process until he got to candle number six. He then began a story about a man who was buried alive in a coffin and to save his life had made a pact with the devil. Every year he had to deliver to the devil a young boy to take his place if he wished to remain alive. This would be his payment. When story number six was finished and before the candle was blown out, the lid of the coffin slowly began to rise. Fingers began to show themselves through the partially opened coffin. The hooded figure then blew out the candle.

There was one more candle left, but the kids watching were in a state of near panic. They couldn't take another story, especially now that they knew something was in the coffin. They were ready to bolt, but they couldn't, as they responded only to orders from the leaders. They had to endure, but psychologically they could endure no more. Just then the coffin lid flew open and out jumped a hideous figure wearing only briefs, his naked body covered with white powder. Screaming "I want a little boy!" he charged into the petrified group of campers.

Seventy-two terrified kids took off running in all directions. Some ran screaming towards their cabins, other simply ran into the dark woods. A half dozen jumped into a few canoes nearby and frantically began paddling across the lake in the near dark.

There was absolute pandemonium, and even though the leaders tried to persuade the kids it was only a joke it was much too late for that. There was no marching back to the cabins that night. Cabin leaders went to their respective cabins to take a head count—many kids were still missing and presumed to be somewhere in the woods. Cabin leaders with flashlights began combing the woods looking for the missing kids, who would not respond to the leaders' calls. They were too afraid that it might be the guy in the story trying to bait them. Eventually, they began to recognize the voices of the leaders pleading with them to come in, and in ones and twos were finally all accounted for. The time was then somewhere around 11 o'clock. Very few campers got a good night's sleep that night.

In all my years at Camp Ocawasin, this was the only evening in memory that I didn't hear taps played.

Church at Camp Ocawasin

Every Sunday just after breakfast the camp director, Ken Reynolds, would take a head count to see who was going to church that morning. Going to church was not mandatory and many kids chose not to go, as this gave them free time to pursue other interests. Those wishing to attend the Catholic Church, which was several miles away, would be loaded into the old Ford stake-body truck for the trip. Wooden benches were provided.

I'm not aware of any arrangements that were made to get Protestants to their various churches, although there could have been.

Mr. Reynolds held a special service for those who did not wish to attend church. I was one of these non-conformists. Led by Mr. Reynolds, a group of us, usually about twenty kids, would walk away from camp to a secluded glen where there was a nice grassy area near a stream. He would then read us stories from his bible. Being a Catholic boy, I had had some instruction by nuns and brothers about Jesus, but I was quite impressed with these stories, which I had never heard before. My mother did not have a bible and we didn't use one in Sunday school when we received instructions. All of the years that I attended Camp Ocawasin I always chose to sit in the woods listening to these incredible stories that Mr. Reynolds read to us.

When I got home from Camp Ocawasin one year, I broached the subject of bibles with my mother, who was a very devout Catholic.

"Ma, how come we don't have a bible with all those interesting stories?" I asked.

"You don't need a bible," she replied. "You just go to church, put your nickel in the basket, and you'll be taken care of."

Cabin 9, last of the original cabins, is still standing

WELCOME HOME, BILL

Bill Schibner was my godfather. He had been my father's best friend and for many years would be a father figure to me and my brother after my father apparently came across those famous words by Horace Greeley and went west, leaving his family behind and never returning.

Bill Schibner and his attractive wife Helen would visit our family often over the years and my brother and I always looked forward to their company. To us they appeared to be the happiest people in the world. They were both mild-mannered, very polite, and not prone to be argumentative. They always lavished their attentions on my brother and me, which was rather rare in those days as children were supposed to have their place and remain there.

In 1942, Bill and Helen had been married for perhaps twelve years and the union did not produce any children. They both loved dogs, especially Scotties, and whenever they visited us they always brought their two black Scotties with them. My mother was not very keen on dogs but when they visited she always had a snack for them, a piece of liverwurst.

Bill always brought my brother and me a small present, usually two small magnetic Scotties, one black and one white. I found out from my uncle Jinx that when you purchased a special Scotch whiskey you would get these little magnetized Scotties. My brother and I would play with them for hours, as the magnets would attract and repel each other and the dogs could be made to move around.

Bill was thirty-nine years old in the latter part of 1942 or early 1943 when he was drafted into the army. I had heard the grownups talking about his rotten luck, as the age of thirty-nine was the last year that you could be drafted. Bill missed not being drafted into the army by four months.

I believe that he did his boot camp training at Fort Dix in the Pine Barrens of New Jersey. When boot camp was completed (in six to eight weeks) he had a few days leave before being shipped to another army camp, after which he would be shipped overseas. While on leave he visited us on Park Row with his wife and their two black Scotties. He looked every bit the soldier in his army uniform and his now fit physical condition. It was evident that his wife Helen felt very proud of him. There was a good deal of small talk as we had other company besides them, and since there was no room at the table my brother and I just sat nearby and listened.

The talk seemed to center around a central question: How long would the war last? For some reason, most seemed to think that it would be over in a year, as Germany was now beginning to lose badly in Eastern Russia (the Battle of Stalingrad).

For the next two-and-a-half years Bill Schibner would serve overseas, eventually ending up in North Africa and participating in the Italian campaign. Our contact with his wife was minimal. Perhaps we saw her twice during this period of his overseas duty.

It was a very cold day in December of 1945 or perhaps it was January of 1946, one of those bitter days when the windows have frost on the insides. The small coal stove in the kitchen could not provide sufficient heat to warm the apartment. There was a knock on the door around 2 P.M. My mother answered and, as was our habit, my brother and I went into the kitchen to see who it was.

We were both surprised and overjoyed to see Bill Schibner enter the kitchen, fully dressed in his army uniform. Even though my brother and I ran over to greet him he paid no attention to us but talked directly to my mother, who was also very glad to see him.

Things changed very rapidly as the following discussion took place:

"Mary, have you seen my wife?"

"Bill, I haven't seen Helen in almost a year. Why do you ask?"

"I just got discharged and I didn't write to her so as to surprise her, but when I went to our apartment someone else was living there. I came over hoping you might know something."

"Bill, I don't know anything. Did you check with the landlord?"

"Yes, he told me she moved out six months ago and left no forwarding address."

Apparently at this point reality began to set in for both of them. My mother began to cry and tears were in Bill's eyes as the magnitude of the situation became clear.

"Mary, I have nothing. My wife is gone, the furniture is gone, the car is gone, and all of our savings are gone." He shook his head. "Mary, I have nothing."

It was a sad scene for two young boys to observe. An old soldier returning home from the war, standing there with tears in his eyes, trying desperately to grasp and possibly save some aspect of his previous life, yet slowly and painfully yielding to the inevitable conclusion: his great love had betrayed him. Without another word, Bill turned and left.

My brother and I had just witnessed a new dimension of war. Not a world of broken bodies and machines but a far more fragile world— a world of broken dreams. Now being aware of the fickle nature of human love and commitment, it became apparent to us that this was not an isolated incident, as more and more of these stories surfaced around the neighborhood.

The ugly face of war would continue for many years after the war itself was over. The Gold Star mothers, the Bill Schibners—for them World War II would never come to an end. Welcome home, Bill.

Bill Schibner (r.) and Jinx

WORLD WAR II SURPLUS

When World War II finally came to an end in the middle of 1945, a whole way of living that we had become accustomed to also came to an end.

Many veterans returned home to Wallington, but with the end of war production, few jobs were available in Passaic's many factories. I heard a few veterans talking one time while sitting on the wooden bleachers behind Washington School. They would often go there to watch baseball games or just to sit and talk to other unemployed veterans. I was sitting near them, carving my initials into the wooden bleachers, when I heard them discussing a club that I had never heard of, called the 52/20 club. Even as a fourteen-year-old I could see that they were pretty upset with conditions after arriving home from the war. When I asked one of my neighbors, a veteran who was also recently discharged, about this club he informed me that servicemen who could not find work after being discharged would receive twenty dollars a week for fifty-two weeks. That sure sounded pretty good to me.

After talking to me for a while, my neighbor told me he had something for me and said he would be right back. Returning from the apartment where he lived with his parents on Park Row, he handed me his Eisenhower jacket.

"You'll grow into it," he said with a smile. On my walk home I thought to myself, Hell, I'm not gonna wait until I grow into it. I put the jacket on, even though it was somewhat warm to be wearing a jacket and the jacket was way too big. Proudly I wore my new jacket as I returned home and went upstairs to our apartment. When I walked in, my mother looked me over with suspicion.

"Where did you get that damn thing from?" she asked. Then she added, "Couldn't you find something that fits?"

Of all the items that eventually became available to the public, the most popular for kids was the waist-length Eisenhower jacket. Years after the war was over, when most of the war surplus material was gone, you could always see someone wearing an Eisenhower jacket—badges and all.

My uncle Paul Wall, better known by the nickname Jinx, returned from his three-year stint in the army loaded with not only his own personal gear but all kinds of sports equipment, the kind we had always dreamed about but never got for Christmas. He was stationed in Louisiana during the entire war as an ambulance driver. The base he was on must have been a recuperation center, which would explain how he was able to get so much sporting equipment.

We were living on Park Row in Kobscenski's house when my uncle arrived after his discharge. He was still in uniform when he began carrying what he called the "government surplus" upstairs to our apartment. There had to be at least eight baseball gloves, plus baseballs and bats. Looking at the bats—no broken bat held together with electrical tape—my brother and I were both overjoyed to see that they were Louisville Sluggers.

We both went downstairs to help him with the next load and he gave each of us a large leather ball to bring upstairs. This ball would have trouble fitting into a bushel basket. We had no idea what it was for or how it could possibly be used in a ballgame. The two balls sat in the attic, where we slept, for years and we only fooled around with them occasionally, as we couldn't figure out how to use them. (Much later we would find out they were called medicine balls.)

The last item that he brought upstairs was a six-foot wooden airplane propeller, saying to my mother, "This is for you, Mary. Where do you want me to put it?"

My mother, who was a very practical woman but often got flustered, replied "What the hell am I supposed to do with that damn thing?"

"You hang it on the wall," replied my uncle. It never did make the wall, and my uncle joined it in the attic, as he needed a place to stay and the only place available was sharing the small attic bedroom with my brother and me. I'm sure his army home had been better than that.

My uncle brought home large quantities of packets containing sulfa drugs. Apparently the sulfa drugs were used on wounds to prevent infection and all soldiers carried the packets when in battle. It wasn't long before all the kids would be carrying these packets and would put the medicine on the slightest scratch or cut.

Shortly after the war was over, Army/Navy stores began springing up like mushrooms. They became a major attraction in our lives and we would visit them just to look at all the marvelous things they were selling.

The quality of the military clothing and boots was apparent even to us kids, and most of us set our sights on getting this stuff. Over a period of time our poorly made sneakers were replaced by combat boots, and those white cotton socks that were always dirty would be replaced by woolen army socks.

Winters were always difficult times for kids wishing to be outside, as our clothing was totally inadequate to cope with the cold and wet conditions of winter. With all of this high quality government surplus, things began to change. We now had combat boots and wool socks instead of those despised galoshes with their long row of metal buckles that always iced up. The galoshes usually covered a pair of low-cut shoes and walking any distance in them was enough to discourage you from continuing. A message that made you cringe was the sound of your mother saying, "Put on your galoshes before you go outside."

Some kids would even wear military leggings in the snow, although they were a pain to lace up and difficult to remove when the metal grommets and lacing became covered with ice. The woolen army gloves were far superior to any gloves you could buy and they even kept your hands warm when making snowballs. If they got wet a quick wringing out would make them usable, and they would even hold their shape.

Military jackets were hot items for kids and many adults to wear. Kids preferred the army field jackets because of the number of pockets and also because they were far tougher than anything available in ordinary clothing stores. Air force flight jackets with their sheepskin lining were quickly picked up by adults, as they had the money to afford them. Another jacket which was fairly common in surplus stores and worn by both adults and kids was the navy foul weather jacket.

Among the most sought after items for kids were the insulated rubber-bottom, leather-topped foul weather shoes called "paks." These paks were used in extreme cold weather by our mountain troops and even had a setup to hold snow shoes. Since we were quite small at the time, it was next to impossible to find a size that would fit you. But it didn't matter that you took a size 7 or 8 and all you could find were size 9 or 10. You bought them anyway and wore a lot of heavy socks or stuffed them with newspapers.

Another common sight was the Alaskan parka with its fur-lined hood. Every Army/Navy store also had its collection of skis and snowshoes, and for those who could afford them army mummy-type feather/down sleeping bags.

Popular items that practically every kid owned were an army canteen and mess kit. Now on every trip to Krug's woods we would bring our own water from home in a canteen. Gone were the days of hiking to the spring to refresh ourselves every time we got thirsty. No longer when camping overnight would we sleep on the ground and look up at the stars—now we had pup tents and ponchos. The baked potato and the hot dog on a stick were obsolete—army C-rations were in vogue.

All this new equipment was changing our world. We were getting spoiled, some ways for the better, some ways for the worse.

THE ROBIN HOOD GANG

The summer of 1944 was fast approaching. Having just finished reading a book about Robin Hood, and being very much impressed, it occurred to me to form our own gang and to use Krug's woods as our Sherwood Forest.

Krug's woods was an ideal location, as it was on the hill and in the hot sticky summers was much cooler. It was also isolated from the rest of the town and adults were rarely ever seen there. Nearby were the sandpits and if we wished to cool off we could easily walk to the Pump House to go swimming. Also, watermelons were always available from the boxcars parked on the railroad tracks just below the hill.

This was the world where we would spend the summer of 1944, just being kids. From morning to evening we would have no contact with adults, except when we returned home to do some special chores or to have supper with our parents. Most of our parents worked and were never home during the week. When we did have contact with them they always seemed to ask the same question: "What did you do today?" The answer was always the same: "We were playing in Krug's woods." This seemed to satisfy them, even though they knew nothing about the woods or what we did there.

Most of the kids made their own bows and arrows. We spent a great deal of time hunting, though a better description might be "shooting arrows at anything that moved." When we were really bored we engaged in a game called "chicken." Each person in the game would wait for his turn to demonstrate that he was not a chicken. The first person would shoot an arrow into the air as high as possible. Then, watching the arrow return to earth, he would position himself as close as possible to the spot where he thought the arrow would strike the ground. With a piece of rope, the distance between him and the arrow would be measured. After everyone had taken his turn, the one closest to his arrow was the winner. The one farthest away from the arrow was the "chicken." Another variation of this was to grab the arrow in the air before it struck the ground. Not too many kids cared for that game.

Most of our bows were made from locally grown wood. We all knew that hickory was the preferred wood for bows but since it was not available we usually settled for cherry or oak. Arrows were generally made from any straight piece of wood but most often they came from the suckers sprouting off tree stumps. The wooden tips would be fire hardened or the arrows would be tipped with nails flattened on the railroad tracks.

Word got around that Bobby Miscuff had gotten hold of some really exotic wood from which he would construct a bow. We had never heard of lemonwood, so we were all anxious to see how his new bow performed. The making of the bow took quite a bit of work as the wood had to be planed and tapered to the correct proportions. Finally the bow was finished, and the next day a dozen kids collected across the street from Bobby's house, which was on the corner of Chestnut and Pine streets. A large vacant area overlooked Park Row and the wall that kept the steep hill from washing onto the road. Bobby passed the bow around and we were amazed at the thickness of the wood and how much effort it took to draw the bow back. We were warned not to release the string when the bow was drawn as this would snap the string.

Finally, all was ready. Inserting a store-bought hunting arrow into the bow string, he aimed directly overhead so the arrow would land nearby. We watched in amazement as the arrow left the bow and continued to climb until we lost track of it. Not knowing where the arrow was going to land and not being able to see it, some of the kids covered their heads with their hands, others began backing away from the area. No one knew where it was going to come down. Finally, thud! We heard the arrow hit, but where was it? A minute passed as we looked the area over for the missing arrow.

"There it is!" shouted one kid, pointing up. The arrow was sticking into the roof of Pandorf's house on the corner of Willow Avenue and Jacob Street.

Time went by quickly and summer was drawing to a close. It was the middle of the afternoon when several of us headed towards Krug's woods where we would hang out for a while, cook our supper, and return home in the evening. A fence that had to be climbed separated Krug's cow pastures from the Star Homes development. This particular afternoon I was somewhat careless in climbing the fence, and in slipping I cut the palm of my hand on the barbed wire that was strung along the top. Butch Kopec quickly came up with a solution for the bad cut. Locating a small stick, he dipped it into some fresh cow manure and came over to apply it to my cut.

I strenuously objected to putting the wet cow manure on my cut, but he insisted that this was how they treated cuts in Poland. He went on to explain how he had heard his parents talking about using dry cow manure as a poultice, and so he reasoned that wet should be even better. Well, I thought, since my grandfather who came from Poland frequently put urine on his head perhaps cow manure was a cure. After applying the wet manure we secured it with a handkerchief, which I always carried.

After hanging around in the woods for a while, I walked to the railroad tracks to check things out around the Pump House. Returning to Krug's woods I found that the other kids weren't back yet, so I built a fire to get ready for supper. After a pile of hot coals had built up, I took all of the potatoes and put them beneath the coals to cook. At this time I noticed a robin about twenty feet away in some tree branches. As a lark, I decided to try a shot from my bow. I did not really expect to hit him because of all the nearby branches, and I was surprised when the arrow struck him and he fell to the ground. What do you do with a dead robin? Nothing I could think of, so I threw him into the fire.

Twenty minutes later the rest of the kids returned, and I informed them that the potatoes were all in the coals and would be ready soon. We sat around the fire telling stories, a few jokes, and just being kids. A green stick was cut to remove the potatoes from the coals. They were too hot to pick up so they were left lying on the ground to cool off. The outside of the potato was usually hard and carbonized, and to eat them we usually broke them in half. John Markovitch picked up his potato and after breaking it in half found that the two halves were still connected. He was puzzled as to what this strange stuff was that was hanging between the two halves. John soon found out that his potato was actually the charred remains of the robin, and it was the bird's guts that hung between the two pieces.

The evening came to an end and so did summer vacation. It was time to return to Jefferson School. This year would be our last year as kids playing in Krug's woods (although as we grew older we would still use the general area for hunting—with guns). We were now approaching the age when the driving force in our lives would not be having fun, but finding work.

The Robin Hood gang,
with Krug's woods in the background

WORK

The place that most kids went to for their first jobs was either Roehr's or Bobbink & Atkins. These were large greenhouses that specialized in growing flowers. One was located on Mount Pleasant Avenue, the other was nearby on the Paterson Plank Road. There were also several large vegetable farms in the area that employed kids during the growing season. One was off of Mount Pleasant Avenue, the other was much larger and was off of Terhune Avenue in Wood-Ridge.

During the summer that the Robin Hood Gang was playing in Krug's woods, I would often see Carol Kroll walking home from her farm job in Wood-Ridge. I had once gone to work on that farm, for ten cents a hour. They had me on my knees thinning carrots, weeding, and bunching celery. I never before realized how slowly time could go by. This was the longest day I ever spent, and when it was over I went to the boss and informed him I wouldn't be coming back. He handed me a dollar, and I could tell by his attitude he was used to one-day kids. Whenever I saw Carol pass on her way home from work at the farm she was covered with dust and grime, and I wondered how this little hundred-pound girl could work so hard all day long for the whole summer.

For kids such as me who could not stand the drudgery of farm work, the second best bet was to get a job as a pin setter in a bowling alley. In Wallington there was Babe's Alleys on the corner of Main Avenue and Alden Street. There was a much larger bowling alley on

Market Street in Passaic near Bergen Street. This alley was somewhat different in that people bowled not only ten pins but also duck pins. Kids didn't like setting duck pins as they were much smaller and when hit hard they flew around too much. For setting pins you received thirty-five cents per frame and you had to handle two lanes. The pinboy sat on a shelf between the two alleys and if a bowler threw a very fast ball you had to watch out, as an errant pin could knock you off your seat. The bowlers usually gave you a tip, so for several hours of hard work you could end up with two dollars or so. It sure beat working on a farm.

Some kids did well shining shoes, but they usually had to go to the area of Main Street in Passaic to make any money. They also frequented bars a lot, and sometimes fights broke out between shoeshine boys over territories.

Things improved a great deal once you turned sixteen, as many more jobs were available. My brother and I both had jobs as ushers in theaters in Passaic. I worked at the Playhouse and my brother worked at the Montauk. Both were on Main Street. In the summer of 1947 my third year at Bloomfield Tech was approaching. My mother brought up the subject of getting a part-time job after school when I returned to fall classes, so I told her that I would begin looking. Several weeks went by and she inquired as to why I hadn't found a job. The truth is I wasn't even looking for a job as I had plans of playing football for Bloomfield Tech, which was fielding a team for the first time. Of course, I didn't tell her of my plans. Another week went by and after supper she informed me that she had found a job for me at the Playhouse Theater in Passaic as an usher. In vain I tried to explain to her that I wanted to play high school football and that it would only be until late November. "You're going to work," she informed me. "You're sixteen and it's time to start paying room and board."

I began working at the Playhouse that Sunday. The movie was "Frankenstein Meets the Wolf Man." I went to work every day after school and sometimes I would also work either Saturdays or Sundays.

My income for the week amounted to eleven dollars. On my very first payday my mother waited up for me to come home, although she was usually in bed by eight o'clock. She asked me how much I made. I wasn't sure, as I hadn't even counted what was in the envelope. I now counted out the money in the envelope and found there were eleven singles and some change. It was then she informed me that room and board for the week was nine dollars. I handed over nine dollars, clenching my teeth so hard I thought they would break.

Around 1948 my parents bought a new Plymouth. This was their first car. And like most people during this period, their life began to revolve around the car. Whenever someone on the block got a new car, all the neighbors would show up and you would end up taking them for a drive. That was okay, but Sundays were dreadful. After church my father would wash the car and get it ready for a Sunday afternoon drive. Leaving for the drive, he would always head for Route 17 near Saddle Brook. Riding north we would hit circle after circle where traffic flowed into Route 17. At this time Route 17 was a very dangerous three-lane road. It seemed to me that everybody in New Jersey and New York took a Sunday drive.

My father always stopped at the Red Apple Rest for lunch, which was always the same: a hot dog. The place was usually very crowded and a half-hour wait for a hot dog was common. My brother and I never really cared for their hot dogs as we always judged the quality of a hot dog by comparing it with those served at Rutt's Hut, which set the standard. After leaving the Red Apple Rest we would continue north and then return home via the back roads around Greenwood Lake. From here we would pick up Route 23 then go on to Route 46 and home.

I got to hate these drives and had to figure out some way to get out of them. I informed my mother that I had an extra job on Sundays setting pins and wouldn't be able to go on those nice Sunday drives anymore. She asked how much I would make. I was getting foxy now and told her I didn't know, it depended on how many people showed up. I cleverly added, "Sometimes no one shows up." I wasn't about to hand over any more money for room and board.

By 1948 I was making some pretty good money trapping musk-rats, which were selling for an average of two dollars each. I'm surprised my mother didn't try taxing me on my furs. I was now able to buy my first car, a 1939 Ford for two hundred dollars. With a car I now expanded my trapping territory to cover Berry's Creek in the Meadowlands and as far north as the Saddle River in Mahwah.

The time was fast approaching for my graduation from Bloomfield Tech. Two months before graduation I received a real shock. The shop teacher, Mr. P., informed me that I would not be graduating, as a result of not fulfilling all of the shop requirements. He reminded me that most of my time was spent fixing things I brought to school rather than doing the required projects. I was horrified at the thought of my mother's reaction upon hearing this kind of news.

"Mr. P.," I pleaded, "my mother's going to be very upset if I don't graduate." He said nothing, so I continued, "I never really did care about my progress here, and I really don't know much about being a machinist, but if you allow me to graduate I promise I'll never go to work in a machine shop."

"You promise?" he asked. "I don't want the reputation of this school ruined by you."

"I promise," I told him.

I graduated from Bloomfield Tech in 1949 and got a job in the Bartmann and Bixer curtain factory as a stock boy. My mother was a sewing machine operator there and got me the job (she was good at finding me jobs). I worked there for a year and was earning a grand total of twenty-eight dollars a week. The government took four dollars, and for room and board my mother took ten. I was nineteen years old and chafing to get out on my own, but with the money I earned and no real skills there was no way out of my dilemma. I was trapped, with nowhere to turn.

Then the Korean war broke out and for a few months I watched the development of the war from the security of the cloth-winding machine that I operated. Then suddenly everything fell into place.

It was eleven o'clock one morning when I turned off the machine, picked up my jacket, and walked out, not even bothering with my time card or notifying anyone that I was quitting.

In one instant I was free from living at home, I was out of a job that I hated, and I became a patriot. All I had to do to accomplish all this was to join the Navy.

Trapping, 1949

MY FIRST DANCE

I had just turned eighteen and my hormones were in a state of overproduction. As the saying goes, I was "feeling my oats." It seemed like only yesterday that I was playing cops and robbers, and now I was going to my first dance at the Polish People's Home on Monroe Street in Passaic. This was the cultural activity center of the area. Dances, basketball games, weddings, and repasts—in addition to political meetings and everything else you can think of—were all held there.

This would be my night to enter a world I had only dreamed about.

After a prolonged discussion, my brother agreed to lend me his red 1939 Buick convertible—that is, if I would fill the tank with gas and mow the lawn for the next two weeks (his designated chore). On my way to the dance, I decided to take advantage of my new status by driving around town a few times. This was 1949, and very few working people owned cars, the common forms of transportation being bus or shoe leather.

I arrived at the dance about 7:30. It was already in full progress and the band was playing the Pennsylvania Polka. Never having been to a dance before, I was somewhat unsure of the procedure to follow. I noticed right off that the bar was packed with males and that the females were all lined up against the far wall, apparently waiting for their knight in shining armor to show up. Of course, my ego and attitude were at the stage of development where the only thing I lacked was a white horse.

Before going over to relieve them of their stressful situation I decided a drink was in order, as the band was playing fast numbers and the only dance I felt comfortable with was a fox trot, which was little more than a shuffle. My aunt had tried to teach me the polka since I was sixteen, but I never could get the hang of it. Another popular dance was the jitterbug, but most people usually just watched as a few talented couples dominated the dance floor, the girls in short skirts with white ankle socks and black-and-white shoes, the boys, called "zoot suiters," in dark clothes with tight-cuffed baggy pants.

I was beginning to get a little nervous. Perhaps another drink would help. The bartender, on the alert for an empty glass, quickly responded when I waved to him. I ordered a scotch and water, which he made and placed in front of me. He picked up the quarter I placed on the bar and made his displeasure known to me by a dirty look, which I interpreted to mean that he expected a tip. Being a senior in high school and making fifty cents an hour as an usher in a run-down theater, I did not have the psychology of a generous tipper. Besides, tipping was not a well-developed practice at this time, as the country had not fully recovered from the Depression and World War II and most people still had the Depression mentality.

Drinking Scotch and water brought back memories of iodine. As kids, our cuts and abrasions were always treated with iodine, and we were always licking our wounds. I think the only reason I drank the stuff that night was because the older guys always said it bucked you up and gave you courage. And I was beginning to feel that I could use some.

A slow number came up. It was now or never. My heart pounded as I began the walk across the dance floor. There was a great deal of smoke, which tended to obscure the far wall where all the gals were lined up. As I got closer, the smoke began to thin out to a light haze. Still, about the only things I could really make out were intense colors. I was attracted by a deep blue dress, and before I knew it I was standing before a girl who was sizing me up in a suspicious manner.

"Would you like to dance?" I asked. I had to look up to make eye contact and it was then that I realized she was six inches taller than me. Her face began to twist in obvious confusion, then disappointment, as I apparently did not fit the image of her imaginary knight. Her hands were nervously fingering some beads, which may have been a rosary. Perhaps she was praying for deliverance. Finally, her pent-up agony released itself with these words: "No! I'm tired and have a headache."

Being unaware of the complexities of female psychology, I approached the gal standing next to her. As I did so, I noticed that she angled her body away from me as if the Devil were approaching to molest her. She looked in the opposite direction, as if she hoped I wouldn't notice her.

"Would you like to dance?" I asked.

She was brutally frank, without even a trace of compassion for the awkward dilemma I was caught up in. "No!"

I was stunned. This was not part of the script my imagination had led me to expect. A strange feeling began to come over me, one that I had never experienced before. This was my first encounter with rejection by the opposite sex, and on my first venture into the psychological world of male and female. Confusion rapidly gave way to self doubt, which quickly resulted in a badly ruptured ego.

With what was left of that ego, I began the long journey back across the dance floor. I was both jealous and angry as I threaded my way between couples fondly holding each other, apparently intoxicated by the delights of touch, smell, and sound.

I finally made it to the bar and ordered a double Scotch and water. Perhaps this would help stabilize my condition and prevent further deterioration. Finishing my drink, I decided to head home. I took a last look at the far wall where my first real encounter with the opposite sex had occurred. The band must have been taking a break, as no one was on the floor dancing and the smoke had dissipated. And there the girls were, lined up along the wall as if locked in a time warp.

At the door, the woman who collected the tickets smiled at me and said, "It's too early to leave." She somehow conveyed that she had been watching me the whole time. "Besides, you have to dance a polka before they warm up to you."

"Lady," I replied, "if you think I'm going to go through that shit again, you're crazy."

I decided to take a long drive so as not to get home too early. I realized that my ego needed some protection, and if I arrived home too early there would be too many questions from my brother.

Arriving home fairly late, I headed to the bedroom where my brother and I both slept. He was reading in bed when I walked in.

"How was your evening?" he asked.

"I had a great evening, Joe," I said, "and thanks for lending me your car. I put the keys under the floor mat."

"Well," he said. "Give me some details."

At this point, I decided to make up a story to cover my disastrous evening and salvage what I could of my battered ego. My brother would be unmerciful if he knew the truth.

"Why, Joe, I had only one dance from this beautiful girl who recently came from Poland. We decided to go over to Rutt's Hut for some hot dogs, after which we went to the Third Ward park and spent some time just talking. After I drove her home she gave me a nice kiss and agreed to meet me at the Playhouse Theatre this week."

"That's it?" he responded.

I didn't bother answering, I just crawled into the bed and hugged the pillow to dry the tears flowing down my cheeks.

A CHRISTMAS PRESENT

I t was some time since the Great Depression and I was at the point in life where I was considered a grownup. However, that term was somewhat misleading as although I was not a child any more, neither could I say that I safely resided psychologically in an adult world. This Christmas would sorely test my dual nature.

Christmas would be celebrated at my mother's house as it was every year, since she was the oldest member of the family group. Our usual festivities of a large traditional Polish meal and the opening of presents would take place on Christmas Eve, as Christmas Day we all went to church.

The tree was beautifully decorated and beneath it were boxes of presents for everyone. We had come a long way since the Great Depression. We were all gathered around the table eating our traditional Polish foods, plus some brisket and other foods that had managed to work their way into our traditions, when I began not to feel too well. I excused myself from the table and went into the living room to sit on the couch.

As I looked over at all the boxes under the tree I wondered how many sweaters I would get this year. After a while, I noticed a most unusual package lying under the tree. It was not the usual box shape and a closer examination showed that the tag said "To Bill from Aunt Anne and Uncle Syl." The package was about three feet long and tapered. The top was only an inch wide and the bottom about six inches. What the hell could that be? I quickly forgot about not feeling well as I began to mentally unravel the mystery of what this strangely shaped package might hold. Making sure no one was looking, I reached down and felt the top of the package. It felt like a piece of steel beneath all the paper wrapping and I quickly came to the conclusion that it was a rifle barrel. I could think of nothing else that would fit the image. My curiosity had now risen to new levels, and there was only one way to be sure. Slowly I shifted my hand to the bottom of the package and began pressing in the wrapping paper to feel the shape of the bottom. It certainly was hard, but not like steel. It felt like a piece of wood. Tracing the outline with my fingers, I felt it follow a curve that resembled the curve on a rifle stock. There was now no doubt in my mind this was a .22 caliber rifle.

I sat back in the couch, wondering what kind of a rifle this might be. I began to hope they had picked the model I had always wanted, a Winchester pump. Somewhere lurking in my mind was the thought that this was crazy, my aunt and uncle would never in a hundred years buy me a gun, these are sweater and shirt people, but I overruled the thought and relied on my sense of touch and my imagination, which said the package contained a rifle.

Patiently I sat on the couch waiting for everyone to finish eating. This would be followed by a general cleanup by the women, the last chore being the washing of the dishes. During this time the thought of my new rifle dominated my imagination. After a half hour or so the women began entering the living room, signaling that all the chores were finished and it was now time to open our presents. Since my mother was the oldest and it was her house, tradition was that she would be the one to hand out the gifts. There was a well-established procedure to follow. My mother would randomly pick a package from the pile then call out the name of the person receiving it, this to be followed by the name of the persons giving the present. The person receiving the package would carefully open it so as not to tear the paper as this would be saved for next year's package (the bows were especially valuable), and after viewing the contents would thank the people who gave him the present. No other present would be given out until this was finished. This process was often very tedious.

It seemed to take forever before my mother came to the odd-shaped package with my name on it, and of course I already knew what the package contained—a .22 caliber rifle. Finally, she announced "To Bill from Aunt Anne and Uncle Syl." I took the package from my mother and, taking my seat, carefully began to remove the wrapping paper. When the final turn of the paper suddenly revealed the contents, I was astonished, bewildered, dumbfounded. As I gazed down upon the object I had just unwrapped, all of my dreams were instantly crushed. It was no .22 caliber rifle. Rather, it was a large black umbrella, the kind one sees Englishmen carrying around in old movies. It had a three-inch steel tip—this was the barrel of my rifle. It also had a large wooden handle—this was the wooden stock I had felt. So much for the veracity of my imagination.

"What the hell am I supposed to do with this damn thing?" I blurted out,

I could see the shock on my aunt and uncle's faces at the outburst. After a short pause my aunt responded, "Your mother told us that this was what you wanted for Christmas."

Turning to my mother, who was also in a flustered state, I asked her, "Ma, what ever gave you the idea that I wanted something like this?"

"Bill," she responded, "don't you remember when I spoke to you in June and asked you what you could use for Christmas and you told me a big black umbrella?"

"Mom," I replied, "who thinks about Christmas in June? You caught me completely by surprise, so when I said I wanted a big black umbrella it was just me being sarcastic. It was the most useless thing I could think of at that moment."

"How was I to know you were jesting?" she replied

At this point my aunt forced her way into our discussion, and getting right to the point announced, "Give me the goddam umbrella and I'll bring it back and get something else."

I handed her the umbrella and that settled the situation.

Soon after the last present was handed out my aunt and uncle left. The last I saw of the umbrella it was under my uncle's arm, and he was carrying a pile of boxes as he left my mother's house. Unfortunately, the curved wooden handle caught on the door jamb and jerked his arm, causing him to drop all the boxes he was carrying. He began swearing in Polish. Even my aunt and uncle now felt the curse of this damn umbrella.

One week later my mother called me to say that my aunt had dropped off a new present for me to replace the umbrella. I informed my mother that I would not be able to visit for a while and she should just tell me what was in the package so I could call my aunt and uncle and thank them. I waited while she opened the package to determine its contents. She returned to the phone, but before she could speak I asked her if it was a brown umbrella.

"Don't be funny," she replied. "That damn umbrella has caused enough problems."

My mother never did understand my sense of humor, which leaned very heavily in the direction of sarcasm.

"What's in the box, Ma?"

"A nice sweater," she replied.

I felt relived. Everything was back to normal.

ANNIE

nnie was my mother's sister and all through the 1930s we lived together with her and her father on Fourth Street in Passaic. My mother was raising two young sons by herself so she had moved in with her family.

One of my earliest memories of Annie was her dislike of guns of any kind. She didn't even like to see my brother and me playing cops-and-robbers and using our fingers as make-believe guns. Of all the toy guns she disliked, at the head of the list were cap pistols. The loud noise they made would really get her dander up, and pity the poor kid if he were close by. He would get a tongue lashing that he was not apt to forget for a long time.

Annie's brother Paul (Jinx), although not living with us, was always welcome company for my brother and me, as he was the only person we knew who had a car. What a thrill it was for us to go for a ride in his 1937 Dodge coupe. We both knew that Jinx was on the wild side, as we heard conversations between my mother and Annie discussing his wild behavior. Whenever he visited us on Fourth Street people would gather around his Dodge to admire it. Sometimes if they were lucky he would even take a few for a ride.

Sometime in the early 1930s Uncle Jinx decided to sleep at our apartment on Fourth Street rather than drive home, as he apparently had had too much to drink. The next morning Annie went to where Jinx was sleeping on the couch to check on him. In his inebriated state, Jinx had dropped a number of items on the living room floor.

One of these items disturbed her so much that she took it, wrapped it in a towel, and hid it away. From what I gather, Jinx never did find out what happened to the object, and it was soon forgotten—at least, by Jinx.

Annie kept the object long after her brother died, which was in 1957. Then one day she informed me that she had something to show me the next time I came to visit.

"I want to get rid of the damn thing," she told me.

"What is it?" I asked, being quite curious.

"You'll know when you see it."

"When do you want me to come around?" I asked

"The next time you come down to visit your mother."

I informed her that it would be several weeks before I returned.

"Just give me a call when you're coming," she replied.

Finally I was able to make the trip to New Jersey. As I drove down the New York State Thruway I wondered what could she have that she had kept hidden for fifty years. When I finally arrived at her house in Elmwood Park, we went through the usual period of greetings and the exchange of information. I had to break the ice at some point and get to why I was there.

"Okay, Anne, let's see what you've been hiding for fifty years."

She beckoned me to follow her. We made our way to the attic where she proceeded to unlock an old trunk. She moved some stuff aside and came up with a towel. Handing me the towel, she said, "It's inside."

I slowly unwrapped the towel and there it was, the object that she was so afraid of. It was a chrome-plated revolver with a beautiful pearl handle. Printed on the side were the words American Bulldog. I could see it was a .32 caliber.

"Take it and get it out of here. I hate those damn things. But," she continued, "be careful, it might be loaded."

Having looked the gun over, I already knew it was not loaded. She was relieved when I told her that there were no bullets in it.

Shortly after, I left and began the seventy-mile drive home. Most of the time I spent trying to understand the psychology of my aunt and uncle and how it related to this gun. Arriving home shortly after six o'clock I poured myself a brandy. Sitting in my favorite chair and slowly sipping my drink I picked up the towel and removed the gun from its wrapping. Upon closer examination of the revolver I received a shock which quickly changed to laughter. I could only stifle my laughter by swallowing more brandy, which in turn was fuel for more laughter. This beautiful chrome-plated revolver with the nice pearl handle was a useless piece of junk.

The first thing I noticed was that the cylinder would not rotate. Next I noticed that the trigger was missing. Examining the barrel I could see that it was plugged; someone had hammered a file into it then snapped it off. Time for another drink of brandy! Was I disappointed? Yes. But nothing that a glass of brandy couldn't cure.

I decided to get rid of it immediately. I drove to the Galeville Bridge which spans the Wallkill River in a remote area and threw it into the river. I had a little laugh as I did this. I could see some bass fisherman finding the gun and bringing it to the police, hoping to help solve some major crime. Why, he might even conceive of getting a reward. Thus the gun would continue to feed the human imagination.

I returned home to the pleasure contained in the small glass and again began toying with the mindset of these two people. One owned a gun that was useless and the other didn't know it was useless, yet both were equally trapped by their imaginations. Now it was my turn to use my imagination—perhaps a new musical, "Annie Get Rid of Your Gun."

Aunt Annie, in the 1920s

INSURANCE

Every Thursday during the entire Depression we had a visitor. Mr. Berry was an insurance agent who had signed my mother up for insurance so that when my brother and I reached the age of twenty-one we could cash in the policy and have a decent start in life.

Mr. Berry would always arrive in the evening, usually about seven o'clock, and he carried a large thick book to record all of his transactions. Mr. Berry must have done well indeed during this difficult period, if the thickness of the book was any indication of success. Before his arrival my mother would always clean the porcelain kitchen table so as not to dirty his book.

Upon his arrival he would open the book on the kitchen table to where my brother's and my names were listed. The whole procedure was like a well-practiced ritual. This would be followed by my mother placing a black coin purse on the table. She would open it and count out twenty-five cents. He would then mark this amount in his book. This was to be followed by her removing another twenty-five cents which he would duly record. When the transaction was complete his last words before leaving were always the same: "I'll see you next Thursday."

My brother and I never knew that these were our policies she was paying on all through this very difficult time.

I was in the Navy when I finally turned twenty-one. During one of my infrequent visits home, my mother took me aside and with a great deal of pride handed me the insurance policy she had so faithfully paid on for so many years. It was evident that she was very proud of her achievement, which was to be able to put aside this small amount of money every week for twenty-one years.

I thanked her and left, as I had to return to Boston where my ship was in port. It was only later, when I was on the train with a four-hour ride ahead of me, that I examined the policy. After looking it over and checking the amount I would receive by cashing it in, I was stunned. The total amount including interest came to three hundred and fifty dollars.

I could visualize my mother back in 1931, while the insurance man was telling her about this large sum of money that I would receive upon reaching the age of twenty-one. Yes, by 1931 standards this was a sizeable sum, when wages were ten to fifteen dollars a week. However, by 1952 this would amount to no more than a down payment on a new car.

As the train rambled towards Boston, I thought a great deal about the Depression and my mother's desire for us to have a better life by sacrificing what we needed now for future security and a start in life.

I got to thinking what my mother could have bought with that fifty cents a week she shelled out for my brother's and my insurance policies.

Since we never ate eggs, as they were too expensive according to my mother, this fifty cents would have purchased five dozen eggs. I do not remember what other items cost but it became apparent to me that if that fifty cents had been spent on good food we would all have been better off.

Several weeks later I returned home on a weekend pass. It was at this time that I took my mother and stepfather out for supper. It was a very nice restaurant and my mother felt somewhat out of place, as she rarely ever ate out and she could see that the place was a little expensive. She very carefully examined the menu and the determining factor behind what she ordered was the price. Even then, so many years after the Depression, she would continue to live in a world of insecurity and caution.

After we finished, the waitress brought the bill over and I removed it from the plate. Taking some money from my wallet, I placed four dollars on the table for the tip. My mother, thinking I had just paid for the entire meal, reminded me to leave a tip of fifty cents.

"Ma," I told her, "that is the tip."

With a worried look on her face, she asked, "How much was the meal?"

With a somewhat humorous inflection in my voice I replied, "One year of insurance payments to Mr. Berry."

My mother as a teenager, in Pulaski Park

EPILOGUE

recently revisited my old neighborhoods in Passaic and in Wallington. I began on Fourth Street, where I parked my car at the Bergen Street entrance to Pulaski Park. Standing on the corner I surveyed the scene. The apartment house I used to live in was gone, replaced by a school named Pulaski. The YWCA across the street was now a Spanish church. The Jewish grocery store on the corner was now a Hispanic grocery store. Yes, the neighborhood had changed.

Next, I walked into Pulaski Park and quickly realized it was only a shell of its former self. Half the park was now apartment houses. The large, beautiful pavilion was gone, as was the wading pool for kids. I walked towards the iron fence that separated the park from the railroad tracks. It was apparent that these once-busy tracks were now only a storage area for graffiti-covered, rusting boxcars. By the amount of filth along the tracks it was obvious that certain elements of society liked this environment. My plan was to cross the tracks via the metal bridge that was built around 1937 to provide access to the river, which was a very popular recreation area in the 1930s. Arriving at the bridge I found that it was no longer in use, as the stairs had all been removed.

I took a seat on one of the few remaining benches and began to remember the stories my mother used to tell me about her life growing up on Fourth Street. One of these stories was about the very tracks I was looking at. One of her jobs as a little girl was to pick coal along these tracks after school was over. She was six years old when she began picking coal here and she did this every day except Sunday.

Next, I drove to Third Street to see the Passaic Boys Club. It was now a Head Start center. I drove onto Market Street and parked in front of the Palace Theater, which had obviously closed a long time ago. I walked to the corner of Market and Mercer Streets. This was where Dr. Weinert had his office, on the second floor. It was now an apartment building.

Going up Jefferson Street, a smile crossed my face as I drove over the now-filled-in Dundee Canal. It was there that my brother had fallen through the ice. I parked on the corner of Jefferson and Columbia and took a few pictures of the day care center which had been such a large part of my early life. Everything was the same except two things: the play yard was much smaller, and the Jewish school next door was now a parking lot. Next, I wanted to see the school that I attended, Lafayette School #6. A new school had been built and it reflected the changing area. It was now Martin Luther King Elementary School.

Driving up Monroe Street towards Main Street I noticed that the Lincoln Theater and the Capital were both gone. However, the Montauk Theater was still there. I really wanted to see the Playhouse Theater, where I worked for two years as an usher, but it, too, was gone. One last stop before leaving Passaic for Wallington: I wanted to see Tidewater Iron and Steel, across the street from the Passaic Stadium. It was gone, replaced by Route 20.

I drove across the Acquackanonk Bridge into Wallington and parked next to a small hot dog stand. Looking over the bridge and the rotten pilings that were supposed to protect it when open, I could see that this bridge no longer opened for barge traffic, which meant that the Market Street bridge and the Eighth Street bridge were also unable to open. The Passaic River was no longer a waterway supplying goods to the factories of Passaic.

My next stop was the war memorial in Wallington, dedicated to the servicemen and women who served their country in World War I and World War II. One cannot fail to be impressed by this small town's contribution—especially in World War II. My son, who accompanied me on this trip, commented, "If this small town had that many people in service during World War II, there must have been no men in town when you were growing up. It's no wonder you got away with all those crazy things you did as a kid."

Close by was Adam's store, which is well known for its excellent smoked kielbasa, so I picked up some rings of kielbasa, three kishkas, and a couple dozen pierogis. I needed some gas so I stopped to fill up on the corner of Wallington and Main avenues. Looking across the street I could see the sign for Wallington Potato King, although the store was now closed and perhaps even forgotten by most. I recalled how I used to lug a large bag of potatoes back home to Park Row and what a struggle it was for a young boy.

At this time, I realized that I needed some good "old country" rye bread. After a quick stop at Banas (formerly Boruta's) Bakery, I was on my way to Alden Street.

Turning onto Alden Street I noticed that Phil Kobscenski's service station and Babe's bar and bowling alley no longer existed. At the end of Alden Street was our old playground, the "canyon." I was disappointed to see that they had finally put a road through the canyon to connect Alden Street to Mount Pleasant Avenue. Driving up the hill I could not fail to notice that the two large old water tanks had been replaced by one tank.

After passing through the canyon I made a left turn onto Mount Pleasant Avenue and parked in front of Dr. Lesko's old house. I took a few minutes to reflect about hunting behind that house as a young boy. I remembered the day I was hunting with Dicky Miskuff and another boy who I shall not name, when a shot was heard awfully close to the house. Pretty soon the unnamed boy came out of some bushes carrying a large black and white rabbit, which we both recognized as a Belgian hare. We all took off running towards the tracks as we knew that he had shot one of Dr. Lesko's rabbits.

Ciliento's dairy farm was now covered with houses, as was the large farm across the street. I drove on to Wagner Avenue and parked, and there it was, just as it had always looked—Jefferson School. I fondly gazed at the school as memories raced through my mind. I was glad to see that there were no longer telltale marks of the paint that Stan Posluszny and I used on the school one Halloween night. Back then they had simply painted over our paint with a brown color that never really did match the bricks.

Looking at the school I felt that something was wrong, but I couldn't quite put my finger on what it was. And all the while I was leaning on it—Jefferson School was now surrounded by a four-foot cyclone fence. What the heck do you need a fence around a rural school for, I thought. Then I realized I was thinking from the viewpoint of sixty years ago, and this was a totally different world. Considering the changes that had taken place, I decided a fence was a pretty good idea.

I turned east looking towards Wood-Ridge, and all I could see were roofs with some trees scattered in between. Yet in the 1940s, to us kids this was the wilderness, a large uninhabited area where we roamed and where our imaginations knew no bounds.

I drove up Wagner Avenue to where Joe Maletsky used to live. I was looking for the dirt road that led to the two water tanks, which was alongside his house. A house had been built over the road. Joe was older than us and our only real association with him was to spend time around his garage, where he built fine model airplanes.

Next, I drove down Chestnut Street, noticing that the Kaiser's store was no longer there. I drove past the house where Walt Wargacki used to live. At that time he was owner of a business called Merchant's Burglar Alarm Co., and whenever our BB guns broke we would bring them to Walt, who always found time to repair our guns. I was always intrigued by the number of chickens that came in and out of the garage as he worked. Many people in the area during the 1940s had free-range chickens (and some, like Dr. Lesko, even had rabbits).

I slowly drove down Chestnut Street to Willow Avenue and up Jacob to Franklin—all new homes covered the area. This was the area of Krug's woods and the anti-aircraft batteries from World War

11. It was here that the Robin Hood Gang hung out, and much later would hunt rabbits. Gone—all gone. Turning around and heading down towards Park Row I couldn't resist lowering my head to look at the roof of Pandorf's old house to see if the arrow was still sticking in the roof (it wasn't).

Halfway down Park Row hill I decided to pull over and park. I looked up at Bobby Miskuff's house, as this was the place where I tried out my first pair of homemade skis. Actually, they were staves from an old wooden barrel that I found on the dump. I nailed a piece of leather onto the staves to put my shoes in and I was ready for my first skiing adventure. Above the six-foot stone wall on Park Row was a sharp little incline which rose about thirty feet to a flat field. Coming down the hill I thought I would stop before the stone wall. Instead, I tumbled over the wall and onto Park Row.

Now I proceeded down Park Row past Dolack's house. His house was located right on the bend across the street from the Krolls. I noticed that the large cherry tree in front of his house was gone, but the telephone pole was still there next to the sidewalk. Park Row hill was [highly] used during the winter for sled riding but we always stayed in the road. On a dare, one kid went down the sidewalk just beneath the wall. He hit the pole in front of Dolack's and ended up in the hospital.

Continuing down Park Row I passed Kudlacik's house, Louie's house, and the Kopecs' before pulling up by the new firehouse. Getting out of my van I looked the neighborhood over. Sura's house and Kobscenski's old house were still there, but they had been remodeled and didn't look the same. As I stood there I felt something was missing. Sure enough, there was no sound of pigeons and no birds were flying overhead.

I drove over to Kossuth Street to where the Pirogs and the Poslusznys used to live. The house where Tommy Pirog accidentally shot Cassey Kudlacik was still there. The very old house next door, owned by the Barneys, had been demolished and replaced with a beautiful new home. Charlie Barney was the fastest kid around and no one could beat him in a foot race, except perhaps Cassey Kudlacik. We used to wonder why one of Barney's toes always stuck out of his sneaker. Then we found out he had six toes—no wonder he was so fast.

I walked over to Miskuff's house, which was next door. It was then that I noticed a relic from the past, the only one I had seen on my visit, perhaps the only one left—an old pigeon coop above the garage.

Next I drove to Stein Avenue to see the house that my parents built in 1947. What a shock to see that beautiful, well-cared-for house missing. It had been torn down and replaced by a modern two-family home. Land in Wallington was just too valuable for small one-family homes. As I sat there thinking about the time when the house was being built, I remember my mother complaining to Liz Kobscenski about how it was costing her more money for beer than for lumber to keep the two local builders working.

Driving down Stein Avenue I remembered the flags with gold stars hanging in the windows during World War II. Several servicemen from the block had been killed in the war.

Directly across Main Avenue from Stein was the Passaic River. We used to hang around the river just below Main Avenue. As kids during the summer we were always thirsty; however, we wouldn't drink river water or even swim in it. One day we noticed a spring we had never seen before coming from beneath Main Avenue. The water seemed clean and it tasted pretty good. For years we drank from this spring, only to find out much later when the city did repairs on the sewers that this was not a spring but water leaking from a broken sewer line.

I turned onto Main Avenue and headed towards the three corners. Gone was Zampacota's candy store. Where Reggie's Tavern once stood was now a Slavic restaurant, and Bednarz's Gulf station had become a Seven-Eleven store.

The Horseshoe Pond, the Sandpits, and the Pump House had all disappeared. In their place was a large apartment house complex known as Jasontown. I remembered the spring that Stan Posluszny and I went swimming at the Pump House. It had suddenly turned very warm in mid-April, perhaps 90 degrees, but when we got to the Pump House it was still covered with ice. We managed to break a hole into the ice, and Posluszny took off all of his clothes and jumped into the pond. On coming back to the surface he quite literally flew out of the cold water, trembling. I decided not to go in after seeing his condition. Of course, I had to live with the title "chicken" for a while.

One last stop and the trip to revisit my past would come to a close. I drove over to the Home Liquor store and parked. Before going in I glanced across the street to the lot where the carnival used to take place. I was not surprised to see a large building instead. Entering the store, I went directly to the vodka section. I knew what I wanted, two large bottles of Luksusowa potato vodka. After surveying Passaic and Wallington in the year 2003 I was going to need a little assistance in making the mental transformation that covered over sixty years and two completely different worlds.

As I was driving up the New York State Thruway I began to settle down and to think more objectively about the past and all the changes that have occurred. This is life, I thought, ever-changing life. Everything here is temporary, including us. I thought about those kids that are no longer with us: John Markovitch, Louie, Butch Kopec, Dick Miskuff, Mickey Mahull, Eugene Bohnarzyk, Yash Bednarz. Perhaps there are others that I'm not aware of. Regardless, we are all in the twilight of our lives and we, too, will end up just memories and a few faded photographs. Just as the Horseshoe Pond, the Pump House, and that wonderful kids' paradise Krug's woods are now just memories—so we will be.

About the Author

BILL MICHALSKI grew up in Passaic and Wallington, New Jersey. After serving four years in the Navy, he attended Paul Smith's College in the Adirondacks, receiving an A.A.S degree in forestry. He earned a B.S. degree in forestry from Utah State University, and worked as a forester for the Bureau of Indian Affairs before deciding to become a high school teacher. He spent the next 23 years teaching conservation, ecology, and earth science at Wallkill Central High School in upstate New York before retiring in 1986.

Bill is working on a book about his experiences in the Navy.

Bill's father, before he took Horace Greeley's advice

NEW COMPANION VOLUME

Edited by Bill Michalski

WALLINGTON - PASSAIC - DUNDEE
A PEOPLE'S NARRATIVE

More tales of growing up in "Poland on the Passaic" submitted by readers

---

250 pages - $14.95
Buy both books and save money
See special offer on the following page

TO ORDER ADDITIONAL COPIES

CALL GREYCOURT BOOKS AT 845-774-6318

SEND E-MAIL TO ORDERS@GREYCOURTBOOKS.COM

OR VISIT WWW.POLAND-ON-THE-PASSAIC.COM

Poland on the Passaic . . . . $ 16.95

Wallington-Passaic-Dundee . . . . . $ 14.95

SPECIAL set of both books . . . . . $ 29.95

10% discount for additional copies of each book

Shipping:	*1 book*	*$3*
	2-4 books	*$4*
	5-8 books	*$5*
	9-10 books	*$6*

**WANT TO SHARE YOUR MEMORIES
OF GROWING UP IN NEW JERSEY?**

VISIT THE "WALLINGTON MEMORIES" FORUM
AT WWW.POLAND-ON-THE-PASSAIC.COM

NEW COMPANION VOLUME

Edited by Bill Michalski

WALLINGTON - PASSAIC - DUNDEE
A PEOPLE'S NARRATIVE

More tales of growing up
in "Poland on the Passaic"
submitted by readers

250 pages - $14.95
Buy both books and save money
See special offer on the following page

TO ORDER ADDITIONAL COPIES

CALL GREYCOURT BOOKS AT **845-774-6318**

SEND E-MAIL TO **ORDERS@GREYCOURTBOOKS.COM**

OR VISIT **WWW.POLAND-ON-THE-PASSAIC.COM**

Poland on the Passaic . . . . *$ 16.95*

Wallington-Passaic-Dundee . . . . . *$ 14.95*

SPECIAL set of both books . . . . . *$ 29.95*

10% discount for additional copies of each book

Shipping: *1 book*   *$3*
              2-4 books   *$4*
              5-8 books   *$5*
              9-10 books   *$6*

**WANT TO SHARE YOUR MEMORIES
OF GROWING UP IN NEW JERSEY?**

VISIT THE "WALLINGTON MEMORIES" FORUM
AT **WWW.POLAND-ON-THE-PASSAIC.COM**